MY BUTCH CAREER

MY BUTCH CAREER

—— A MEMOIR ——

ESTHER NEWTON

DUKE UNIVERSITY PRESS   Durham and London 2018

Printed in the United States of America on acid-free paper ∞
Cover designed by Courtney Leigh Baker;
Interior designed by Heather Hensley
Typeset in Chaparral Pro by Copperline Books

Library of Congress Cataloging-in-Publication Data
Names: Newton, Esther, author.
Title: My butch career : a memoir / Esther Newton.
Description: Durham : Duke University Press, 2018. |
Includes bibliographical references and index.
Identifiers: LCCN 2018016914 (print) | LCCN 2018019936 (ebook)
ISBN 9781478002727 (ebook)
ISBN 9781478001294 (hardcover : alk. paper)
Subjects: LCSH: Newton, Esther. | Lesbians—United States—
Biography. | College teachers—United States—Biography. |
Butch and femme (Lesbian culture)—United States.
Classification: LCC HQ75.4.N49 (ebook) | LCC HQ75.4.N49 A3
2018 (print) | DDC 306.76/63092 [B]—dc23
LC record available at https://lccn.loc.gov/2018016914

Cover art: Photograph by Nancy Rae Smith, 1967.
Courtesy of Kathryn McHargue Morgan.
Frontis: The author, 1967. Photograph by Nancy Rae Smith.

For LOUISE FISHMAN:
my first great love

for F. B.:
Le papillon qui tape du pied
[the butterfly that stamps its foot]

and for HOLLY HUGHES:
steadfast and inspirational from
beginning to end of this book

CONTENTS

ix | Acknowledgments

1 | Introduction

18 | CHAPTER 1: A Hard Left Fist

33 | CHAPTER 2: A Writer's Inheritance

56 | CHAPTER 3: Manhattan Tomboy

72 | CHAPTER 4: California Trauma

81 | CHAPTER 5: Baby Butch

102 | CHAPTER 6: Anthropology of the Closet

119 | CHAPTER 7: Lesbian Feminist New York

160 | CHAPTER 8: The Island of Women

183 | CHAPTER 9: In-Between Dyke

198 | CHAPTER 10: Paris France

237 | CHAPTER 11: Butch Revisited

249 | NOTES

261 | BIBLIOGRAPHY

265 | INDEX

ACKNOWLEDGMENTS

In 1996 I received the honor of presenting the David Kessler Lecture from the Center for Lesbian and Gay Studies (CLAGS) at the Graduate Center of the City University of New York. I was thrilled to receive the invitation to this once-a-year event honoring a queer scholar, and I threw myself into it, using text and even music to create a PowerPoint version of my life. I was rewarded with a standing ovation, and many people urged me to develop the material further. Without the Kessler lecture, this memoir would not have happened.

I was still working full time until 2006, and progress was halting and slow, but in 1999 two grants allowed me to take time off from teaching. Once again, CLAGS supported me with a Rockefeller Fellowship in the Humanities, and I received a small but helpful boost from the President's Research Support Grant at Purchase College, State University of New York.

In 2001, a version of the first chapter, "A Hard Left Fist," was published in GLQ: Journal of Queer Studies 7, no. 1. And in 2003, the original lecture was published as "My Butch Career: A Memoir," in Queer Ideas: The David R. Kessler Lectures in Lesbian and Gay Studies (New York: Feminist Press).

Hardly any LGBT writers could be "out" in the modern sense of letting their sexual orientation be known publicly during the years described in this memoir. That began to change in the 1980s, and I thank the editor Michael Denneny for recognizing and promoting so much queer talent, including mine; my agents Frances Goldin and, later, Ellen Geiger of Goldinlit Literary Agency; and Ken Wissoker of Duke University Press for believing in me and my work.

The project before me was to transform the Kessler lecture, memory, journals, and letters into a coherent narrative, and without serious editorial help, this story, had it ever been published, would have been lumpy and indigestible.

On the recommendation of my partner, Holly Hughes (we married in 2015), I turned to her friend Cynthia Carr for editorial help. I had admired Cindy's writing since her days as a cultural critic for the *Village Voice* under the byline C. Carr, and this was a most fortunate choice because Cindy understood what I was trying to do and yet was tough with me. She did the heavy lifting of turning a much longer manuscript that even I perceived as shapeless into something coherent. In more recent years, five anonymous but perspicacious and dedicated readers for Duke University Press led me through three rounds of painful cuts and revisions until *My Butch Career* reached its final form. At the very end, Holly Hughes and Ellen Lewin both read versions of a balky chapter 11 and helped me drag it over the finish line.

On a personal note, I thank my brother, Robert Newton, for giving me our father's transcribed recollections on which much of chapter 1 is based, and my cousins Barbara L. Cohen and Betty Levinson for the photograph of the Cohen family and for helping identify them; Jane Rosette, who gave me important technical support in putting the Kessler lecture together, and staff at both the Social Science Department of Purchase College and the Women's Studies Department at the University of Michigan for going out of their way to help with scanning and copying; my French friends without whom chapters 8–10 would not exist; and Bena Ball and June Fortney, my friends at the Resort on Carefree Boulevard for insisting that I keep working through the revisions. Thanks to all those Ann Arborites who visited and encouraged me through the four hospitalizations that have impeded my progress on the manuscript for the past two years. You know who you are. And most especially, I thank my in-laws, Trudy Hughes and Jeff Bieszki; my friends Stephanie Rowden, Vicki Patraka, Lisa Nakamura, Christian Sandvig; and, most of all, my life partner Holly Hughes for putting up with twenty-two years of angst over this project and for her gutsy and beautiful writing that inspires me every day.

ANN ARBOR, MICHIGAN
NOVEMBER 5, 2017

INTRODUCTION

This is the story of how I came into this world a "Commie Jew bastard"—
my grandfather's slur—and became an anthropologist who helped create sexuality and gender studies. That is the career of my title. It is also
the story of how I came to see myself as butch, a stigmatized identity
quite at odds with the concept of a career. By "butch" I mean an identity
within LGBT communities that describes someone who identifies as a
woman but whose sense of self is deeply rooted in masculinity.

This narrative centers on the first half of my life, from childhood to
age forty. These were years when I suffered torments, as did most gay
people of my generation. We were hated, hounded, arrested, and slan-
dered without being able to answer back. Through it all, I finished high
school, college, and graduate school suppressing, and lying about, my
masculinity and homoeroticism even while naively daring to write
Mother Camp: Female Impersonators in America, the first anthropological
description of the American gay community, which was published to
no notice and didn't prevent me from getting fired from my first academic job.

What does it mean to have a career, and why did I want one? The idea of career is bound up in class and gender. To have a career means education and training in business, politics, armed forces, medicine, law, or academia and like professions. A career is supposed to be a spur to ambition and a calling that gives shape and meaning to a life. Having a career almost always depends on expectation—because of your class privilege you are expected to do so; family stability—so that you can concentrate on your goals over a period of time and earn at least a middle-class family income.

In the nineteenth century, well-situated or unusually enterprising men entered professions. Only a few elite women became professional anythings; the rest were ladies, housewives, or laundry washers, maids and farm or factory workers and slaves, and most women were mothers, too.

My great-grandmother was one of those exceptional women in being a nineteenth-century journalist for a major New York City newspaper, and she established the possibility of a career for women on my mother's side. My father, the son of Jewish immigrants, also believed in careers for women, not because he had such role models, but because the Communist Party theoretically believed in gender equality (though it was far more active in the struggle for racial justice).

I was born in 1940, on the eve of World War II. By the time of my adolescence in the 1950s, it was a given in upper-middle-class families like mine that girls would go to college, although the usual rationale was that a bachelor of arts degree made them better wives and mothers.

My career path was not level and smooth because from childhood on I had a boyish demeanor and was attracted to girls and women. As a teenager I told a psychiatrist I thought I was homosexual, as we said then, and at eighteen a strange and sexy woman seduced me and showed me lesbian bar culture, where women were either butches or the partners of butches, femmes. Within that scheme I was butch, no doubt. Back in college, though, lesbianism was not acceptable, and femininity was mandatory. Wanting to finish college, I went into therapy in a vain and damaging attempt to "fix" myself.

By the 1960s, Cold War government funding meant that many graduate schools were admitting far more women than they ever had before.

But the pressure to marry was so great that advanced training produced more marriages than female professionals. Such women more often married male professionals than went on to such careers themselves.

Although I had had (problematic) sex with men in college, I could not bring myself to marry. So in the absence of a trust fund, I was going to have to support myself. Two brief stints at menial jobs had convinced me that career was the better option. But one could not be openly homosexual as a professional; there was no choice but to lead a deceptive public life and a separate and secret private one. And as a gender "deviant," as we said then, hiding my sexual orientation was even more challenging, since any mannish ways were supposed to be the mark of a lesbian.

From high school through a full professorship, my persona, interests, and, later, feminist/gay politics blocked my advancement so much that by the 1970s I was almost completely alienated from the whole notion of having a career just when I should have been notching accomplishments.

During the part of my life described in this memoir, my research and writing had no context and no audience. As a professor, I was lucky to survive, much less thrive. But by the 1980s, on the energy of feminist and gay liberations movements, eager readers emerged outside the universities, and mainstream publishers started to take notice. Women's studies programs and departments and gay academic conferences were providing the beginnings of supportive institutional structures. These movements, more than academic support (I was the only out gay or lesbian professor at my college from 1974 through the early 1990s), gave me hope, and all of my work since then has been written not just for academic colleagues but also for the national LGBT communities that were taking shape.

Around 1980, working-class lesbian intellectuals were creating a new and more generous conception of the butch-femme roles and sexuality of my youth that were a revelation and liberating. Since *Mother Camp* I had done little academic work. "The Mythic Mannish Lesbian: Radclyffe Hall and the New Woman," which I wrote in 1981, was my return to scholarly work, and it made masculine lesbians my subject. Finally I could pull my career and my queer life together.

/ / /

The butch is either the magical sign of lesbianism,
or a failed, emasculated and abjected man.
—SALLY MUNT, *Heroic Desire*

We live in an America where long held assumptions about sexuality and gender are dramatically shifting. Until the beginning of the twentieth century, most people believed that same-sex attraction was caused by gender "inversion," a man who was too feminine or a woman who was too masculine. These inverts were thought to be the aggressors in same-sex liaisons with more "normal" people, which was the basis for the stereotype of the sexual predator, both male and female.

Sigmund Freud, who started publishing in the early years of the twentieth century and was hugely influential, especially in America, argued that sexual orientation and gender identity were both shaped through childhood experience (the famous Oedipus complex) and that neither determined the other, although in his essay "The Psychogenesis of a Case of Homosexuality in a Woman" Freud noted the patient's refusal of traditional femininity, noting, "She really was a feminist."[1] In using the word "homosexual," Freud brought about a new way of thinking about same-sex desire, as a specific (and morally neutral but socially undesirable) form of eroticism. As Freud's ideas gained traction, the sexuality aspect of same-sex desire grew dominant over the "gender inversion" hypothesis.

"Butch" is a gender identity within lesbian culture that fuses female masculinity with homosexual desire. Butch became compulsory for even slightly masculine women during the 1950s and '60s in the one semi-public space in which lesbians could have fun, dance, and meet partners: bars.[2] Other subcultures and even countries have related gender identities with different names: within African American communities, for instance, some masculine lesbians call themselves "aggressives," or AG, as in the 2005 film of that name. But whatever name they use, such women emerge from every American class, race, and subculture.

A rather masculine lesbian friend of mine, who does not identify as butch but, as she puts it, always knew she was gay, teased me one day, "If you are so butch, where is your tool belt?" When I have practical problems in my Florida home, I call her. In fact, she built the desk on which I am writing. But her father was a mechanic while mine was a psychologist who never wore a tool belt or fixed anything. Postmodern butch is not necessarily about tool belts or who is more dominant in a relationship; it is not even about what you do in bed (or elsewhere). It is about a gender expression that combines some version of the masculinity that you saw around you as a child with same-sex desire.

Butch is not, as is often claimed, just a copy of manhood. Although Gertrude Stein said, "Thank god I was not born a woman," she always wore skirts. One's gender presentation is, among other things, a projection of your personal and cultural imagination. Stein was saying that because of her masculinity she was not and never had been like other women. And she had the expatriate lesbian community around her in Paris to support her claim. Although butch identity appropriates certain aspects of normative masculinity, it is an invention of the lesbian community.

Whether caused by biology or experience (and more likely a combination), feeling innately masculine or feminine is not a choice, but how people mesh that sense with their adulthood possibilities is, within the available avatars in any culture. Because the world of my childhood presented only conventional gender possibilities, I had no way to make sense of my discordant sense of self. Even after accepting that I was gay, my intimate and sexual relations were confusing and conflicted when I could not fit them into a lesbian-feminist template. At forty-one, then, I claimed this butch identity because it made sense of my sexual and personal experience and because, to paraphrase Stuart Hall, to claim an identity is to place oneself in a narrative of history.

/ / /

Tonight in the lesbian retirement community where I spend the winter I was flipping the TV dial and happened to come across a rerun of *Dirty Dancing*, a 1987 film set in a Jewish Catskills resort. I loved it even more than when I first saw it. But online I learned that Jennifer Grey's Jewish nose, which I had especially loved, had later been mutilated by her choice to have a nose job. Grey is supposed to have said that she went into plastic surgery a celebrity and came out anonymous. In other words, she chose to alter a characteristic she was born with and wound up compromising her beauty.

Although I have ideas but not certainties about why I grew up, despite relentless opposition, a mannish woman who wanted intimacy with other, mostly feminine women, I can't remember a time when this wasn't true. If these parts of me were not innate, like Jennifer Grey's nose, they might as well have been.[3] As an adolescent I wished for what might be called a "gender job"—some magic that would make me feel like other girls and everything that went with it, including heterosexuality. I felt ugly and awkward, and it was only through the affirmation of my female lovers that I gradually came to see myself as they did: a woman more masculine than feminine, with good looks and charisma who could live in her own body.

Judging by current newspaper and Facebook wedding photos, feminine-looking lesbians now sometimes marry others like themselves, and although for some reason I don't see their wedding pictures in the *New York Times*, I know about quite a few masculine-masculine couples. We appreciate now that both gender and sexual orientation are not either-or propositions; that they are, rather, continuums that are much more fluid than I was led to believe as a child and young adult.

Many—probably most—lesbians are more in the middle, and many who appear to be more masculine or feminine don't accept a "label" or look down on butches, so by no means is this the story of every lesbian, although many queer people of my age will recognize the toxic atmosphere of my youth.

/ / /

You are not what you want. You are what wants you back.
—GARY SHTEYNGART, *Little Failure*

In the 1950s and '60s the partner of any butch had to be feminine and preferably identify as femme. The femme lesbian looked more feminine in dress and mannerisms, but she had antipathy toward aspects of the conventional female role, and she was attracted to butches. I presume that many of my readers, both today's young "queer" women and others, may not know (or know that they know) any lesbian femmes, even though the identity is still evolving and vibrant. The majority of my partners have been femmes, although some did not call themselves that, and in their loving gaze I saw who I could be.

Feminine women in mainstream media are not legible as femmes because they never get to say so and are always represented as attracted to men. Although I cannot speak for them, in trying to characterize femmes as I have known and loved them, I return to *Dirty Dancing* and its portrayal of a (heterosexual) femme-like attitude: Jennifer Grey's performance of Frances "Baby" Houseman, the young Jewish heroine. From the early scene when Baby purposely spills water on a sexist jerk and walks away, you know that she is gutsy and determined. When her doctor father tries to order her around, you can see by the set of her mouth that she won't obey. Baby pursues Johnny, a blue-collar gentile dance instructor and she keeps at it until she gets him in bed. There's no ulterior motive. Her heart is true, and she's not a conniving bitch. She wants him because everything about him gives her pleasure, and she's not ashamed of it, and this is what their thrilling dancing embodies.

But there is no glossing over the fact that Johnny is a working-class guy who works as an Arthur Murray dance instructor/rent boy, while Baby is the Jewish upper-middle-class daughter of a doctor. The film acknowledges that their class differences are a powerful part of their attraction and will ultimately separate them.

OK, so Johnny's a man. But we gays have had to project ourselves into heterosexual narratives. Working-class Johnny can't believe that this doctor's daughter wants him, and his attitude is not one of conquest; it is always of gratitude and tenderness. They don't slurp open-mouthed kisses and hump in offbeat locations and positions, as in today's conventional representations of heterosexual lust. Their masculine-feminine attraction is played out in partnered dancing and in tempo, in gestures, her hand running over his ass, the electric moment *before* they kiss. As Grey plays her, Baby matches Johnny's sexy masculinity with her powerful femininity. This is definitely a queer film in the current sense, disrupting normative gender roles and heterosexuality.[4]

The only couple I knew of who had what could be called an intellectual femme-butch relationship was in books about the lives of Alice B. Toklas and the modernist writer Gertrude Stein. Toklas willingly devoted her life to Gertrude's comfort and success, but if this was ever the pattern of most feminine lesbians, it is no longer. As I was to discover, femmes often are not interested in domesticity and are looking for an equal relationship. They are feminine yet determined and more headstrong than submissive by temperament.

/ / /

Lived identities are complicated fictions essential to our social function.
—SALLY MUNT, *Heroic Desire*

There is a contentious and sometimes painful debate going on in the queer world about the relationship of butch identity to transgender. I first became aware of this when the female-bodied Brandon Teena was raped and murdered in 1993. On hearing about the atrocity, I assumed that Teena was butch, but suddenly there were voices claiming her for transgender and insisting on something that butches don't do: referring to Teena as he instead of she. (A similar controversy has erupted over the famous author Radclyffe Hall, who used the older term, "invert," to describe herself.) According to the Wikipedia entry on Teena, he began passing as a man in his late teens, and wanted to transition but either could not get access or could not afford it. Every entry I saw recently online referred to Teena as "he."

My first personal encounter with a transman was at an LGBT academic conference, when a good-looking young person who appeared to be butch introduced herself and told me she was going to become a man. Without thinking I said, "Why?" This person, who was then a graduate student, answered, "Because it takes too much energy to be seen the way I want to be seen." A part of me was shocked and alarmed, and the other part knew instinctively what she meant.

I share a double gender-consciousness with drag queens and with transgender people who choose to end the discrepancy between their bodies' sex and the gender they deem themselves to be, and I know how strong and indelible is the sense that one's socially ordained gender is a performance that feels put on. Like transgender men, butches have been the targets of medical intervention—in our case, to correct our grievous mistakes, our impermeable certainty about how we should look and move. My body commits every one of these movement "mistakes"—

for example, *hands on hips, fingers forward*—that are used to diagnose gender identity disorder, a category of mental illness listed in the DSM-IV, the shrinks' diagnostic handbook.

The aristocrat Michael Dillon is the first transman in the modern sense that we know about. In the nineteenth century there had been women who successfully passed as men and sometimes had female partners who were the cultural ancestors of both butches and transmen, but the technology of altering your body to more closely resemble the gender you felt yourself to be did not exist until the discovery of hormones and the development of plastic surgery techniques during World War I. Dillon began to transition (which was then called "sex change") around 1939 with the then experimental hormone testosterone and later had multiple plastic surgeries to create a phallus.

As a young adult I knew vaguely about Christine Jorgensen, the army soldier who'd transformed into a woman in 1952, but following that example never crossed my mind as a possibility, even in the 1960s when I first met transitioning drag queens. (It seemed like one more opportunity open to men and not to women.) But beginning in the 1990s the option of renouncing womanhood and becoming, (or, as is now said, affirming being) a man has opened to many more female-bodied people. Quite a few have been former masculine lesbians, including a number of my students, which has raised the alarm from many lesbians that "we are losing our butches!"

Hostility to me as a lesbian is now greatly reduced, but my gender presentation remains problematic. I am still called "sir" in public, and in women's bathrooms I get strange looks or am even challenged, including once at the annual meetings of the American Anthropological Association. Why, then, do I still identify as butch? Why not transition?

Generational and autobiographical factors are the most important reasons. As a child I did not think of myself as a girl trapped in a boy's body. I knew full well that I was not a boy, perhaps because I had wished that I were one so intensely. Recently I saw the excellent PBS Frontline film *Growing Up Trans*. The option of blocking puberty with hormones has become medically available, and the filmmakers captured the viewpoints of the conflicted parents and doctors in the face of determined children who, thanks to mass media and the Internet, already called themselves trans. I had to face the fact that I was seeing myself in these children and realized that if I were a child now, I likely would have wanted that testosterone.

In my childhood, though, I was OK with a body that was healthy, capable, and strong. What I hated was compulsory girlhood and the inferior everything status of my gender. I think that most girls share these feelings, but there are varied ways to deal with the disadvantages of girlhood, including within the femininity I rejected.

Puberty was drastically worse. Now I hated both being a girl in a man's world that was basically hostile to women and those parts of my body that to me were girliest: having a period and breasts. (The cessation of the former has been one of the benefits of old age. As to the latter, until recent years it would have been impossible to talk some surgeon into removing healthy breasts.)

Later I was swept up in feminism, the gay liberation movement, and lesbian feminism, which changed my relationship to my gender because (after a struggle against homophobia) these movements expanded the boundaries of womanhood to include me. Up to that point, despite being raised almost exclusively by women and going to a girls' camp, I felt attraction to but little solidarity with other females. My interests and persona seemed to diverge so radically from theirs. But since feminism, I no longer wanted to be part of dominant masculinity. Young people do not see being butch as "transgressive," but lesbians challenge the gender hierarchy just as much, or more, by *staying* women. I am opposed to pressure being put on masculine girls and women to "go all the way" by transitioning, just as I dislike any one-upsmanship over who is or is not more butch.

In my experience, the majority of people who become transmen were younger than forty when they made that decision. I do know one butch lesbian who, in her sixties and only after her elderly mother died, became a man. But for the majority of butches of my generation, "that ship had sailed," as my friend Gayle Rubin, the great butch intellectual, said. After sixty-five, most people don't want major surgery for any reason except in matters of life and death. You are glad your body is recognizable to medical personnel while hoping that, in the future, trans men and women will be treated better by doctors and nurses.

Will transmen supplant butches entirely? We have no way of knowing. Just as butch and femme have evolved, the trans movement as it

Self-portrait,
around 2012.

matures will also. Perhaps butch and trans will merge into a broader or changed definition of female masculinity. Or of trans masculinity. Or of gender queer. Already, older terms such as "transsexual" and "sex change" are passé, and people with more varied self-definitions are asserting themselves. Some see themselves as men, and others see themselves as transmen, whether they have had surgery or not.

So far, butch as a way to understand yourself and be in the world has survived. Ellen Lewin, another dear friend who is a lesbian feminist academic, summed up her political, sexual, and aesthetic reasons for preferring to partner with butches this way: "I like a girl in boy's clothing."

PROLOGUE

Coming out stories have long been important to queer narratives, and so I invite you to see me as a freshman in college, in a dorm room in Mary Markley Hall at the University of Michigan in the spring of 1959. This first sexual encounter with a woman was bizarrely wonderful and so scary. If Betty Silver, as I'll call her, had not existed, I would not have been able to make her up.

A skinny blonde girl named Shirley Walton and I were assigned as roommates, we speculated because we both smoked. We seemed to have nothing else in common. For fifty-six years we remained best friends until the cigarettes we both had loved did us in. Shirley died of lung cancer three years ago. I subsequently was stricken with asthma and COPD.

Shirley was originally from a small town in Washington State, but her middle-management father's corporation had moved the family to Evanston, Illinois, north of Chicago. We'd both spent our high school years in plushy, privileged suburbs that we hated. Shirley's older sister had belonged to a sorority, and she was expected to join it.

I didn't even try to rush the sororities and couldn't face college mixers, but when Shirley arranged blind dates, I accepted. The fraternity men bored me, but I liked double dates with Shirley because we could hash them over afterward. A thirtyish bisexual librarian, whose impotence I mistook for sensitivity, had an apartment and a Karmann-Ghia convertible. Girls in the dorm were impressed with my older man, and I thought my homosexual longings were safely hidden.

But not from Shirley. Coming from a conventional home, she knew a lot more about conventions than I did. She never understood my wanting to be like everyone else. My New York background fascinated her. I was an oddity trying to pass for normal, while she was a conventional girl run wild. For instance, in high school she had been arrested in a car, making out with a black classmate, and her horrified parents had to bail her out. After she was rejected by the sorority, Shirley took to wearing bohemian black and hanging around the student union, where the graduate students and kids outside the Greek circuit gathered.

"Have you ever met a lesbian?" she asked me one night in our dorm room.

I put my hand over my mouth to hide a crazy smile. My chest tightened.

"You have!" she pounced. "Come on, admit it."

"No," I said weakly. How had she come up with this? We had already discussed—down to the size of their sex organs—several men I'd dated.

"You're lying," Shirley said matter-of-factly. "I've just met one." She'd been sitting in the Union with some of the art students and met Betty Silver—or, as Shirley described her, "A real weirdo who everyone says is a lesbian."

I asked her whether Betty looked like a man. Since reading *The Well of Loneliness* I knew that lesbians were women who should have been men, and looked it, like I would if it weren't for my vaguely bouffant hair and clumsily applied lipstick.

Shirley shook her head emphatically. "She doesn't look anything like a man. She's very sexy. Stacked. And she wears tons of black eye makeup."

"So how could you tell she was one?"

"The kids swear Betty Silver even boasts about it." Shirley stubbed out her cigarette and picked at some cracked red nail polish on her left hand. "I thought you'd be interested. Don't you even want to meet her?"

"Why should I?" I sat down at my desk, facing the cinderblock wall, so Shirley couldn't see my face. Our room was the size of a walk-in closet.

"You don't have to be so fucking defensive." I could hear her lighting another cigarette, and automatically I did, too. The silence stretched out, accusing. Was I going to lose her friendship now? She had listened sympathetically to the edited version of my high school breakdown. Having rejected the school, my mother, and the bland weather and smug wealth of the California suburb made me worthwhile in her eyes. But lesbian tendencies were just disgusting, I knew. That others might find them titillating was way over my head. Dating men was cool; sneaking around the curfew in our women's dorm to spend the night with them was being grown-up.

But finally curiosity and hope overcame fear, and I stopped by the Student Union cafeteria, picking Shirley out from a group of older-looking students by her bleached blond hair. Books, sketchpads, ashtrays, and coffee mugs covered the wooden surface of the table.

"What are you doing here?" Shirley smirked.

"Lost my meal ticket, OK? Just lend me some money."

She handed over her change purse. Everyone was watching a game show on black-and-white TV. Shirley didn't introduce me to the others, but I knew they were the wild crowd she'd been running with by their black turtlenecks and an unshaven, uncombed air that shouted "bohemian" against the crew cuts and khakis at every other table.

After a while Shirley dug her elbow into my ribs. "Hey look," she whispered. "That's her."

"Who?" But I knew.

"Betty Silver, over there. Staring a hole right through you."

The cafeteria, the size of a bus station, was crowded, but Betty Silver was unmistakable. Dressed all in black, even black tights, colored beads cascading over a large bust. Betty Silver. Was she really staring at me? Her eyes were almost lost in rings of black eyeliner.

"God, she looks like a raccoon," I sniggered defensively.

"Stop giggling, you jerk," said Shirley. "She's going to come over."

Betty Silver had a nervy stare and a sexy smile as if she were acting in a lesbian movie that didn't exist yet. After all, she was an artist, and they are visionary. As she threaded her way through the tables, I bent intently over my cold cheeseburger. Betty pulled a chair over from another table and squeezed brazenly between Shirley and me. Although I jerked away as our thighs touched, I knew then that she was going to seduce me, that Betty had seen right into me and knew I was "that way."

"Do you mind if I sit here?" Betty asked in a low, breathy voice. Marilyn Monroe crossed with Lauren Bacall. An unlit cigarette dangled between her fingers. Could she be waiting for me to light it? A forbidden act, like wanting to carry a girl's books, something I had never dared. A naughty smile played over Betty's lips. I felt in the pocket of my oversized man's white shirt, then in style, and came up with some ratty paper matches. My hands were shaking, and the matchbook dropped onto the sticky floor. Betty was still waiting, and all eyes were on her. "Give me a light," she said to a guy with a thin beard and pimples who deftly snapped open a Zippo.

"Betty's been up to some tricks," he announced. "This girl's been giving the art school a name. . . . I won't say what kind, 'cause there are freshmen here." Everyone snickered.

"Asshole, you're just jealous," Betty replied indolently. She seemed composed to the point of being completely indifferent. Later I realized she had been high, but until she introduced me to it I had never heard of marijuana. She had a cute little round face, framed by a cap of straight brown hair. But her large green eyes and husky voice gave her such airs! One of those bad glamour queens who drive men to desperation.

"Where's that photographer you've been hanging around with?" the Zippo boy asked. "The one with the crew cut?"

"He got to be a bore." Betty blew a perfect smoke ring. "Wanted to marry me. *In church!* Can you imagine?"

"Uh-uh. My imagination can't keep up with you."

"I liked the idea of the wedding dress," she mused. "All white, with a train. But," she waved one hand languidly in the air flashing several silver rings, "I just couldn't see myself in the part."

So she isn't one, I thought, both relieved and disappointed. As I pulled my books together to leave, her other hand slid down my leg under the table. She introduced herself to me as if her hand weren't stroking my thigh. We exchanged a few stilted words about our dorms, studies, and hometowns. She came from a wealthy Detroit suburb.

"I've got some errands this afternoon," she said abruptly. "Want to come with me?" I was already fifteen minutes late for my zoology class. The bohemians still at the table were staring. I stood up in a trance, whispering to Shirley, "Make yourself scarce this afternoon, OK?"

Betty's only errand was the loss of my lesbian abstinence. We walked back to my dorm. Nothing was said, not one word. I had the presence of mind to lock the door behind us. It would look suspicious, if anyone knocked, but better that than someone walking in on us. We would be instant pariahs. Get kicked out of school. My life would be ruined. And I was still going to do this.

Betty took off her colored beads, strand by strand, and laid them on the bureau top. Too excited and scared to speak, I wondered what I should do. How should I act? The boys I'd known were clumsy, the librarian with the sporty car more talkative than hot. Clark Gable never got beyond the kiss.

She broke the silence. "Have you ever slept with a girl before?"

I shook my head no, thinking she'd know if I lied.

She pulled her sweater over her head, revealing a small, plump torso and a large, well-filled black bra. "The moment I saw you, I thought, 'Now there's a cute butch.'"

I had never heard the word "butch" before and could only guess at its meaning. I still stood frozen. Although I had pulled the vinyl curtains, there was still plenty of light. Wasn't sex supposed to happen at night, in the dark? Betty didn't do anything by the book. "Well," she laughed, "aren't you going to light my cigarette?" I fumbled in my shirt pocket. Impatient, Betty snapped the cigarette in two. "Come over here. Don't you want me?"

Yes I did. Wanted to run the palms of my hands over the insides of her plump thighs. The ample breasts pressed together inside the black bra. To hear a woman speak to me in a swollen voice—"Oh, yes, oh, God, yes . . ." It was so obvious, suddenly, what I wanted, had always wanted.

Betty tilted her face up as I moved toward her. She meant to be kissed on the mouth, I knew, because she closed her eyes. Between her lips and my kiss were huge black newspaper headlines: "PERVERT." Her face swam out of focus as I pulled her closer. Betty put her hand on the nape of my neck. She was shorter, smaller, so feminine, and I loved this. A moment after our lips met she put her hand on my face and twisted our heads so we were cheek to cheek, facing Shirley's mirror. "Look, look!" she whispered. There were our two young faces—eyes wide with terror and the thrill of it. She still got the adrenaline jolt she lived for from doing something so *Wrong*. There we were, the unthinkable, the abomination: two girls kissing. I squeezed my eyes closed and tasted the sweetness of her lipstick, the fragrance of her breath. "Take off my bra, baby, go ahead," Betty urged. My legs shaking, I pulled Betty, laughing and sighing, down under me on the narrow dorm bed. Peeling up her straight skirt, then fumbling with the black tights. Each move was more taboo, more spine-tingling. My hand felt the intense heat of her cunt. Her legs opened wider as her nails dug into my neck.

"Oh, yes," she whispered. "Go on, don't stop now." Obeying her, I'd never felt so powerful. "More, more," Betty cried out with a note of anguish. I tried to wedge my fingers further up, but she didn't open, inside. Ignorant as I was, I sensed her excitement had already peaked. Whatever she wanted, she'd already gotten, or already given up.

Exhilarated and afraid to disappoint her, I still handled her clumsily. She squirmed away. "Wow!" she said, out of breath. "You got it."

What did I have, what did I get? A rush of power and affirmation that had seemed more out of reach than the moon. Betty was getting dressed in an unnerving silence. "Did you come, honey?" I said, thinking you were supposed to ask. With a last look in the mirror, she checked her makeup and fluffed her cap of hair. I waited, confused, my thumbs hooked in the pockets of the women's jeans I'd never even unzipped. "Uh. . . I love you," I offered. Wouldn't we be together now?

She hoisted her purse to her shoulder and strolled toward the door. "Come with me to New York this summer," she said. "Lots of girls in Greenwich Village."

/ / /

And so my introduction to the concept of lesbianism (via *The Well of Loneliness*), lesbian sex (thanks to Betty), and gay life (with the "Greenwich Village girls" I indeed met that summer) all began under the sign of butch. In what follows, my father's and mother's stories set the cultural and emotional context into which I was born and became a New York tomboy. My youthful gender dysphoria and longing for women finds a shape in that 1950s butch identity, but massive social pressure and my developing academic career push me into trying to "go straight" and, later, into the gay closet. In graduate school, I studied the cultural significance of female impersonators and got away with it, thanks to a powerful mentor, but the initial failure of *Mother Camp* and getting fired from my first job soured me on academia. Saved by second wave feminism, the anti butch-femme ideology of 1970s lesbian-feminism, though never whole heartedly accepted by me, still led to conflict and confusion in a passionate Parisian love affair. And then, at the age of forty I begin to achieve personal and scholarly coherence in the company of the first politicized generation of out lesbian and gay scholars, we who helped create gender and sexuality studies.

CHAPTER 1

A HARD LEFT FIST

My "fathers": I had three of them, all Jewish, the men who turned my mother on. My mother's first husband was a photographer, a Jewish refugee named Laszlo Gluck, much older than she, who died of a heart attack several years before I was born. A year or two after his death she met another Jew in the Communist Party named William H. Miller, but when she became pregnant he refused to marry her because, he said, she wasn't Jewish. To escape the then severe stigma of bearing and having an "illegitimate" child, my mother named the dead Hungarian as my father on the birth certificate.

In my sixties I asked my mother why she had named me Esther-Mary (which I shortened as soon as I could insist; I was strange enough without a double name). She said these had been names of Laszlo Gluck's dead relatives; she had wanted to think of me as Gluck's child, and growing up, she made me believe that I was, despite his being only a ghostly absence.

My mother withheld information about Gluck—never showed me a photo, for instance—because she knew someday I would learn that Miller had been my biological father. As it turned out, I was nineteen before she told me, and like Gluck, my bio-dad, as a person, is part of my mother's story rather than mine.

My third father, Saul Newton, was the only one who directly shaped my sense of a masculine self. Saul was a Communist Party organizer, an antifascist warrior in the Spanish Civil War and World War II, and, eventually, an unethical therapist who demanded sex from his female patients and told them who they should have children with. My mother was his third wife; eventually he married six times.

I've wondered why I always came back to New York City, a place my mother disliked, since for her it was just a devastating interlude. But I was drawn to the milieu of those Jewish fathers, fire-eating Communist dragons who belched smoke into the New York City air that I breathed growing up, so that I was never comfortable in my mother's chosen state, California, with its big blondes and bland Republican attitudes.

I consider myself a quintessential twentieth-century American, the offspring of a Mayflower WASP mother and three Jewish immigrant men. My existence is the biological and cultural proof, the flotsam, or achievement, take your pick, of the friction and attraction between the old Anglo-American stock and the immigrants who came toward the end of the nineteenth century. That is, I am the prototype of what whiteness became after the Irish and Jews and Italians and Poles elbowed and charmed and fucked their way in.

At the same time, of course, like every American, I am a "unique individual," so why not just start at my birth? Well, we invent ourselves, but not just as we please. My birth occurred inside the situations of my parents and even their parents; without this context, my story makes no sense to me. In this as in other ways, my historical mind-set rubs against the grain of popular thinking. The "primitive" peoples I studied in graduate school were right, it seems, in their ancestor worship if, by "worship," one means giving full due to the ways the ancestors set the parameters, though not the particulars, of our lives.

After Saul Newton's death I began to ask myself why I'd thought of him as my father. I did not have his "blood." My mother and I had lived with him as a nuclear family for only a couple of years; I was eight when he divorced her. How authentic was my mourning? How appropriate?

Saul had claimed me as his daughter, given me the legal recognition of his name. His brothers and sisters and their children had warmly welcomed me into their homes, never making me feel the outsider. His money paid for my first jalopies, for my higher education, for my college graduation trip to Europe. Even after my mother and I moved to California, I continued to see him at Christmas and every summer until I was in my twenties. Perhaps only now, writing this, have I fully accepted that although he could never be my only father, Saul Newton was the only man who inhabited, who lived, the role of father, however deficiently. The other two were the shadow fathers, the ones my mother wouldn't talk about, important figures who were never present, mysteries.

So let's say that my American history through my father Saul Newton starts back on Ellis Island in the nineteenth century, when somehow Saul's father's name was changed from Aronoff to Cohen. I don't claim this Aronoff/Cohen as my grandfather. This is not just because I am not Aronoff's "blood" descendant (I never knew either of my biological grandfathers). My disentangled paternal line is too twenty-first century to support any role so unambiguous as a "grandfather" without the quotes. Despite the fact that both Aronoff/Cohen and my mother's father, General Bash, were dominating, patriarchal figures, their links to me were compromised. In fact, I can hardly say I have a "family," especially on my mother's side. Rather, I have relatives, a postmodern kindred.

In my first memory of Saul, he is wearing a U.S. Army uniform. Suddenly World War II was over and he came into my life—around 1945—with a captured German revolver and a battered helmet, telling scary war stories. Almost to the day of his death he was a compelling storyteller. He had a dark, sexy energy that had bowled my gentile mother over when they first hooked up, back in 1933 (he didn't bother to tell her he was married), when they were part of a network of young left-wing radicals around the University of Chicago.

Throughout his life Saul lusted after women, and many of them reciprocated. Even during his final illness, he was just as glad to see friends who accompanied me on visits, whom he had never met, as he was to see me, perhaps gladder. Simply because they were pretty, personable, and female, my friends brought him pleasure and made him forget for a few minutes that he was tied in a wheelchair and constantly anxious, because although he could not remember any of our names, or where he was, he knew he no longer had a home.

When Saul's fourth wife, Dr. Jane Pearce, whom I called my stepmother, was succumbing to cancer back in the summer of 1994, two years after Saul's death, she let me know that for her, too, years after their divorce, Saul was still magical, perhaps an evil warlock whose spell she could not break. She dreamed, she told me, that she was floating down the river Hades in a boat that went aground. When she climbed onto the shore she made her way toward an old barn that had been converted into a theater. Inside, Saul was bossing around the cast and crew, directing the rehearsal of a musical comedy. In the dream she said to herself, "If Saul is still in charge, even in hell, I don't want to die yet."[1] Then she pressed on me a sheaf of badly written and abstractly tortured poems she had written when she and Saul were falling in love, back when he was still married to his wife number three, my mother. He had cheated on women all his life, which to him demonstrated his superiority to men who had settled for monogamy, and the older he got, the more he rationalized it with his Marxist-therapeutic theories. He once told me about attending an annual reunion for veterans of the Spanish Civil War, underlining his contempt for the broken-down old men who, he said, were dominated by their wives.

Along with his terrible temper and disregard of others' feelings, Saul had irresistible charm and, improbably, a quality of sly sweetness, which appeared suddenly at some of the most unexpected moments. During his final illness, many of the hospital workers remarked on the vitality and appeal of his personality even as they complained about his violent outbursts, when he would throw things at another patient or curse out a doctor. One nurse's aide was bemused rather than outraged when, after he leaned out of his wheelchair to pat her behind and she objected, he said sheepishly, "I just couldn't resist." She cut short my apology on his behalf saying, "I wish I had known him in his prime!"

One of the ways that Saul perpetuated the myth that he had invented himself was that he rarely talked about his past, and in the years after their divorce, my embittered mother didn't talk about him at all if she could help it. So when my half-brother Rob, who is Saul's son with Jane Pearce, mentioned that he had more than three hundred pages of interview material with Saul—"Yours if you want them"—I jumped at the chance while thinking about how Rob had offered me Saul's ashes ("Yours if you want them") and I refused, not knowing what I'd do with them. Nobody wanted his ashes. His only memorial was organized by my cousins, the daughters of those brothers Saul had picked fights with and kicked out of his life years before.

Before the dementia took him, though, nobody ever could or did ignore Saul. After he adopted me he had nine legal children (a couple of the youngest were rumored to have had different bio-dads). He had kicked fascist butt in the Spanish Civil War and World War II, and he co-wrote a book that became gospel and verse for hundreds of people in a cult-like community that, as my partner Holly quipped, "combined the worst aspects of therapy, Marxism, and musical theater."[2]

Reading the manuscript Rob had given me I was fascinated by the almost biblical bitterness of my father's childhood milieu. His early life had been as mysterious to me as if he'd emerged from some misty Paleolithic, but in those transcriptions of Saul's memories, I learned for the first time that he'd been born on June 22, 1906, in St. John, New Brunswick, Canada. And both his parents were ferocious.

Saul's mother, Minnie, always boasted how she'd slaved to put her brothers through medical school. She herself had left school at eleven when their father, a Hassidic rabbi, apprenticed her to a seamstress. Although she hated her father all her life for this, she visited the same fate on her oldest children. Saul's older brother George was forced out of school at the end of eighth grade and put to work, though the family was prosperous by then. In Saul's view, his mother acted out of bitterness and envy.

Minnie bought books in lots at auctions "to put them on a bookshelf so that people would assume that she was educated and cultured" but also to hear them. Since she never learned to read or write English she would badger her children to read to her, and in this way Saul came to know the novels of Dickens, Turgenev, de Maupassant, Jane Austen, and Emily Brontë. As Saul put it, in his unaccented but Yiddish-influenced way of speaking English, "My mother was a particular kind of culture vulture who on the one hand refused to learn to read and write English and had learned to speak a rough-and-ready English which was spotted by big words that she didn't quite understand and therefore misused. . . .

A frequent phrase out of her mouth during my growing up was 'If I only knew how to read and write English, what I couldn't do!'"

Despite her handicaps as a woman and an immigrant, Minnie was a leader in the Jewish community of about a thousand souls in St. John. She was an officer of the Ladies Aid Society. Saul heard her interrupt a boring rabbi at the synagogue with a rousing speech regarding a Polish pogrom that "normally" (if a man gave it?) would have earned a standing ovation. By anyone's reckoning, this Minnie, whom I remember as a tiny, bent woman with a strong Yiddish accent, had been a powerful figure. My cousins Betty and Barbara remembered her as "intrusive." For example, when Saul's youngest sister, Dobie, had boyfriends over to the house, Minnie would sit down between them. But both cousins had a far less harsh view of Minnie than did Saul, saying she had had a tough life and had done her best. As for Saul, by the end of his life, when he dictated his memories, he was convinced that his mother had harbored vicious enmity for all of her five children but especially for him, her supposed favorite. When as a small child he snuck away from the house, hopped on a raft, and almost drowned, he blamed his mother, sure she wanted him dead. What an egotist he was! His mother was always, he imagined, thinking about him. "What kept me alive," he said. "I began studying the art of problem solving very young. . . . She [Minnie] was good training for surviving two wars."

Saul believed that his mother was out to undermine his manhood. As a teenager he hated her for a remark he overheard her make to a female friend that, unlike some, Saul was a good boy and would not take advantage of girls. Years later, moving to New York with his second wife, he had a panic attack while looking at a two-bedroom apartment, thinking his mother would demand to move into the second bedroom, and "What could I say?" Later still, the three brothers—George, Saul, and Maishe— put Minnie into a nursing home. One night, Saul got a call from the doctors that Minnie was dying and calling for him, her favorite son. This seemed to provoke another panic, because he had to think about it overnight. By morning he had concluded that it was a scheme: Minnie was trying to lure him to the home so she could die in his arms. If he refused to go see her, he reasoned, her plot would be foiled and she'd recover—and she did! When she finally did die, he boasted (or so I assume, in light of the theories Saul developed about the evils of motherhood) that he didn't even go to the funeral (something that cousin Betty refutes). He got his comeuppance: Saul never even had a funeral. Perhaps his most lasting memorial, aside from his ten children, is the obituary I helped arrange in the *New York Times*. Until I decided to write this memoir, that is. Isn't it strange that I, the adopted child, have become his scribe?

Saul never mentioned his father's first or last name in his memoir, referring to him only as "my father" or "my old man." Now nobody in the family even remembers his first name. (Isn't it true that in Judaism the name of G_d must never be spoken or written?) My cousins recently told me that Saul's father was known in the family as S. K. He was born around 1873 in a village in "white Russia," probably Vitebsk. Orphaned in childhood, he had three older siblings whom he hated for cheating him out of his inheritance from a brewery. All but one of S. K.'s siblings came to North America, where S. K. outdid them all.

His oldest brother was a peddler named Yoshe who was reportedly so cheap he tried to train the horses that pulled his cart not to eat. Then the horses would die, and Yoshe would show up at S. K.'s house, hat in hand. "This father of mine," as Saul said, would continue reading the Yiddish paper *The Forward* and would ignore his brother for an hour or so. Then, without even looking at Yoshe, he'd say, "How much is it this time?" And he would hand the cash over without a word.

I was astonished by stories like this that came right out of the *shtetl*, especially because Saul had seemed to "stop being Jewish," as my brother Rob put it, when he changed his name from Cohen to Newton sometime in the 1930s. Yet these stories of my father's, and the way he told them, were not theoretical; they were a part of him, though a part he had rarely shared with me. Although his sperm did not make me, his character, his ideals, and his masculinity did, and reading his memoir made me feel how much of a Jew I partly am.

(I told my former lover Jane Rosett, who taught me to light a *yahrzeit* memorial candle for Saul, that I didn't feel like eating the pork chops someone had offered us, adding, ironically, "I'm Jewish, you know." Jane laughed. "If you were really Jewish, you would have wanted the pork chops.")

Saul despised all religion. Cousin Betty told me that he almost wrecked her wedding, by fighting with another guest who had asked Saul if he'd joined the Abraham Lincoln Brigade because he was a Jew. Saul belligerently said no, he went strictly as a Communist, and being Jewish had nothing to do with it. They started yelling "Jew!" and "Communist!" at each other, almost came to blows, and had to be separated. Saul had been an old man at that point, but, as he liked to say, "I never back away from a belligerent situation."

Although my father never observed any aspect of Jewish religion, he never denied that he was Jewish, either, and his looks—he had a prominent hooked nose that had been broken in a fight and dark skin (he had been known in his family as the *schvartze*, the black one)—would scarcely have permitted him to pass for gentile even if he had wanted to. Probably being Jewish was such a given for him that he felt no need to state it. I recall only one time when he affirmed that he was Jewish. "Never forget that you are one of the chosen people," he said to me, although I don't recall what provoked this completely atypical admonition.

S. K. had gone to New York first, probably in his late teens, around 1890, where an indifferent immigration officer had changed the family name to Cohen. He learned the skill of cutting clothing in the women's garment business and then gradually saved up to get his factory in St. John. The relatives didn't help him at all, he claimed. By his mid-twenties he had a thriving clothing factory, selling his wares to modest department stores in the Maritime Provinces. He was able to build a large house for his family and send them upriver or to the seashore in the summer.

Saul described his father as having had "a sort of paranoid turn of mind and a belligerent character. . . . [He] was taciturn, reasonably generous. . . . He was a rather good-looking man with a face that was characteristically withdrawn and distant. But when he smiled, there was a kind of charm that would melt ice." Apparently, he didn't smile often. Saul recalled his father picking up a disgruntled customer and bodily throwing him out of his retail store into the street, so, Saul concluded, "If I wished to be like my father I had to be slender and powerful. I couldn't afford to panic with such a father." Saul's younger brother Maishe was more critical. In a brief autobiography written as a college freshman, Maishe recalled that "father's deep-seated irrationality slowly became a tangible horror in my mind. He would have violent fits of temper, blustering and shouting like a wild man for such things as the tendency to oversleep of my oldest brother George." Both parents, but especially S. K., abused George, constantly calling him stupid and punishing him even for things he didn't do. George came up with a non-verbal response. He once shit into S. K.'s boot, knowing his father would step in it the next morning.

The decisive event in Saul's young life was his father's struggle with the local synagogue. There were two in St. John: an upper-class one to which the Cohen family belonged, and a lower-class one that they shunned. When Saul was about five his father accused the officers of their synagogue of misappropriating funds. When they responded by appointing S. K. to a high position in the synagogue, he took this as a sign that they wanted to buy him off and accused them even more loudly of being corrupt. In retaliation, the entire family was expelled from the synagogue.

Having been a homosexual before Stonewall and therefore dependent on an embattled community, I can appreciate what kind of disaster this must have been for an immigrant Jewish family in a provincial Canadian town. Saul recalled that his father "wast[ed] his best energies on an utterly stupid six-year lawsuit to force his reinstatement in the synagogue." After his family's ejection from the sacrum and social center of the Jewish community, Saul became an atheist, furious at god and at adults in general, believing them to be a pack of liars and hypocrites. He was five years old. From then on he would refuse to say the Lord's Prayer at school. (The teachers never challenged him, and afterward he thought it was because he was Jewish.)

Having created a vacuum by rejecting the religion of his fathers, little Saul expanded to fill the space himself. At six, when he announced that he wasn't afraid of the dark, his friends dared him to prove it, so he went alone to a graveyard and said out loud, "Well, if there are any ghosts down there, why don't you c'mon up? I'm waiting for you." He decided to run everywhere instead of walking and once, so he claimed, collided with a vicious pit pull when neither of them would give way on a path. He taught himself to swim after the incident in which he had almost drowned, and when his father refused to buy him a bike, he swiped his father's bike and learned to ride on his own.

When I was about seven, my father took me to Central Park with my new balloon-tire bicycle, the exact one I had begged him for and that he had given with evident paternal pride. My feet barely reached the pedals, and there were no training wheels in those days. I was giddy with delight, excitement, and fear. He ran along with me a couple of times, holding me steady by the back of my seat. "Don't let go, Daddy, don't let go!" I said. "I won't," he answered, but after running behind a few steps, he shoved me off. I soon wobbled and crashed. He ignored my whimpers and skinned knee. "Get up," he ordered. "Get back on now." I did, and soon I was riding all over Central Park and loving it. It was worth being afraid, and even worth learning I couldn't trust him, to win his approval.

Saul was a leader in the gang of little boys that formed in his neighborhood. He learned to fight from his older brother George, who later became a noted amateur boxer in Quebec and used Saul for a sparring partner. "In various contexts," Saul remembered, "being a Jew was enough reason for a fight. And in others, not being a Roman Catholic was enough reason for a fight."

Saul taught me to box. He crouched down to my seven-year-old level and showed me how to hold my hands up, to jab with my left and follow through with my right. If I let down my guard, he slapped me—not hard—with his open hand. "Don't telegraph your punches," he advised. "Don't let 'em know what you're going to throw."

We played a game called "henchmen." "I've got two henchmen," he sang out, and I answered, "I've got three henchmen." "Daddy's got four henchmen," he said. "How many do you have?" "I've got five henchmen," I said, jumping up and down with excitement. We both laughed, but no matter how many henchmen I had, he always had more, and sometimes the game ended with me in tears. Fifty years later my mother told me, "I thought Saul should have let you win sometimes." But I was thrilled that he let me have any henchmen, that I was worthy of the game.

We spent part of one summer in northern Maine. I was six or seven. Saul and I often drove into town in his new Dodge sedan to buy groceries or get ice cream cones. A winding, bumpy dirt road led up to our rented cabin, and sometimes he let me sit on his lap and steer the Dodge up the hill while he worked the pedals and gearshift. I knew he wouldn't have done this if my mother had been there. I remember the struggle, the ache in my arms from wrestling with that behemoth of a car—no power steering—and the thrill of the jolts and swerves, the road before me, the mastery, the danger, our shared adventure and his confidence in me.

/ / /

Saul loved the Boy Scouts and was the head of his class in school, but he frequently had problems with authority. He did not dare involve his parents in any school problem for fear they would make things worse. I had always assumed, knowing how physically tough he was, that Saul was rebelling against the image of Jewish scholarly manhood, all white soft flesh, but Saul described his father and even his mother as violent and combative. Once when she thought that a teacher was picking on Saul, his mother, Minnie, went to school and beat the teacher with her umbrella.

Saul's violence was among my earliest memories of him. One of my jobs was to change the cat's box, which in those days before kitty litter was made up of torn strips of newspaper. I could never figure out whether the paper should be torn vertically or horizontally and always wound up with uneven fistfuls of paper instead of the long, neat strips my mother kept demonstrating. One day I was whiny and frustrated with this task when my father came home, and I told him petulantly that I couldn't do it. He erupted, screaming at me and finally kicking me as I cowered on the floor while my mother cried, "Don't hurt her, don't hurt her!" My father wouldn't tolerate incompetence and weakness, and against his rage my mother was ineffective. I didn't want to be like her, standing in the corner, screaming. I wanted to be like him: dominant and scary.

During Saul's adolescence the fighting between Minnie and S. K. intensified, and he concluded that his father always lost because of losing his temper, while Minnie's "quiet, even, rational style" would reduce him to impotently calling her bad Yiddish names. So Saul decided never to lose his temper, and according to him, he never did until he reached his forties. He admitted, however, "I think I have somewhat made up for it in the subsequent thirty-five years. And if someone now says to me, 'Did you have to lose your temper?' I have a simple answer, which is, 'Yes, for my health.'" He thought the fighting with his mother drove his father insane and ultimately killed him. My cousins told me that S. K. was actually committed to Rockland State Hospital for the Insane, where he died; they thought he had bipolar disorder, what used to be called manic-depression.

Just because the family had been kicked out of the synagogue didn't mean that Saul would be excused from having a bar mitzvah. But because the family eschewed the lower-class synagogue, Saul never went to Hebrew school. At thirteen, after some weeks of memorizing the Hebrew, having no idea what it meant, he had his bar mitzvah at the despised lower-class synagogue. After the ceremony, Saul declared in his interview transcript, he was "in the most violent rage that I can ever remember experiencing. I cannot remember enough of what was in my head at the time to know whether the focus of the rage was my own submissiveness or my parents' hypocrisy, but I made myself a vow that I would never ever again walk through the door of a House of God." He was to break this vow only twice, once to visit a beautiful cathedral in northern Italy, and another time to go into the disused synagogue in Toledo, Spain. He found it "sufficiently fumigated" after being empty for a couple of hundred years.

Once he spoke to me scornfully about what he saw as the pettiness and hypocritical lewdness of the synagogue members he had known in St. John. "They would study, study," he said, mimicking how they would *daven*, or pray, by rocking back and forth. "And the kind of question they would debate. . . . See, a guy is up fixing the roof, and he falls. There's a woman passing below in the street, and when this guy falls, his penis goes into her. Is it rape?"

In the summer of 1919, just after his bar mitzvah and while Saul was finishing the eighth grade, his father finally won the lawsuit against the synagogue. Having proved his point, S. K. sold the factory in St. John's and moved the whole family to Montreal, where he went into a spats manufacturing venture with a cousin from Halifax. Uncle Maishe saw this as the beginning of the family's decline. "There was always some new scintillating get-rich-quick scheme to make [S. K.] completely neglect his already well-established business." In Montreal, Saul and his siblings were introduced to a wider world. The Jewish kids were treated as gentiles and sent to the English-speaking schools, where Saul was popular because he was a good basketball player and again at the head of his class.

But just as Saul was finishing high school in May 1922, his mercurial father suddenly sold the spats business to another cousin and bought a dairy farm in the Catskill Mountains near the small town of Wurtsboro in Sullivan County, New York. The farm was seventy acres of arable land and one hundred acres of woodland and had two dozen milk cows. Saul and George were peremptorily summoned by S. K. to drop everything and move to the farm. Saul had hoped to go to college; he wanted to concentrate in theoretical physics, and it would have been better for him and so many others if he had done so.

Although he recalled loving the "look of the land, and the far perspective down the valley, and the changing of the seasons," the Wurtsboro farm was a disaster. There was no heat in any of the bedrooms, and all of the older children had to work seven days a week while S. K., who had the mistaken belief that he knew about farming from having grown up around peasants in Russia, still viewed himself more as a "manager" the way he had been at the factory. While Saul milked cows and tried to get balky bulls to mate, he brooded about his lost college opportunity and fumed under his father's authority. He said he never dared to ask his parents why he couldn't go to college, yet "I think that's what I never forgave him: telling me, 'I didn't go to school; you can't go to college, and you'll work eighty hours a week for me for no pay.'"

The family was subject to more overt anti-Semitism in the Catskills than in Canada. A neighbor shot one of their dogs because she was a "Jewish dog." Saul claimed that he and George took this guy out into the woods and "beat him up as viciously as one could without crippling him, and turned him loose." In an even more traumatic incident that seems to have expanded my father's resentment of patriarchal authority into hatred of the state, a Trooper shot the other family dog for barking at him while Saul stood helplessly by. "I never forgave the State Troopers for killing my dog," he said. "Before that point, making a big issue of anti-Semitism had never been my thing. But I seem to have been utterly outraged that they didn't ever try to come directly after me but got at us through killing my dog who, from her birth, had been French, not Jewish." (Saul often spoke of himself in this weird passive tense or in the third person.) Saul claimed to have had no fear of the Troopers,

Jewish Okies: the Cohen Family in the Catskills around 1923. First row, left to right: Minnie, Sarah (Saul's favorite sibling), George, family friend. Second row: Maishe, Dobie (in plaid dress), Saul (leaning against the post), family friend. And, of course, dogs. S. K. is not pictured.

despite being unarmed and slightly built. "I think they were puzzled," he speculated with eerie grandiosity, "by this kid who, without a hand-gun, yelling down the State Trooper, might have some unknown-to-them political strength that it would not be advisable to challenge." In his crazy courage, my father thought that he imitated his own father, "who, if his cause was in his mind just, would take on anyone of any weight. I always thought he was convinced that his cause was just."

The Troopers' cruelty had one unexpected effect on my father: it made him determined to keep dogs. Perhaps his rejected Judaism resided in them, or even his family loyalty. After Saul left my mother and me and established new households with new wives, he kept a succession of standard poodles: Lucy, the smartest, sweetest black poodle I ever knew; Jack and Jill; Rambi and Beau. The last time I saw him before his final illness, he had two brown miniatures. I wouldn't say these poodles were neglected, exactly, but they were untrained and ungroomed, and he never seemed to bond with them. They were like his ten children: greatly desired but rarely embraced.

/ / /

Back in the Catskills, Saul's resentment against his difficult and tyrannical father hardened into rebellion. Sick of doing unpaid labor on a failing farm in a backwater and longing to go to college, Saul conceived sometime in 1924 of what he ironically describes as "the most graceful plan I could think of" to escape the farm:

> My father was standing, musing, in the farmyard. I walked up to him. I struck a rather hard left fist smack in the middle of his chest. He was so violently—as I expected—outraged that a Jewish son could even conceive of striking his father, let alone carry it out, that he ran around looking for the largest size stone he could locate that would crush my skull with one blow.

"Borrowing" his brother George's suit and the family car, with nothing but ten or twelve dollars he'd managed to save, seventeen-year-old Saul drove to the Wurtsboro station and boarded a train for Greenwich Village.

/ / /

Once when I was in my late thirties and confident that I had finally escaped from his crushing predominance, I had dinner with my father Saul near his home on the Upper West Side of Manhattan. As we stood on the corner of Broadway and 91st Street, waiting for the light to change, I noticed that we were dressed nearly the same—running shoes, jeans, and plaid shirts—both standing with *hands on our hips, fingers forward*, a couple of tough Jewish guys.

CHAPTER 2

A WRITER'S INHERITANCE

After the failure of her second marriage, to Saul, breeding and showing purebred dogs became my mother's ambition and her sole preoccupation. In an obedience training class we met Richard Bauer, a lonely neighborhood boy, also destined to be gay, who had adopted Duke, a mismarked, rambunctious Boxer. I had Davy, the Shetland sheepdog that was supposed to distract me from Saul's departure. When Richard and I began showing our dogs in the new sport of obedience competition and in junior handling, where kids learned how to show off purebred dogs for their beauty—what is called "typiness"—we were becoming future "dog people."

Just having a dog doesn't make you part of the dog *world*. Most of the millions of Americans who have dogs are "pet people," as my father was. Pet people may love their dogs dearly. They may even attend a couple of dog training classes, but they don't go any further. In the eyes of most average people, dog people are loonies who have gone too far, who have chosen to "marry" not "their dogs," since dog people would not have sex with their dogs (it wouldn't be fair to the dogs) but, rather, their love of dogs.

As my mother, Virginia, did. (After the divorce, in fact, she would neglect me for the dogs, leaving me angry and deprived.) For gay people, "breeders" used to mean heterosexuals. But for dog people, a breeder is someone who brings more "purebred" dogs into the world, especially if they enter conformation competitions, or dog show beauty contests, hoping to "put championships on" their dogs and become known as top-notch to others in the know. Mercenaries who breed dogs purely for money or to supply pet shops with puppies bred in dubious or dirty conditions are not dog people. One's primary motive for breeding dogs has to be aesthetic or functional: to improve the breed.

Being a dog person is a matter more of attitude than of dog ownership as such. Yes, the dog person probably collects dog *tchotchkes*, such as china figurines of her chosen breed, and covers up her breasts with dog T-shirts showing, for instance, a person and several dogs in bed ("Never Sleep Alone Again"). But those are only symbols of the underlying fact that the dog person makes life decisions (for instance, getting over a devastating divorce) based on her love of dogs and involvement in dog-related activities. Being a dog person is an identity.

My mother's chosen dogs were papillons, tiny "lady dogs" that appeared in old and expensive paintings, dogs of the aristocracy who prided themselves on their own "breeding." I would say that my attraction to dogs as a group, "pure" or not, is not just *in* my DNA but actually *is* my DNA. In theory, I don't approve of this "purity" concept. I don't need anyone to tell me that I am not myself "purebred." Although my mother was descended exclusively from Northern Europeans, I was aware that Hitler and his blond Aryans would have sent me off to Auschwitz, and that, conversely, by Jewish law I am not Jewish because my mother was a *shiksa*. But no matter how inconvenient, facts must be faced. The beauty of certain purebred dogs floors me. I am devastated, thrilled, as before the shape and movements of certain feminine women.

/ / /

My first standard poodle was a consolation for turning forty. I'd had no contact with dog training since I'd left my mother's home at sixteen, but I decided to train her at an obedience school. A friend I made there bred black standards and offered me a poodle puppy from her most recent litter. I hesitated and agonized, knowing this was a life-changing decision. The dog trainer tried to convince me to take the pup. "With two dogs," she said, "you wouldn't be a pet person; you'd be a *dog* person." Just what I feared. To the adolescent me who had wanted to appear normal to my blonde suburban classmates, my mother and her dog friends had been an eccentric embarrassment, with their endless chit-chat about biased judges and promising male puppies whose testicles were tragically undescended.

My friend with the litter of poodle pups soon invited me to her apartment. Black curly creatures like balletic sheep were lounging in artistic poses on every chair and sofa; they rose to check me out with their elegant muzzles and almond-shaped eyes and suddenly I wanted dogs like that on *my* furniture. I wanted poodles, plural, to greet me at the door, their luxuriant curls like astrakhan under my fingers. I took the pup and became a poodle person, combining my father's breed of choice with a version of my mother's avocation.

For years my mother read through the *American Kennel Gazette*, for which she wrote a monthly column, keeping up on genetic problems and big show wins in other breeds and in other venues, such as tracking and herding. She trained many of her dogs in obedience, which had been our point of entry into dogdom back in the late 1940s. In 1992, when she was partially wheelchair-bound, I took her to England so she could fulfill her lifelong ambition to go to England, meeting up with breeders she had known only by mail and attending Crufts, the world's largest dog show, where we spent happy hours cruising the dogs, fingering leather leashes for sale, and watching the new sport of agility, which in my sixties would become my greatest pleasure.

Eventually Virginia became a preeminent breeder of papillons, with something like forty dogs. Paps are elegant lap dogs; their name comes from the French for butterfly because of their spectacular cantilevered ears. I grew up appreciating the importance of black ear fringes on a papillon and knowing why the liver-colored papillons that a foolish woman in Texas was breeding should be excluded from the gene pool. I went with my mother to so many of the national specialty shows, where papillon people gather once a year, that they all knew me, though I wasn't one of them. My mother joked that she never approved of my being a poodle person, because poodle people were annoyingly snooty, convinced that their poodles were more intelligent and capable than other breeds. But she showed her appreciation for my pushing her wheelchair around England by offering to go with me to the poodle national specialty. At that time, I had not been to a poodle specialty—I wasn't *that* nutty (that would come later). As my mother fell and bumped her way toward death, the poodles became more and more precious to me, as if I could read my mother's mute love in their almond eyes. A mediated, unspoken love was more comfortable to us both.

Whatever else I was to my mother, I was not her confidant. Her decisions were never discussed with me, and in 1952 I learned that we would leave New York (my neighborhood, my school, and my father Saul) for California only after all the plans had been made. (I was eleven.) Significant gestures infused with passions had to be crudely interpreted because they were never explained, as if Virginia and I were a deaf couple deprived even of sign language. Such was the stuff of our intimate and painfully intense mother-daughter life.

/ / /

In 1987, Richard Bauer, my childhood dog friend, called me: "Virginia needs you." I had been worried about her for several years. During my infrequent trips from New York to California in the 1980s my mother had insisted on meeting me at restaurants. Then her telephone broke, and she refused to repair it or to see me at all, communicating only by increasingly messed-up letters—her beloved IBM Selectric typewriter was gradually breaking down—leaving me anxiously out of touch. Richard, though, after a long career as a professional dog handler (mostly showing poodles), had become an outstanding dog show judge and continued to move in the same "doggie" circles as my mother. "Esther-Mary," Richard said sternly, using my childhood name, "that dog that Virginia shipped to R. was filthy and covered with fleas. R. thinks that your mother is in trouble; you'd better look into it."

Days later, defying her express orders to keep away, I showed up at my mother's front door, seven miles up a eucalyptus-lined two lane road in the hills above Stanford University. Neighbors I had hunted out by telephone had told me she had been seen wandering up and down the road, unkempt and smelly, so I was shocked but not surprised to find that my mother, at seventy-five, had become a bag lady with only a leaky roof over her head. The yard was littered with dog shit and rusty crates; her small wooden house had seen no upkeep or repair in years. She peered at me through the torn screen door from inside the house. She refused to let me enter while from inside came the frantic yapping of the trapped little dogs. At last I was presented with the project that my personality had been formed in relation to: rescuing my mother.

/ / /

My mother came from old Yankee stock. All her ancestors but one had come over before the Revolution, one of them on the Mayflower, and she was proud of it. We were descended, according to family lore, from Preservèd White, the elder brother of Peregrine, the first European American-born baby. How could I feel connected to Preservèd White, and why would I want to be? The Pilgrims were cultish religious fanatics. But then, our pasts must be owned.

My mother was fair-skinned, but my fathers were all dark, and as luck would have it, I am, too, though not as dark as they were. A mutt is what my students call us American mixed breeds. Eventually, I began to think of my butch self as bicultural and to appreciate my hybrid vigor. Because I grew up in New York among my father's Jewish relatives, I'm at home among Jews, though ignorant of the religion. Because I was raised by my WASP mother, though, my sensibility is more akin to that of the WASPs I don't resemble. Yet I came to understand that I wasn't as white as they were. My mother once corrected a hospital nurse who remarked on our resemblance as mother and daughter, "But her father was of a completely different race!"

When I started writing this memoir, I bought a genealogical software program and set about filling in my parents' family trees. My mother by that time was sliding into dementia, so she couldn't help much. Her side wasn't ambiguous the way my father's side was. I knew who my mother was—there was only one. But it was ambiguous in other ways. What was my relationship to these people I had no memory of, except for my mother's mother, Bertha Runkle, with whom we had lived during the 1950s? We could join the Daughters of the American Revolution, my mother always said, though it was understood that we wouldn't want to because of their racist policies. She had told me stories—"We're descended from the Mayflower"—that had no names attached, or if there were names, they were free-floating, affixed neither to historical events nor to my mother and me. Were they ancestors on my grandmother's side or my grandfather's? Were we really related to a president of MIT? To Adlai Stevenson? The ancestor who struck out from the Shaker colony in Kentucky and founded Peoria—was he four generations back? Five?

For a couple of weeks I worked on the genealogical chart every day and haunted the family tree forums on the Internet, trying to match up the fragments of stories to which I had never paid close attention with lines of descent and collateral branches. I filled in a lot of the blanks and learned the names of all four of my great-grandparents on my mother's side and most of the great-great-grandparents, all from the solid upper middle class of America. Most of the men were attorneys or army officers.

On the web I found a copy of an oil painting of my mother's father's mother's Peoria family, the Ballances. My great-great-grandfather Charles, the very one whose father, my mother had told me, had freed his Virginia slaves and joined the Kentucky Shakers, stands against a murky background—nightfall in Peoria? inside a Victorian parlor?—surrounded by his wife and seven children in poses that are stiffly artificial and otherworldly (most of the children gaze upward). All except for a blond babe on my great-great-grandmother Julia Schnebly's lap look cranky or depressed or both.

My mother's father, Louis Hermann Bash—whose male relatives on both sides fought in the Civil War on the Union side—graduated from West Point and made a career in the army, fighting in Mexico, the Philippines, and World War I. Eventually he became a four-star general and the quartermaster-general of the army. In 1904, he met and married my grandmother, Bertha Runkle. They would seem to have had few tastes, values, or beliefs in common.

/ / /

When it fell to me to clean up and sell my mother's ruined house in the hills up Page Mill Road behind Stanford, where she had moved to get away from Palo Alto's dog-restrictive zoning after I left home, I found that only one room was clean and orderly: the one that had been my grandmother Bertha's. Evidently, Virginia had never slept there or allowed the dogs into it or used it for any purpose other than to safeguard the memory of her parents and their ancestors. There she kept the pictures, books, and other heirlooms my grandmother and grandfather had treasured most. My eye was drawn immediately to a good-size watercolor painting of a white-haired woman in a floor-length white dress, sitting at an old-fashioned upright writing table. Although her back is to the viewer, the angle and position of her right arm suggests that she is writing. The room in which the woman sits is rustic but bright, the heavy exposed beams set off by light coming in the open doors and warmed by Oriental rugs. My mother explained this was a painting of my great-grandmother Lucia Gilbert in the family summerhouse at Onteora, New York, in the Catskills, not that far from the location of the Cohen family's failed dairy farm.

In each of the three retirement "homes" offering increasing levels of care that my mother lived in after we sold her house, the charming watercolor held pride of place, always set somewhat apart from the many paintings and photographs of papillons; a couple of large studio portraits of me as a child with a litter of Siamese kittens; and a hand-tinted photograph of her father, the general, also with a litter of kittens, which was the only one of him she liked because, she said, it showed his warm side. Stiff uniformed photographs of this grandfather I had never met had dominated my grandmother's house on Santa Rita Avenue in Palo Alto.

Finally, after a series of falls, my mother had to move out of the last suburban "home" with an airy room looking out on a garden that she and I had both hoped she would die in. Her room there, despite the stacks of "diapers" and the aluminum walker, was still kept personal by the watercolor and some books and the antique French wind-up clock that had accompanied my mother's parents on their honeymoon to the Philippines, where my grandfather had been stationed. The nursing home discouraged having many personal possessions, and, confused and angry, constantly telling me and anyone else that she just wanted to die, my mother no longer was able to care about them. At last I wrapped up the watercolor painting and took it back to New York on the airplane. In my apartment, quite a bit of wall space was devoted to photographs of me handling the poodles and framed copies of their obedience and agility titles. Somewhat apart, my talented great-grandmother Lucia Gilbert sat alone, writing, in a high-backed wooden chair in her solid country house more than a hundred years ago.

My female forebears were unconventional women, strong enough to follow their hearts and desires. (And, in my mother's case, to be punished for it.) Lucia Gilbert had been an abolitionist and a feminist, and she was the ancestor my mother always talked about the most. Lucia; her only child, Bertha; and her only child, my mother, had lived together in San Francisco when my army grandfather had been commandant of the Presidio, at the time a large army base on San Francisco Bay. The 1920 federal census recorded them as a household. Louis Bash was frequently absent on his warrior duties. (Thirty-some years later, my grandmother, mother, and I would live together in Palo Alto.)

"In my grandmother's eyes I was a child who could do no wrong," my mother said with evident satisfaction and gratitude, making it clear that her grandmother was the only family member who saw her this way. Lucia Gilbert Runkle had heart trouble and, in one of the many misfortunes of my mother's life, died aboard ship during the trip from San Francisco through the Panama Canal to Fort Hamilton in Brooklyn, where Louis Bash had been made commander and was bringing his womenfolk. My mother was ten, and she never forgave her parents for keeping her away from the burial at sea.

Lucia Gilbert had been born in West Brookfield, Massachusetts, in 1837 to a lawyer father and a mother who was the daughter of a clergyman. She graduated first in her class from high school at seventeen, but virtually all higher education for women was religious (she was not). Oberlin College, founded in 1837, was distant and co-ed (risky), and Vassar College, which her family might have seen as acceptable, wasn't founded until 1861. Still, after high school a teacher who lent her books from his own library encouraged her to read and write.

In the late 1850s, the family moved to New York City, settling in Waverly Place. When the Civil War broke out, Lucia's new husband, a man named Calhoun, and her brother Curtis both joined on the Union side. Calhoun was killed, but Lucia wrote letters to Curtis every week during the war, summarizing world and local events and reading the letters aloud to her family and their circle of Abolitionist friends, one of whom was the publisher of the *New York Tribune*, Horace Greeley, later a presidential candidate, who mentioned her writing to the editor of the *Tribune*.

Greeley persuaded Lucia to report on a grand ball that was being given for General Grant, assuring her that she would be picked up by carriage and escorted by a staff writer in evening clothes. Greeley was so pleased with her report that he asked her to write regularly for the paper. He overcame her reluctance—was journalism a respectable career for a Victorian lady?—by arguing that in opening this door, she would open it to all gifted women.

For many decades afterward, my great-grandmother wrote a regular column for the *Tribune*, as well as for *Harper's* and other journals, and I found many of them carefully pasted into two huge scrapbooks in my mother's unused and pristine bedroom. Lucia's authorial voice was not personal; even when, as rarely, she wrote in the first person, she never described details of her daily life or intimate thoughts. But despite being descended from what she admits were "generations of Presbyterian ministers," her work is somehow warm, tending toward both compassion and conviction. To me, her epistolary columns from a rail journey to the West Coast in 1869 are the high point of her work. The newly elected President Ulysses S. Grant dispatched Vice President Schuyler Colfax with seven other notables to celebrate the opening of the Transcontinental Railroad. The overall title of Lucia's series, "Letters from Next Door," implies the novel nearness of the western frontier.

Although the "fact" that Lucia had reported on the driving of the Golden Spike was a staple of my childhood, this doesn't seem possible, as the spike was driven in Promontory Point, Utah, on May 10, 1869, and the group didn't set out until the summer of that year. Although the railroad had just been completed, Lucia did report at length on the "Promontorese," whose thrown-together shacks "[command] a prospect whose foreground is railroad sheds, whose middle distance is a garbage ground where the Noble Savage with his little family cheerfully diversifies the plain, and beyond which a scrubby waste bristles off into space."

My commitment to social justice descended to me not only from Saul's Jewish communism but also from my mother's Abolitionist forebears. (Both my parents bragged that they had never crossed a picket line.) For instance, in her first cross-country column, after extolling the "capacious rolling splendor" of Mr. Pullman's new railroad cars, Lucia Gilbert skips lightly over the scenery in favor of the workers who made this feat possible:

> It is impossible to understand how enormous a triumph over physical defeats is this great Pacific Railroad till one has gone over it from end to end. To me, the scaling of the mountains with all its grading, and blasting, and tunnel-making, is not one bit more impressive than the slow, miserable toil that laid the rails along the horrible alkaline desert, its suns smiting, its winds piercing, its cruel dust sowing disease and death . . . I confess to a profound respect for the hard hands and bending backs that laid the one rail at a time. We owe Irishmen and Chinamen a debt of toleration and patience. There are not in America Yankee hands to do the work that Yankee brains devise. What if we stop railing for awhile at the condemned Irishman and consider whether, since he was both inevitable and necessary, we have made quite the wisest use of him.[1]

In February 1870 Lucia married a second time, to Cornelius Runkle, who, like her father, was a lawyer. (The president of MIT that my mother told me about was Cornelius's brother Daniel.) She wrote increasingly about domestic and women's issues from an upper-middle-class perspective: how to treat servants with respect, defending women's colleges. As the 1880s progressed, she wrote more, and more fervently, about women's rights. She continued to be active politically and was a founder of the League of Women voters.

Her views on marriage in general were not dewy-eyed. She advised wives who complained that their husbands had grown inattentive that "the simple truth is that most men neither expect, nor desire, nor intend, to be agreeable after marriage in the same way which commended them to acceptance during courtship." The wife should make life interesting to herself with artistic and intellectual pursuits, even if that does not rekindle the husband's interest:

> She must, of course, make the most that she can of her house and her table, herself and her children, whether her husband knows it or not, because that is so nominated in the bond between herself and

her conscience. That being done, let her not worry as to how she shall recover the vanished lover. Ten to one she cannot restore him. He is probably dead as the PHARAOHS; more probably, even, he never lived, save in her imagination.[2]

My grandmother Bertha was born in 1877, a late and only child. She grew up lonely and bookish, and although "the Runkles were hospitality itself and loved to fill their house with visitors, their friends' children were young men and women, while Bertha was in short frocks."[3] These visitors were distinguished writers and intellectuals of the post–Civil War era; the child acquired bulging portfolios of what is now called cultural capital:

> She never played with dolls, being unable to imagine them real, and seeming at this age to possess no maternal instinct whatever. . . . She was well supplied with fairy tales, but her critic mother detested the sloppy style and namby pamby sentiments of the average "child's book" and forbade their coming into the house. At a very early age, the small daughter was turned loose among the English classics. Her early adoration of Sir Walter Scott was probably largely responsible for her own efforts in the romantic vein.[4]

For some reason Bertha, like her mother, did not go to college, instead turning her hand to writing popular romantic novels. The first, *The Helmet of Navarre*, was published in 1901—by dint of her family connections—and became a best seller. Although the book is dedicated to her mother, I wonder what the high-minded Lucia really thought of it. Over the years, Bertha followed up with four more, which were somewhat less successful. My mother believed that Bertha stopped writing because General Bash thought it was inappropriate for his wife.[5]

My grandmother Bertha was a tall woman, and in early photographs she looks awkward and plain. Perhaps she was grateful to Lieutenant Louis Bash for rescuing her from old maidhood: she was twenty-seven when they married. Regardless, by my mother's account it was a lifelong love match. Bash was fiercely possessive of his wife. He did not want children, because, my mother said, he wanted Bertha all to himself. In this, though, Bertha finally prevailed, giving birth to my mother in 1913 in San Francisco.

Virginia hated this photo of herself with her military father. The Presidio, San Francisco, around 1921.

Bash had wanted a boy. From the beginning he carped at and criticized his daughter, so cruel to her about a minor weight problem that, as she was wasting away in her late eighties, she was still worried about being fat. Childhood pictures show a little blonde with an angry, defiant expression stifling in layers of old-fashioned children's clothing.

She disdained the society matron's life to which her father would have consigned her; refused to have a debut as he wanted; was bored by the young army officers he brought by to court her; and insisted on going to college, despite his belief that higher education would be wasted on a woman. She wanted to be a biologist, which he thought absurd. But he let her go to Rollins, a small, elite liberal arts college in Winter Park, Florida, hoping she'd meet a suitable mate.

My mother loved the Florida Everglades. Near the end of her life she confusedly repeated how proud she was of having been one of the few girls to take field trips there, fascinated by the exotic swamps, alligators, and birds. She was adventurous, with a naturalist turn of mind. In another clear sign of her future attractions and allegiances, she quit her sorority in protest when a pledge that everyone liked was blackballed after some alumna discovered she was Jewish. After two years, a professor she was especially close to was fired for his leftist political views, and she convinced her father to let her go to the University of Chicago to study zoology. Had he known where it would lead, he would have made her come home at once. It was 1933, during the Great Depression, and the kind of social unrest that Louis Bash detested was fermenting. (Once when a date of Virginia's ventured at the dinner table that he didn't see the point of religion, Bash replied, "Young man, religion is needed to control the masses.")

At Chicago my mother went wild. She drank too much and partied a lot. I gather she slept around. (When I asked why she hadn't aborted me, she said crisply, with evident discomfort, "I wanted a baby, and I had reason to know I couldn't get pregnant easily.") She hung out with a student group with ties to the Communist Party, where she met and fell in love with Saul Newton (then Cohen).[6]

Saul had already had his bohemian period in Greenwich Village, where he argued with self-taught philosophers and seduced arty women, supporting himself with whatever work he could get. The farm in the Catskills had failed; his crazy father was committed to Rockland State Hospital for the Insane; and Minnie and the kids had moved down to New York City. Saul chafed at his mother's proximity and at his obligations to the younger siblings. His yearning for higher education had led him to hitchhike out to the University of Wisconsin, where he enrolled and graduated. After college, he joined the Communist Party, which sent him to Chicago to organize shoe factories.

Nowhere in his taped ramblings does my father mention Virginia, but to her, their affair in the 1930s was hot. Once he told me how pretty she'd been then, how full of life. But when she found out he was married, she broke it off.

The disaster that my mother had been flirting with befell her in Chicago. I knew that she had been arrested in a demonstration while an undergraduate at Chicago and that her father had found out through an article in the *Chicago Tribune*. I had always wanted to see the article and in June 2007 I found that the paper had been archived back to 1885 and was available online. In seconds I found four articles that told the paper's version of the story. The hook was not that students had been arrested but that the daughter of the quartermaster-general of the U.S. Army was a "pink" who had been arrested several times at demonstrations for the rights of "negroes"; was the editor of the "pink" student newspaper *The Upsurge*; and had gone to court—dressed in a mink coat!—to defend a fellow radical. If the quotes attributed to her are accurate, she was prudently evasive about her communism and insouciant toward her father. When the reporter asked what her father thought of her Communist activities, my mother replied that she hadn't heard from him on the matter and said, "I am not responsible for anything that my father says." Despite her social justice politics, my mother always had a careless sense of entitlement that led her to speak her mind, often heedless of the effect or whom she hurt.

It is difficult to describe the *frisson* that seeing these newspaper articles—both chronicles and agents of my mother's tragedy—gave me. I had heard a vague and understated version from my mother for as long as I could remember. It was part of our intimate shared world, private. To find the external verification of this, and to discover that my mother was not just a bystander but a student leader of the struggle for "negro" equality, to see her disastrous brush with authority displayed alongside the real world of the Depression and of Chicago politics, was both thrilling and a shock. I felt so sad for her, this "plump girl with blue eyes and brown hair" dressed in her mink coat, who saucily answered the reporter's question about her Communist affiliations: "I'm not a Communist and I'll sue your paper if you call me one. Of course there is Communism at the University, but it is all unofficial."

The economic insights about money and power that she may have gained from her Communist friends did not extend to her own life. She was thumbing her nose at the person who was paying her bills, and he took it personally. Furious, General Bash rushed to Chicago and pulled her out of school to end the publicity. Although she was a senior within a month of graduating, she never got her degree. Instead she fled to New York, where she had two supportive older feminist "aunts"—surprisingly, Florence and Harriet were both cousins of Louis Bash through his Peoria connections.

My mother, Virginia.
New York City,
around 1937.

Her father having cut off her monthly allowance, Virginia went to work as an advertising writer for the Brooklyn department store Abraham & Straus. Around 1937, she married Laszlo Gluck, the man I long thought had been my father, the opposite of the man her father would have picked for her. Probably they met in the Party, because she had continued to belong in New York. They shared a love for Siamese cats, as I still do. Judging by the photographs he took of her, Laszlo Gluck adored her. They are the most becoming likenesses I've ever seen.

In his self-portraits Laszlo looks gaunt, very *mittel* European, with big, dark, haunted eyes and high cheekbones. When he died suddenly of a heart attack, Virginia was bereft and adrift, but she was only twenty-six, a pretty, intelligent, and damaged woman.

This is where William H. Miller, a Communist and big dark Jewish "hunk" (as my mother described him), charmed his way into the picture. He had attended college on a football scholarship and become a labor lawyer. This was a man my mother couldn't resist. She had liked and felt accepted by his immigrant parents, but when she became pregnant, he backed off, saying he couldn't disappoint his parents by marrying a *shiksa*. He came to see the infant me once, but within a year he had married a Jewish girl named Pearl, and my mother never saw him again.

Pregnant and alone, my mother turned to her paternal relatives for help. She was twenty-seven and a widow with a low-paying job. As she told it, they helped her arrange somehow for an abortion. Her bags were packed to go to the hospital when she was overcome by desire to keep the baby, despite everything. She called her feminist relatives Florence and Harriet, who encouraged her to do as she wished. They would stand by her.

When General Bash found out, he disinherited my mother, his only child, and me, his only grandchild. He is supposed to have ripped up the baby photos my mother sent, saying that he wasn't going to help support the "bastard kid of some Jew Communist." Ironically, although I never noticed the resemblance—my mother preferred to say I looked like my Jewish father—a friend of mine, upon seeing Bash's photograph, remarked that I looked a lot like him. The fickle finger of fate, as we used to say in college and as the ancient Athenians pointed out, was not to be denied. Legitimate or not, as the only child of the only child of the only boy of the oldest child of Charles Ballance of Peoria, I did finally inherit many family papers and photographs, including lovely quilts from Peoria and all of Louis Bash's love letters to his wife, Bertha; his war records and journals; even his silver stars and tie pins and Legion of Honor rosette, bestowed by a grateful French nation for his efforts in World War I. A meticulous expense record that my grandfather kept shows that in November 1940, the month I was born, he sent Virginia money through a relative, then again in January and February 1941. Yet he never relented, never spoke to her again, and never, as long as he lived, allowed Bertha to meet with her daughter and granddaughter.

How often does the woman whose body bridges antagonistic worlds fall into the chasm below? My mother was rejected by her lover for not being Jewish enough and then rejected by her father for being a Jew-lover.

Photograph from Virginia's address book of Saul, my father, around 1940.

The man who stepped in was Saul, who had moved to New York after fighting and being wounded in the Spanish Civil War. He was single now, and they resumed their romance, writing to each other during his second enlistment, in World War II. When he came back, they married, although she knew he was the unfaithful type. After all, he had cheated on his first wife with her and had had a mistress over in Europe. She was fatalistic: "He was just that kind of man."

Toward the end of her life, my mother, like Saul, had dementia. Inside her address book I was astonished to find a romantic snapshot of young Saul. When I asked my mother about it, she looked up from her wheelchair with a sly smile. "He was the love of my life, you know." They'd been divorced since 1949. "Oh Mom," I blurted out, "he was a terrible man." Underneath the photo of sexy Saul was one of Saul the father, *kvelling*, glowing with pride as I showed off the cast I got breaking my wrist on the jungle gym, and underneath that, three pictures of me, ages maybe five to eight, all in boys' bathing trunks at a public playground. Presumably my mother had arranged those photos in the order of their importance to her.

/ / /

By the second year of my parents' marriage Saul was having a secret affair with Dr. Jane Pearce, a big-name psychiatrist at the William Alanson White Institute, where by this time my mother was an administrative assistant to the well-known psychiatrist Clara Thompson. They had all hung out during the University of Chicago days, where Jane had gotten both a Ph.D. and her medical training. Saul was done fighting the fascists. Although he only had a bachelor's degree he wanted to become a therapist, and Jane Pearce represented his entrée and his future.

The summer we went to Maine, when I learned to steer the Dodge sitting on my father's lap, he sneaked off to meet Jane at a motel, where she gave him an ultimatum: she was approaching forty and wanted kids. My mother must have sensed the marriage was shaky, so when Saul said he wanted to adopt me, she was reassured that he was committed. He was, just not to her. Maybe he saw me as the first of what would become his ten children, his patrimony. It seems that he loved me, because he always kept me around, the way the moon, also a chip off the old block, is kept around by the earth. As soon as the adoption was final he announced he wanted a divorce and would marry Jane.

For my mother the divorce was a train wreck and to my knowledge she never had another date with a man for the rest of her life, though she was only thirty-five when Saul dumped her. Not that Jane was younger, or prettier, but she had the University of Chicago degrees my mother had never finished. She was the doctor that my mother had thought of becoming, the important figure at the institute where my mother was only a glorified secretary.

No wonder Virginia was despondent. She left the institute to get away from Saul and Jane, taking a job she disliked managing an art gallery. She had no eye for painting, and the boss was difficult. The brittleness, paranoia, and resentment that had been a legacy of her melancholy childhood came to the fore. She stopped cleaning our apartment.

I rarely heard her laugh, she whose wit was one of her best qualities. She shut herself into the bedroom that once had been theirs. I was in her way, always underfoot or doing something wrong. Once when I talked favorably about Saul and Jane she slapped my face. From her horrified expression I saw she hated herself for such a revealing outburst and for striking me in anger.

Our Upper East Side apartment gathered dust underneath the tattered furniture. Instead of her reading to me from *Dr. Doolittle* and *Winnie the Pooh*, instead of her witty and usually disparaging remarks on the world and its inhabitants making me laugh, she would come home from work, put dinner on the table in silence, and retreat to her room, the door slamming shut with a finality that repulsed contact. It was all she could do to go to work, to shop for food, to cook. No longer her darling, I was now a burden.

This rejection was a disaster for my eight-year-old self. For better or ill, I had been raised only by her during the six years before her marriage to Saul, and although my big brown eyes must have reminded her of her feckless lover, Miller, she had paid dearly to keep me. During those early years our bond was like emotional superglue; we were stuck on each other. She was proud of my cleverness, good looks, and vigorous good health, while everything about her enchanted me: her kisses, her touch—in those early years she was physically affectionate—her beautiful inflections and awesome vocabulary, the smell of her Tweed perfume, her quick wit. When she picked me up from kindergarten I puffed up with pride at having the prettiest mother.

I can see the core of my future lesbianism in this early passion for my mother *and* what I felt as her rejection; the violent rupture of our mutuality, which had already been compromised by Saul's arrival in our lives. From this point onward, she was withdrawn, and I was angry.

My mother's friends, pointing to the ill effects on me of her depression, advised her to seek therapy, but when she did, the outcome was neither a new man nor a return to our old intimacy. Her new life, as she began to want to live, would be made with dogs. We soon acquired two Shetland sheepdogs, but soon she had decided to breed papillons, and she bought a breeding pair.

In 1952, General Louis Bash died in California. Within weeks, Virginia and her mother resumed contact, and within months Virginia had agreed to move to Palo Alto to care for her mother, who was in her seventies and not in good health. For my mother it meant leaving her burned-out life in New York, reconciliation with her mother. She would no longer have to work for a living or even keep house, as my grandmother had a maid. Virginia would be free to breed dogs on a bigger scale. She would never have agreed to leave me with Saul, as I always suspected my grandmother would have wished. But she also didn't consult me and seems never to have considered how difficult the change might be for me, even discounting the fact that I did not know that my birth had caused the family rift. I belonged in New York where being half-Jewish wasn't a problem and where preferring stickball to dolls and blue jeans to dresses was OK with my progressive elementary school. For me, living in a California suburb wasn't going to be an adventure; it was going to be a catastrophe.

/ / /

If her mother's and grandmother's literary accomplishments and outspoken feminism set my mother on a path to distinction, her father's harsh judgments and crankiness made her doubt her right to even try. That my mother was deeply influenced by her matrilineal literary heritage is something I knew, however imperfectly, all my life. My most enduring memory of her after we moved to Palo Alto was of her writing by hand in what she called her journals, gray high school notebooks. After she died I inherited all twenty-one volumes. With difficulty—we are supposed to be private people—I made myself read the first three books. They are consumed with the minutia of dog breeding and showing: the puppies weighed this much on Friday; she sold that tricolor puppy on Wednesday. Her mother and daughter appear only when we were involved in dog matters. After a while she began writing the papillon column for the *Kennel Gazette* and for her local dog obedience club.

Reading and writing were like breathing in her. Before dementia starting taking her, I tried to get my mother to use a computer. She sat down tentatively in front of the screen, just to try the keyboard. Where most people would have typed "the quick brown fox jumped over the lazy dog," my mother whipped off a few paragraphs that still make me laugh and that only she could have written:

This has been a most unpleasant afternoon. There have been UFOs over the patio and gremlins on the balcony. And this is driving me screwy.

Lucile has been most unpleasant about the whole gremlins thing. She keeps stuffing her shoes into the closet to save them. When I told her gremlins are allergic to shoes and would never touch them she threw the rice pudding at me.

Henry came just then fresh from his bath and he said gremlins eat shoes and she should go down to the cellar and get some turnips which would be sure to repel any creatures from outer space. By this time Lucile was hysterical and insisted that one of the gremlins was her long lost lover whom she met in New Zealand twenty-five years ago.

Henry said some aliens are lovable and Lucile should just learn to accept them. That is not very likely. Martha said that Lucile has never accepted leprechauns so how can she be expected to accept ordinary aliens?

After improvising whimsically for a few more paragraphs she ended,

We all miss you very much, John. The weather is beautiful here in this season and I hope you can visit us before your trip to Namibia.

Namibia? My mother's brain could cut and turn like a border collie herding sheep, and until the dementia she could usually win at Scrabble. Except for board games and cards, she never played with me, as parents do today. She was not athletic and pretended no interest in my Lincoln Logs and toy soldiers. The most pleasurable bond between us flowed through words. She starting teaching me to read with the Burma Shave Road signs, typically six red-and-white signs placed sequentially by the roadside: "Our fortune / Is your / Shaven face / It's our best / Advertising space / Burma-Shave."

We competed to see how many license plates from different states we could identify, rolling the names around our tongues for fun. At dog shows she taught me the names of all the breeds: Keeshond, Chow-Chow, Golden Retriever. After the divorce we went to almost every Gilbert and Sullivan operetta put on by a neighborhood company. My mother wasn't at all musical; it was all about the clever dialogue and the patter songs. I wonder what she thought of "I am the very model of a modern Major-General . . ."

/ / /

In the beginning of 1988, three winter months after Richard had called me, my mother, who had adamantly refused all of my offers of help except for a few groceries, collapsed on the floor of her unheated hovel crippled by what turned out to be three herniated disks. "I lay there for twenty-four hours," she told me later from her hospital bed, "deciding whether I wanted to live." (Later still, when she had recovered and was settled in a retirement community, she added dryly, "I decided you would be upset if I died.") Eventually she had crawled through the house to her car, and, releasing the emergency brake after a prolonged struggle, coasted down the hill to the nearest neighbor, who called the paramedics. Before friends in the Northern California Papillon Club could get into the house, several of the weaker dogs died; the survivors were snapped up by breeders eager to have one of my mother's Mariposa papillons.

My mother had crawled out of her house along a path through walls of garbage three feet high—not just papers but empty dog food cans and hundreds of gallon bottles of cheap wine, for she had fallen (back, I understood later) into alcoholism. Not one appliance was still working. The toilet "flushed" by pouring a bucket of water down it. Cobwebs looped in festoons from every ceiling lamp and cabinet. The dogs had chewed the legs off furniture, and the males had lifted their legs all over. When a real estate lady came to look over the property, fleas jumped up and clung to her nylon hose. A crew of sweet-faced, hardworking Mexican immigrants filled four dumpsters with the wreckage of my mother's life. In the years afterward, my mother and I never discussed how this creeping disaster overtook her, or even acknowledged that it did.

When, after her collapse, I walked into my mother's room in the San Jose county hospital, she threw her arms up toward me from her bed and cried out, "Lover!" It seemed her predicament made her drop her guard, and all her filters were temporarily gone. Suddenly we were the too close mother and child again. Only now I would be the protector she had raised me to be. On her lap was the yellow legal pad on which she had been writing, despite her self-inflicted poverty, drunkenness, and physical misery; despite the needs of the little dogs she was each day less able to meet.

My mother's *stuff*, which were the dogs but also the dog hair dust bunnies that began, in the months after Saul left, to gather like free-floating anxiety under a couch whose edges were scratched into pulps by the cats, had defeated her finally. Yet one more time she decided to live, for her daughter "lover" and that yellow legal pad that eventually would become *The Papillon Primer*, a lovely little book for first-time owners that she designed and published herself and for which she won an American Kennel Club dog writer award in 1989. It would turn out to be her only book.

What did I inherit from my mother, Virginia? She gave me half of my genome and much more than half of my educated, upper-middle-class mind. Like her, I have a sense of entitlement of which I was not aware as a child. And then I had the sweet though cold revenge of receiving the family heirlooms and what was left of my grandparents' money. She also passed on her love of dogs, her ingrained feminism, and the pleasure of making words out of thoughts and experience. My great-grandmother Lucia had been a journalist; my grandmother Bertha, a novelist; and my mother, a dog writer. Would I carry on, and how?

—— CHAPTER 3 ——

MANHATTAN TOMBOY

> I spent much of my childhood trying to distinguish iden-
> tification from desire, asking myself, "Am I in love with
> Julie Andrews, or do I think I am Julie Andrews?"
>
> —WAYNE KOESTENBAUM, *The Queen's Throat*

Everyone thought me a beautiful baby, Virginia always said, and she was probably stunned when the general rejected my smiling studio baby portrait with a slur. My mother's disinheritance and single motherhood made us poor during the war. We lived in a small walkup tenement apartment on East 33rd Street almost under the racketing elevated train. In one of my earliest memories, my mother and I were riding on the Second Avenue bus when she burst into tears over losing her ration book. Meat was rationed, as were butter and sugar. I comforted her, already her would-be protector.

My love for my mother was lodged in the deepest part of me. My earliest memory is of an idyllic sunlit afternoon in the country. Near a pretty brook, my mother and another woman are eating a picnic lunch on the grass, chatting and laughing. I watch from a little distance, out of the picture, longing to be near her. Some of my partners have told me their mothers were intrusive, watching, policing. *My* mother commanded my gaze, as later would my lovers. Later on, when Virginia and I were in painful conflict, she developed an unconscious tic of touching her pubic area, a habit that embarrassed and angered me. As a teenager trying to break away, I experienced this pointing to her vagina as forcing me to look at her. The creation of a lesbian; shrinks make of it what you will. Like my dark fathers, I was attracted to my mother's fair skin and light eyes. Is this a form of self-hate, a delicious eroticism, or both?

/ / /

In my favorite photo, the setting is urban: a kids' playground. In the background are a 1940s baby carriage and a grim brick building—public toilets. My wasp mother and her little guy. Her chestnut hair is braided around her head like a laurel wreath or a halo. She wears a plain cotton dress, modestly holding her legs together and smiling into the camera. One knee is exposed, though. The edge of her skirt partly covers my thigh.

I must have been four or five. My mother thought bathing suit tops for little girls premature, a commercially motivated imposition of femininity, so I wear a boy's bathing suit, feet swinging free. You can tell I'm a girl because my brown hair covers my ears. I am leaning into the crook of my mother's arm. Protectively, she circles my shoulders from behind. The outside hand pulls me into her, the closer one seems to ward off some danger to my chest. I stare out—unsmiling—as if to say, *this is my spot.*

/ / /

My child body was a strong and capable instrument somehow stuffed into the word "girl." I was the first kid up the jungle gym, as good as any of the boys at stoop ball. All my friends were boys—girls were dumb. I had nothing in common with them. But because of my XX chromosomes, my body is female and I was stuck in the girl gender, linked worldwide to hard work, low pay, disrespect, and cheating husbands. Impossible to refuse girlhood, so I refused femininity.

When Saul came back from the war and moved in with us, everything

Her mother's "little guy." New York City, around 1946.

changed. He monopolized my mother's attention, and I was intensely jealous of him. Yet I also idolized this tough, sinewy fighting man who doted on me, hoisted me on his shoulders to watch the Macy's Thanksgiving Day Parade, and gave me boy's toys for my birthday. After the penury my mother and I had suffered during the war we now had— thanks to Saul—butter, coffee, a telephone, even a car. And Saul's siblings George, Dobie, and Maishe opened their homes and hearts to me and made me feel that, for the first time, I had family beyond my mother. Collectively, the Cohens and their wives were mainly responsible for my lifelong attraction to Jews and Jewish culture and my own (partial) sense of Jewishness.

At that time, East 33rd Street was a working-class, mostly Italian neighborhood. In the first grade, I went to the local public school, where we marched down the halls in line. The steel-brassiered Catholic and Jewish lady teachers hit our hands with rulers and made us keep quiet unless called on.

As both my parents worked, I was what was later called a latchkey kid and at a loose end after school. My father found out that a neighbor man was sexually molesting me. I have no memory of this misadventure, whose only visible trace is a bite scar on my left hand where the neighbor's little terrier is supposed to have bitten me. But when Saul found out—("He was licking your cunt" was how he later put it)—he threatened in a rage to shoot the neighbor if he ever touched me again. (At that time, I doubt that police were called in such cases.) Saul had killed men during the wars I thought. He showed me the scar from the bullet wound in his foot; his khaki uniform hung stiff and starched in the closet, along with his German Luger captured from a dead soldier. People were afraid of him, and I was impressed.

My best neighborhood friend was Frankie, a tough ten-year-old boy I idolized, a guy I was playing sex games with, thinking that we were buddies, that I was a younger version of him, that I could even be him. Then came the day he tried to use me as a sexual favor for his real buddies. I refused to play sex games with them or ever speak to Frankie again, and my rage and shame over his betrayal threw me into traumatic shock. The guys had made me understand that they were the boys, and I was just a body they wanted to use. After this, I knew I was not and would

This photo of Saul and me captures some of the ambiguities of our early relationship. New York City, around 1947.

not become a boy. But that didn't make me a girl. That way meant weakness, shame. Somehow it was my fault that men exposed themselves to me in the park; that they rubbed up against me in the trains; that boys tried to take advantage. I became an anti-girl, a girl refusenik, caught between genders.

These experiences of vulnerability and terror were surely part of what made me so conflicted about men sexually. But many, maybe most, girls are violated in these and far worse ways, with diverse outcomes. There are girls who become angry or reasonably contented wives, girls who become nuns or whores, girls who become recluses or eccentrics, scientists or protectors of wildlife. Have not many of them had their sense of bodily and moral integrity threatened or seriously damaged by boys and men whose power to hurt or help females is so great?

Whether because of these incidents (if my parents knew about them) or because they now had two incomes or because my mother was tired of correcting the working-class accents I was copying, in 1948, when I was just turning seven, we moved uptown, from the tenement, to East 78th Street and a two-bedroom apartment in an elevator building. Much against their principled belief in public education, my parents pulled me out of public school in favor of the Downtown Community School (DCS), founded just three years previously by left-wing parents and educators who believed in racial equality and bringing out children's presumed potential. Among adults involved in the school at different times were Lillian Hellman, Margaret Mead, the African American folk singer Josh White, and Pete Seeger (who taught music there). Most children were named Noah and Peter instead of Frankie and Vito. Along with Elisabeth Irwin and the Little Red School House, DCS was training the future generation of New York leftists.[1]

I loved DCS and was as comfortable there as my prickly skin would allow. My cousin Betty, the daughter of Saul's brother George, went there in a higher grade and looked out for me. It was just off the corner of 11th Street and Second Avenue, across from St. Mark's Church, that bastion of left-wingers. I played catch with Noah Bernhardt on the St. Mark's cobblestones. Around the corner were the Yiddish theaters and the Lower East Side, still home to thousands of Jews. Lodged in a six-story brick building, DCS was emblematic of my parents' progressive worldview. The artistic, social, and political values I absorbed there are still mine. My mother always blamed "that progressive school" for my poor spelling skills, and I did not learn to write script or conjugate verbs. Instead we sang along with Burl Ives and Pete Seeger records ("Streets of Laredo," "I'm Stickin' with the Union"). The arts were emphasized; we were taught that the Indians were here first and that there was nothing wrong with "Negros," though if any of my classmates were black, I don't remember them. (My fourth-grade teacher was black, and I disliked her intensely, probably because she taught math, for which I had no gift.)

As an eight-year-old, my everyday school outfit was sneakers, jeans, a polo shirt, and a blue Brooklyn Dodgers baseball cap. (The rivalry between the "progressive" Dodgers and the pinstriped "capitalist" Yankees

The Short Ranger, New York City, around 1948.

was serious in my youth.) For dress-up, I was the Lone Ranger, whom I called the Long Ranger, so my father called me the Short Ranger.

An urban urchin, I grew accustomed to taking the elevated train, the subway, the buses on my own between home and my school, sixty-six blocks away, threading through the drunks on skid row in the shadows under the elevated train near my 11th Street school, unfazed by traffic and already a jay walker.

Oscar Wilde said that life imitates art. More than finger painting at DCS, the images that formed the particulars of my gender identity came from radio, books, and photographs of football players I cut out from my parents' *New York Times*. Books about horses and pirates' lost treasure, baseball, anything with adventure. On radio "Hi-yo, Silver, away!"

and Sergeant Preston of the Yukon and his dog, King. Movies at the kids' Saturday matinee in the local movie house, dreaming myself into Tyrone Power; Errol Flynn the buccaneer running his sword through villainous Basil Rathbone. My intrepid body and dominating (though needy) personality seemed to others—and to my child self—to be masculine. On the street and on the elevated train I was often mistaken for a boy. I spent endless hours outside playing stickball and stoopball and, later at summer camp, tennis, basketball—competitive physical games.

Women were as good as men, in my mother's opinion, and she vocally resented men's privileges and presumptions. You could even say she was a female chauvinist, a kind of woman's woman. Predictable in her attraction to domineering men, she defied convention in many other ways. Besides having been a Communist and having an illegitimate baby, she was brainy and proud of it. She disliked shopping, and I don't know how she acquired her WASPy tweeds and classic tailoring. She wore perfume (Tweed, which, according to Amazon, is "an elegant and sophisticated fragrance with a classic English branding," which describes my mother's upbringing) but little makeup beyond lipstick, which was obligatory for women then.

She wanted me to be intelligent and articulate like her, but tended to discourage my few feminine inclinations. Two of my most vivid memories regarding femininity occurred after the divorce, when my mother was at her most short-tempered and unresponsive. There was an epidemic of head lice at DCS, and the mandated remedy was to cut off all long hair, the better to shampoo away the parasites. My mother took me to the beauty salon at a department store to have my braids cut off. I sniveled and cried at losing my braids, much to my mother's annoyance. Confusedly, I felt that this was my one claim to being like other girls but could not articulate this to my mother, who would have surely dismissed it as nonsense.

Then there was the time my father—who enjoyed shopping for the women in his life and was more affluent after his marriage to Jane Pearce—bought me a frilly white dress. When I brought it home my mother was furious. "He doesn't care that I'll have to bleach and iron this thing," she shouted (as a WASP, "shouting" meant raising her voice). I never wore it. Not that I wanted the dress like I'd wanted the braids, but lesson learned: frills are a pain in the ass and not for you.

My father was more inconsistent. I was supposed to be tough, to know how to box and ride a bike on my own. It was OK for me to reject dolls and play with toy soldiers. But I should also wear frilly white dresses, especially as I got older, a preference on his part that I increasingly resisted. My father's abstract but genuine feminist beliefs—women should get higher education, work, and be able to drive and get abortions—was more than tempered by his macho arrogance and avid pursuit of compliant and even reluctant skirts.

What they had in common as parents, besides their left-wing politics, was the commandment "Don't make emotional demands." I was never babied, expected to fend for myself and deal with my fears on my own time. By eleven, I was flying alone from California to see Saul in New York and back (with a mandatory stop in Denver or Chicago), and although my mother would take me to the airport, my father never considered it necessary to meet me or drop me off for the return flight. In fact, he often forgot which day I was arriving, and the household was surprised when I turned up. My emotional problems, if they were noticed, were met with exasperation or deflection: send her to a shrink, to summer camp, or to boarding school.

My love for my parents grew in rocky soil, with deep and tenacious roots. I both admired and feared them. My father held ferocious opinions that could not be contradicted about every conceivable subject, from the righteousness of Chairman Mao and the backwardness of Tibetan monks ("feudal oppressors," according to him) to the inadequacy of all parenting except his own. He spoke slowly, and, except when he lost his temper in screaming tirades, softly, with long pauses between sentences, during which you were not to interrupt.

My mother also held fixed beliefs of her class—for instance, that colored ink, hair dye, and the two-tone cars popular in the 1950s were vulgar. When I repeated the latter assertion, my father said, "There's nothing wrong with two-tone cars. A car is not a solemn event." My mother thought that television was trivial (we didn't own one). My father had the biggest televisions made. To him, money was to be enjoyed and spent. My mother, understandably, did not trust men, and none of the boys and men I later dated were, in her view, good enough for me. My parents were both confident talkers, my father holding forth like the dictator of a banana republic and my mother with her crisp inherited authority. (After finally getting a television set, she could beat most contestants on *Jeopardy*, her favorite program.) But after my youngest years, when it came to expressions of emotional connection, loving concern, or signs of tenderness, my father and mother were at a loss, at least with me. We signaled our deepest feelings toward and about each other, if at all, in a semaphore in which none of us were fluent.

In 1949, our little family was split apart by my parents' divorce. Saul wanted joint custody, but my mother fought him, and he got only visitation rights. At that time, adultery was one of the few grounds for divorce, and men had to arrange for a photographer to "happen upon" the carnal scene, which may have put him at a disadvantage in the custody fight. Unlike many divorced fathers, he sent alimony for my mother (though she complained the checks were often late) and child support for me until I went to boarding school, at which point he took over my entire support. He paid for my college and the first year of graduate school and sent me a small allowance, sometimes late but always there, enough to afford me a bike in college. True to our first bond driving the old Dodge car, he bought me several used cars, starting when I was sixteen. He paid for both of my abortions. We would go out to his favorite Chinese restaurant when I visited New York. I always knew that in his disconnected way he had my back. About once a month I dream of him still, and despite everything, he is always helping me go somewhere or achieve something.

In a Manhattan seafood restaurant, while I ate myself sick on oyster crackers, Saul introduced me to my "stepmother," Dr. Jane Pearce, his new wife with whom he would soon have three children. I slumped sullenly in the booth with my baseball cap pulled down over my eyes, refusing to meet Jane's gaze or speak to her as they both blew cigarette smoke into the space between us. He was leaving my mother and me for this woman.

Jane was an ample woman with a round face, a Texas accent, and slightly bulging light-blue eyes, a well-known therapist at the William Alanson White Institute for Psychoanalysis, where Saul was studying to be a shrink. They bought a five-story brownstone building on West 77th Street, almost facing the Hudson River. Despite my fears of abandonment, Saul, who was now my de jure as well as my de facto father, made it clear I was always welcome, and I frequently journeyed over there by crosstown bus.

Jane, unlike my princess of a mother who perhaps had never truly expected to work for a living, was an unequivocal professional woman—she held both a Ph.D. and an M.D. from the University of Chicago—while at the same time she adored Saul and would do anything to keep him. (He stayed unfaithfully married to her for twenty years before leaving her for wife number five, the late Joan Harvey, a younger, prettier woman who had been a soap opera actress and probably his patient.) The basement of their brownstone was a large kitchen and dining room, where the black housekeepers Ida Mae and then Daisy, who were much more emotionally generous than the shrinks above, held sway. Jane did almost no childcare and never cooked so much as an egg.

The first floor of the brownstone held two offices, one for each of them, separated by a lobby. The largest room on the floor above was their master bedroom. As a teenager I once walked into it to see Saul's naked back pounding up and down on Jane, much to all of our embarrassment. But this was one of Saul's episodic generous moments. "That'll teach you not to knock," he said wryly. Jane never referred to this incident. It was also in this bedroom where I realized that Jane was a drunk. Being always hung over she often slept late, and as I passed down the stairway from the smaller bedrooms above, she would try to get me to come and lie in bed with her, her speech slurred and her whole body exuding vodka. These advances were not sexual but intended to be affectionate. She later told me—while writing me a check for $1,000 toward a down payment to buy my first apartment—that she had always felt guilty for not mothering me more. I thanked her sincerely; there was no point in saying that I already had a mother and had not wanted another.

/ / /

After World War II, New York City had been in a good mood. In 1947, my progressive school was united in rooting for Jackie Robinson to succeed with the Brooklyn Dodgers and integrate Major League Baseball. But the school and my parents' social world divided over Henry Wallace's presidential campaign in 1948.

Wallace, a former vice president under FDR, ran for president at the head of the Progressive Party against the Democratic candidate, Harry Truman. Wallace opposed Truman's hardline policies toward the Soviet Union in the Cold War, and just as important to my parents, he advocated an end to segregation—he refused to appear before segregated audiences. He favored black voting rights and universal health care.

But many liberals and conservatives believed that the Progressive Party was a Communist front. I don't know exactly when Saul left the Party under whose banner he had fought in Spain, but I think it was after he came back from World War II. My mother had been expelled from the Party in 1940 for giving birth to me, an illegitimate child. When, after the war, a woman from the Party's Women's Bureau called to express her outrage over my mother's expulsion and beg her to come back, my mother declined, telling me later, "I had kind of lost heart." Yet Henry Wallace's campaign represented the values of social and racial equality that they both believed in, and for reasons that I accepted rather than understood, my parents were staunch Wallace supporters. This is my first political memory. Much later I learned that the Mattachine Society, the first gay rights organization, was founded by a group called "Bachelors for Wallace."

From fights and shouted insults at school I also knew that some of the kids and their parents—whose views proved dominant in the election—fervently disagreed. There was tension and suspicion all around, and it had the feel of a decisive moment. My parents' belief that victory for Truman would be disastrous for the left was proved correct when the Cold War set in and Senator Joseph McCarthy began persecuting former Communists and their "pinko" sympathizers. (My father lost his passport during that period.)

In the months that led up to the divorce and after it I was subject to dark moods. Wallace's loss and the political tension at DCS combined with my parents' rupturing marriage to create an aura of dread. I was terrorized by the dead black cat that I saw in the gutter, wedged between a car tire and the sidewalk near the local candy store. I became fearful and aggressive, cutting into my wooden desk with a kitchen knife and bullying a younger neighbor boy until his parents complained to my mother. A preview of a Frankenstein movie terrified me into barricading my bedroom with chairs. One night I knocked on my mother's bedroom door looking for comfort, and when she didn't respond, I cowered in the foyer closet crying. When my mother came out and found me, she was furious; she had to go to work the next day. My father arranged for me to have a Rorschach test, and I saw all kinds of monsters in the inkblots.

I was angry that Truman was president and the future seemed dangerous; angry that Saul had disrupted our lives, got me to love him, and then left; angry that my supposed "real" father, Laszlo Gluck, had died; angry that I wasn't a boy; angry that my mother was cold, removed, and cranky. That churning inside comforted my loneliness and let me know I was strong and that I would survive no matter how hurt. Throughout my life this sense of being strong through anger—my one reliable defense—has stayed with me. I wouldn't be pushed around; I would fight back when I was wounded and lash out—like my father—or sulk. Anger, though not as strong as suppleness, is better than being crushed by adversity. Often I have wondered at people who seemed defeated by circumstances less daunting than mine.

In the summer of 1949, to have time for herself and to give me a change of scene, my mother decided to send me to Belgian Village Camp for Girls in the Berkshire Mountains. Never having been away from my mother before, I was horribly homesick. But the counselors showed me concern and sweetness that my mother could not. During the seven summers I spent at Belgian Village, my scope enlarged beyond the stoops and traffic lights of New York City. I played tennis, rode horses (that cost extra which my father paid for), learned to swim, sang around the campfire, and gathered wild berries. I met attractive girls and women: friends, crushes, and role models.

Mary Beasley, the founder of Belgian Village, was a physical education teacher at the Dalton School. Bertha Rankin, her companion, was also a teacher, a chubby woman whom we campers thought silly, especially for her fanatical devotion to the American poet William Cullen Bryant, a Cummington native son whom none of us had ever heard of and whose poetry went right over our heads. Mary's position at Dalton gave her connections to well-off New York parents who wanted to get rid of their kids for the summer or give them new experiences, or both. Going to summer camp was common among the New York kids I knew. Although there were no girls from my school—my only friends there were boys—the campers could have been students at DCS, most of them. There was no jarring transition, and pretty quickly I liked not having men and boys around. Many campers were Jewish, and many probably came from left-wing homes like mine. (Kathy Boudin, a couple of years younger than me and later of the Weather Underground, was a camper there for a couple of summers. She also went to the Downtown Community School.) But there were no union songs, no political discussions. Mary and Bertha were more patriotic and WASPy than left-wing. Every day we had formal flag raising and lowering and were taught how to properly fold the flag and that it must never touch the ground.

In choosing Belgian Village, perhaps my mother began declaring her independence from her Communist men: kids from DCS often went to Camp Woodland in the Catskills, which was co-ed and had the same left-wing values as the school. Belgian Village was more in the mold of my great-grandmother Lucia Gilbert's nineteenth-century feminism, believing in physical and mental education for girls to give them confidence away from the corrupting and distracting influence of boys. I suspect my mother hoped vainly that sending me to girls' camp would make me more feminine. What it did was show me a female world that I enjoyed.

All the counselors were women, mostly vigorous young physical education students from places such as Alabama and Georgia. Although they were from backgrounds opposite to mine, the counselors, like me, were physically confident and well-coordinated. Peggy taught me the overhead tennis serve and Tex showed me how to handle nervous horses. I had a mad crush on Peggy and wanted to be just like Tex, who rolled her own cigarettes and drove manure around in a pickup truck. They never said there were things girls couldn't do.

I loved the afternoons on the hot dusty tennis courts, learning to serve. My first year there, at age eight, I was the baby, and everyone felt sorry for me, coming to camp so young and my parents divorcing. But I didn't think about that as I stood with my side to the net, practicing the serve. Mary, the camp director played tennis; all of the glorious, muscular, tanned counselors played tennis. Their white outfits, singing southern accents, open healthy faces, and muscled arms and legs demonstrated a possible future.

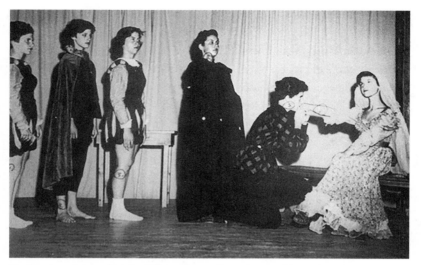

Playing the prince at Belgian Village Camp. Cummington, Massachusetts, around 1953.

Spending every summer with girls made me feel more at ease with them. Maybe there was a way to be a girl that could sort of work. For the first time I had tomboy friends and even wound up liking regular, feminine girls more, despite their teasing because even in my bunk I always wore my baseball cap. The girls called me "Cornel" because when I played the prince in the camp theatrical the girls would exclaim, "Oh, you're so good-looking, you'd make such a good-looking boy! Just like Cornel Wilde!"

At the end of July 1949, Virginia picked me up from camp, and we drove to Provincetown for August. All the William Alanson White shrinks, including Clara Thompson, for whom my mother was still working, vacationed there. Years later my mother complained that we'd had to go to a lake fifteen miles away because I had refused absolutely to go down to the beach that was adjacent to our house, a beach that was covered with "hundreds of hermit crabs that had been washed up." She said this with the clueless exasperation that reflected the irritation she had felt toward me at the time of the divorce.

I remembered this quite differently. The beach was always scary to me because of the many dead horseshoe crabs, hard-shelled creatures the size of dinner plates and the color of cockroaches that have changed little since the dinosaurs. But one day on the narrow path from the beach I encountered a dead seagull, with broken wings and sand-blown feathers riffling in the light wind, as if to simulate flight. My heart pounded with unreasoning panic. Looking back, I think I saw in this pile of decomposing feathers, this shapelessness, the death, disorder, and loss that haunted my childhood.

Horror gripped me, and I scrambled back toward the ocean but then couldn't remember on which of the two paths back to the house the dead seagull lay. No one could or would help me, and I felt utterly alone. My mother confessed decades later that her harsh reaction to my freak-out over the seagull ("Don't be silly!") was because her former lover, my biological father, William Miller, had had the same phobia, and she was shocked at the resemblance.

After that day, despite loving the sea, I refused to go to the beach, and we would drive to the lake that my mother complained was too far away and sit on the shore like brokenhearted lovers, neither of us speaking while all around an unnamable abjection mirrored my mother's despair.

--- CHAPTER 4 ---

CALIFORNIA TRAUMA

Eleven is said to be the age when girls lose confidence. That was when my mother and I moved to Palo Alto, California, then a sleepy suburb an hour from San Francisco. The grandfather general I had never met had died, and my mother and grandmother agreed to reunite, a bargain that was to change my life. On the drive across country in a tiny second-hand car stuffed with suitcases and dogs, I kept thinking over and over that if I'd been a boy this exile from everything familiar in New York City could not have happened. The Great Plains, Grand Canyon, impoverished Native Americans at Acoma whom we reached after bumping along a dirt road for endless desert miles all passed by in my sullen silence. I was absorbed by self-pity and anger at my mother, whom I saw as a sell-out to my grandmother's money.

Since to my grandmother I was the living, breathing, dark-eyed reminder of her daughter's rebellion and her own failure to come to her daughter's aid, she probably would have wished me away from her stucco and timber neo-Tudor house on Santa Rita Avenue. But my mother would not leave me with Saul, and just as she had been torn between him and me during her marriage, now she was the pivot of a power struggle between me and her own mother Bertha. "Try to remember that Mother"—she never referred to her as grandma or even grandmother—"is not used to having children around," Virginia said. But I was too young and too injured to see another perspective. My only point of view was resentment.

My mother made no allowances for the difficulties I faced adjusting to Palo Alto. She knew that New York was my home, but her decision was final. Though she may genuinely have wanted to care for her elderly mother, she was ruthless in her determination to make a new life. Probably the biggest single sacrifice she imposed on me was the loss of my beloved Shetland sheepdog, Davy. In New York I had trained Davy in obedience and attained a CDX, the middle level of difficulty in obedience work. Before we left for California she gave away her own Sheltie, Brucie, to a dog friend, but Davy came with us.

Palo Alto had zoning restrictions; only so many dogs were allowed per house. Because my mother wanted to breed multiple litters of papillons, and would need to keep some of them for her "breeding program," Davy stood in her way, and finally, unable to quite take him away from me, she put him in a boarding kennel, over my strenuous objections. He was my only friend, the only familiar face in the new and frightening suburbs. I had never seen pomegranate orchards like the one across the street from us or eaten an artichoke. The kids I was meeting at David Starr Jordan Junior High School, with their Peter Pan collars and saddle shoes, were like people out of the TV sitcoms that I rarely saw, since, as a matter of principle, we still had no television. After a few weeks, Davy scaled the kennel fence and was never found . . . this is what I was told. As much as I loved my mother, I have never forgiven her for this act of cruelty.

My grandmother was a frail woman in her seventies with a dowager hump from osteoporosis, though she could still, as my mother bragged, bend down and touch her hands to the floor. As a younger woman she had been taller even than me; now she was stooped from the coughing associated with chronic bronchitis, what is now called COPD, an illness that sent her to bed for most of each winter, but she never lost her clout, whether on her feet or enthroned in her room on the second floor. Pride, authority, and a comfortable income were evident in her dark silk dresses, silver-mounted antique amethyst and pearl jewelry, and the hand-knit shawls that covered her bent shoulders. She had very long white hair, which she always wore in discreet braids wound around her head that framed her severe, intelligent face and old-fashioned gold-rimmed glasses as if to say, "There, everything's in order."

She would sit for several hours in the afternoon in her rocking chair, reading and crocheting or doing needlepoint at the same time. She, like my mother (and me), was an avid, dedicated, disciplined reader, but my mother always felt she was inferior because she could not knit or sew *while* she read.

My grandfather had allowed three or four of the novels she had written before their marriage to remain on the lower shelf of the big mahogany bookcase in the living room, which filled up one large wall with leather-bound editions of the classics. The living room was the darkest room in the house and the one least changed by our arrival, so I hated it most. Heavy brocade draperies blocked out the sun; grandmother saw no reason to open them because the living room faced on the street on one side and the neighbors on the other. Only windows that faced on her well-tended garden in the back were left exposed. The room was filled with imposing upholstered furniture, which never changed position. In fact, nothing on the ground floor had been rearranged since the general's death, and to oversee the status quo, a large, framed black-and-white photograph of his stern face and stiff uniformed body held pride of place.

Our main contact was at the nightly dinner, which was always served by Mildred the maid or by my mother on Mildred's days off, the table covered by a white linen cloth and plates flanked by monogrammed silver settings, which my grandmother showed me how to place correctly. My mother would discuss the genetics of her breeding program or how the new litter of puppies was doing (my grandmother listening politely), or my grandmother discussed what was happening in Army Daughters, the organization where she saw her retired military friends (my mother nodding politely), and I sulked, pushing my food around the plate or wolfing it down. I was not allowed to leave the table until they were finished.

Sometimes in the evenings we would play Scrabble or gin rummy or Bezique, a nineteenth-century card game, my grandmother with one of her hand-knit afghans around her shoulders and her reading glasses perched on her long nose that was always dripping because of her colds. She loved cards, and knew hundreds of variations on solitaire, which I still play today on my computer.

My grandmother's complaints about my churlish or ignorant behavior were relayed to me through my mother. The two of them always had an afternoon drink—port for my grandmother, sherry for my mother. I presume that, among other things, they complained about me. Too noisy, or clothing and old banana peels lying around my room, or on the phone too much, and why wouldn't I take an interest in gardening? These were things that irritated my grandmother.

The door to my room became a blockade against their judgments; I stayed there night after night and on weekends, reading, and listening to classical music. Later I smoked there in secret and refused to make my bed for weeks at a time. The gap between us was just too great, and the violent family ruptures that had led up to and followed my birth, circumstances unknown to me then, were unhealed wounds. My grandmother didn't love me, I felt, and just put up with me because she had to, and the only thing she liked about me was my intelligence (I got good grades and could sometimes win at Scrabble and Bezique). She died when I was a freshman in college, and I skipped the funeral.

Now, in my old age, I can try to see it from her perspective. She was an elderly woman in poor health, suddenly invaded by four or five yapping dogs and an unruly preteen. Her only child's life was a failure. Virginia had neither married well nor had the medical or scientific career she had longed for. She was not the noted writer her female forebears had been. Not even a successful rebel, my mother the black sheep had come back home with her tail between her legs, so to speak, dragging along an unhappy little goat as the only thing to show for her mistakes.

But as powerless as I felt in my grandmother's home, I was also a tough customer. My supposedly dead father, the molesting neighbor, the divorce, and my mother's depression had injured me, but nothing had crushed the rebellious spirit I had inherited, and by nature I was stronger than my mother. "You're the type who always takes the bed closest to the bathroom in the motel," she said drily, years later, explaining why she had to defend herself from being pushed around by me. By then, I was able to see the truth of it and even smile as I promised to be more considerate.

/ / /

In Palo Alto, all the stultifying conformity of white 1950s America that I'd been sheltered from in New York City by my eccentric parents and permissive school began to box me in and, worse, became part of me. My masculine self was crushed into hiding. No more baseball cap—I wouldn't have dared, faced with the gendered dress code. I could not go to school without bobby socks and crinolines under my skirt. Then there was a strict caste system: whites on top, blacks and Latinos on a bottom so low that I, who was near the bottom of the white hierarchy, never even knew these "lower" students' names or gave them a thought. Among the whites, "popularity" was everything, and it was determined by the athletic prowess, looks, and self-confidence of the boys. Girls' popularity was a function of the boys they dated. These popular kids enjoyed their power, verbally tormenting those below them, like me. "Weirdo!" they would shout as they floated by on a cloud of arrogance. At the very bottom of the white group were the "queers," a grab bag of the socially inept, the disabled, and the not quite white. For instance, the popular kids would enliven their lunch hours by taunting a painfully shy epileptic girl, who ate her lunch alone by the swimming pool because no one would befriend her, including me. The person who should have been my best friend was Louis Mendelowitz, an intense Jewish boy with acne and a stutter, who seemed to be the lone other intellectually minded kid in the school, although he also loved hot rods, which recommended him tentatively to the hoody boys who had slicked-back hair and dated trampy girls. But I would talk to him only at his house because to be seen with him publicly would have ruined what little "reputation" I had. Compromises like these filled me with self-disgust, though not enough to prevent my making them. It was during these years that a desire to be normal, to fit in, came to dominate my thoughts and actions. I was ashamed of my all-female household, ashamed of my dog breeder mother, ashamed that I wasn't blond like a cousin who went to an exclusive girls school in a nearby suburb that was even wealthier and WASPier than Palo Alto. Why wasn't my name Linda or Ann instead of Esther-Mary?

These experiences of being mostly a victim and occasionally a victimizer in a cruel social hierarchy gave substance to my inherited left-wing skepticism toward the powerful, but these were *my* experiences, and I lived them with resentment and rage. Athletics, in which I had excelled at summer camp and on the streets of New York, were closed to me in Palo Alto. We girls dressed for phys ed in modified bloomer outfits and pretended to play half-court basketball while boys loitered around the court sneering and snickering at any girl, like me, who could shoot or dribble. I had a wicked smash in badminton and went to the state junior championships, but that was something to downplay rather than boast about. A few times I played tennis with another misfit, but she had had lessons and was better than I was, and there didn't seem any point in taking lessons myself.

As much as I tried to fit in at school, I was more comfortable alone in my room. I got good grades (except in math and compulsory home economics) and enjoyed reading, as I always had, with no prompting. I loved science fiction, losing myself in alternative futures and worlds. In some of my darkest hours in Palo Alto I lay on my bed in tears repeating to myself, "Everything is relative; everything is relative." The anthropological inclination in me runs deep. Being able to step back, to distance myself from pain by looking toward social forces rather than blaming myself, was a survival skill.

I enjoyed music and wanted to play an instrument. I would have loved the trumpet, but that would have been too masculine. No girls played horns. So I took up the flute and practiced long hours in my room. I got into the school band—I loved wearing the green quasi-military marching uniform. Nobody cool was in the band, but it gave me a sanctioned role, and I developed a crush on a clarinet player, John Ballantine, the son of the notorious Bay Area attorney Marvin Belli (who later defended Lee Harvey Oswald's assassin, Jack Ruby). John never noticed me, and my next crush was on a trumpet player, David Packard Jr., the son of *the* David Packard who founded Hewlett-Packard. I was attracted to these boys not because they were sons of famous men but because they were both good musicians and tall, since I now believed that any boy I dated

Forced into the mold of a teenage girl. Palo Alto, California, around 1955.

must be taller, stronger, smarter, and a better musician than I. Lacking any but a brief and unhappy model of a heterosexual relationship in my own experience, I adopted the most conventional ideas from films and from my high school.

At the center of my pain was the confused revulsion I felt toward my new body and its sexuality, which emitted strange smells, fluids, body hair, and, worst of all, breasts. I did my best to hide inside white blouses and bouffant skirts, bobby socks and flats. The only way that girls achieved status was through the boys they dated. But my crushes weren't simply dreams of upward mobility. I sincerely and desperately came to *want* to be normal.

Alongside the fantasy boys I dated actual boys I looked down on because they liked me—notably, Paul, a boy with a blond crew cut whom I had met at Mr. Bowdoin's social dancing school that my grandmother thought would teach me better manners. Paul was more popular than I. Dating him gave me a status boost, but, although I tried to hide it, he bored me. I was aware that all of my actions—in fact, my entire public persona—was a lie. But what was I covering up? My mother didn't know that I had started sneakily smoking and that on my infrequent dates I let boys touch my body, since it seemed mandatory—not going too far, though. I didn't want to be known as one of the "cheap" girls who would let a boy "go all the way."

To my girlfriends, other bright losers like me, I pretended to be wild about Elvis when in my room I listened to Edith Piaf and Les Companions des Chansons, trying to understand the French I was studying in school. Most kids took Spanish, which was supposed to be easier—the fact that we lived in California, with a Spanish history and sizable Hispanic population, didn't figure in. My mother insisted I take French instead. (While her preference for French was a legacy of her class, I would be grateful for it later.) I listened to lots of chamber music: Mozart and Beethoven symphonies and concertos, Gilbert and Sullivan, and even the noted counter-tenors Alfred Deller and Richard Dyer-Bennett, tastes my New York City friends had introduced me to on my summer visits.

My mother dismissed my misery at school—"You are much too given to brooding"—or would dust off our class superiority. When I complained that I could never attain the social heights of the busty blond cheerleader who was the most popular girl in the class ahead of mine, my mother replied, "When she has three whiney kids and lives in a trailer park, you'll be excelling in graduate school."

Every summer my father would fly me back east to go to summer camp. I lived for this and would leave Palo Alto keen with anticipation to become, once again, a New Yorker. In line with conventional Palo Alto wisdom, at fourteen I decided that it was time for me to leave the all-girl Belgian Village and go to a co-ed camp. I picked Putney Work Camp, in Vermont, where I spent two happy summers shoveling gravel on the road crew among the kinds of kids I had known at the Downtown Community School, including Jewish kids who weren't ashamed of being brainy or talented, whose parents were college professors or social workers instead of business managers and who voted Democratic instead of Republican.

Spending a couple of summer weeks with Saul and Jane was expected. I visited them in Sag Harbor and then in Santa Fe, where I learned to ride western—Hi-yo, Silver, away! Then they built their dream house at Barnes Landing in Amagansett, right on Gardiners Bay in the Hamptons, which at that time was more of an artists' hangout than the millionaires' playground it is today. The whole entourage was there: Jane's three little kids, Sarah Jane, Robby, and Paul, plus the wonderful general factotum Daisy and another black woman to help her with childcare, plus the poodles that nobody paid attention to.

Saul and Jane had split off from the William Alanson White Institute and founded their own training school, the Sullivan Institute, based purportedly on the theories of Harry Stack Sullivan, an American Neo-Freudian psychiatrist. Their colleagues, students, and analysands gathered on Long Island's South Fork in Amagansett and Springs, buying or renting houses, the forerunner of what eventually became a cult ruled by Saul and his fifth and sixth wives based on Marxism, Sullivan's theories, compulsory promiscuity, and, eventually, musical theater and antinuclear activism. Although I looked down with an adolescent's supercilious Puritanism on their drunken parties, I also found some of the adults congenial.

By far the most important of these was Nancy Rae Smith, a painter and a former patient of my father's who had recently graduated from Bennington College. I met her the summer of 1954, when I was thirteen and she was twenty-three. Under her wing was the one place besides summer camp that I was happy during these years. It was she who introduced me to counter-tenors, to coffeehouses, to bohemian Greenwich Village. She had a tiny walkup apartment on Barrow Street with an old bathtub in the kitchen and oil paint on the floor. This became the first place I would rush to on arriving in New York. And years later, it was with her, that I would gratefully and with stunned surprise experience my first orgasm.

CHAPTER 5

BABY BUTCH

SECTION I

Before Stonewall, "coming out" was an interior and secret process. After you acknowledged to yourself that you were gay—coming out to yourself—you had sex with someone of your gender, like Betty Silver, the art student at Michigan, who would "bring you out." Finally, you would enter—"come out into"—the underground society of other gay people, who would keep your secret as you kept theirs. The gay world lurked in whispers and shadowy places behind unmarked doors, between knowing glances and suppositions, longings and dreams. Middle-class gays kept it that way for their own protection. Coming out to the straight world was never voluntary but only brought on by disaster, such as capture by the police or a parent or roommate reading your diary.

From at least junior year in high school, when I started keeping a journal, I suspected that I might be homosexual, though I hoped that it wasn't true. I was confused by my crushes on boys as well as girls. My crushes on girls were, I rationalized, merely my desire to be like them. I knew I was attracted to masculinity—I loved that Paly band uniform, and my eyes would go longingly to the heavy silver ID bracelets that the boys wore—but did I want that bracelet for myself or did I want to wear Paul's ID bracelet as the sign that we were going steady?

What was it, to be feminine? How did the girls do it? Practicing in front of the mirror, tugging the stiff crinolines this way and that, the rolled-down bobby socks, charm bracelets, flared skirts, straight skirts, Peter Pan blouses, Pendleton outfits . . . What was it? No clothing, no borrowed gesture ever performed the magic, made me right.

The other girls just were it. Sue, for instance. She sat next to me in honors English. She was busty and inactive, definitely feminine—the kind of girl that boys liked. She asked me over to study for a test. Sue's room was right out of *Seventeen Magazine*. Her bed even had a canopy that we sat under, with stuffed animals on the pillow. As she ran through a plot synopsis of *Cry, the Beloved Country*, my eyes kept going to her blonde hair and to her breasts. Just the top of her cleavage showed when she bent over the book. I began to sweat, and my body felt grotesque, bulky. My ears were hot. Was I getting my period? My arms and hands seemed so huge and separate, almost out of control. I saw myself as a plague of locusts swarming all over her smooth creamy skin. Did she feel this tension, too? She gave no sign. Terrified of my feelings and afraid I might give myself away, I fled with an excuse.

There was no denying the fierce impulse to shake her up, to kiss her mouth, even to squeeze her breasts. It was sexual; it was how I imagined that men got turned on to women. The girl I had played tennis with passed me *The Well of Loneliness* in a brown paper bag, so I knew there had been a masculine girl like me in England. The kids called it "lesbian," and if you wore green on Thursday you were one, which I was careful never to do. "Lesbian" might as well have been "leper."

I expected Sue would avoid me, after that. I avoided everyone. Several weeks later, coming home from the dentist full of Novocain, I stared dispassionately in the bathroom mirror at my sullen, strong-jawed face. This face looked gross, ugly, and wrong. The big, dark eyes scared me. What was inside there? Reaching into the medicine cabinet I unwrapped a razor blade and cut a slash by the side of my mouth. "I can't feel anything," I said aloud as the blood dripped down my neck. Yet I wrote in my diary, "I satisfied all my desires."

My grades didn't suffer, but I spent even more time alone in my room and picked fights with my friends. My mother tried to ignore my long silences and intensified sulking, and typically she and my grandmother chose to believe my lies about how I came to have recurrent cuts on my left arm and my face.

One of the bathrooms on the second floor was for the exclusive use of my grandmother. The other could be accessed only through my mother's bedroom. I needed to pee, and although there was a toilet downstairs, I stubbornly wanted to use hers. Virginia was in the habit of taking an afternoon nap, which seemed to me then to signify her lack of a worthy purpose in life. I knocked on her door. The yapping dogs told me she was in there, but she did not respond. Like a grotesque boil, the anger and frustration inside me erupted. The whole situation—my dependence, my grandmother's private bathroom, bobby socks, hair rollers, dating, all of Palo Alto in its palm tree niceness and unattainable blondness—collided with terrible memories of my mother making me love her so and then shutting me out; killing my dog, Davy, because he was inconvenient to her plans. All this anger and hurt spun inside me into a roaring. I started shouting at her through the door, "I need the bathroom! Let me in!" And then, "Fuck you! Fuck you! I know you're in there!" My sweating, hurting, yearning teenage body confronted my mother's locked, cold, rejecting bedroom door. No response. Dashing to my room I broke a window pane with my bare hands, smeared her door with my blood and ran down the stairs, leaving bloody handprints on the banister and driving away in the little secondhand car my father had given me for my sixteenth birthday. My seventy-six-year-old arm and hand still bear scars as witness to this spectacular meltdown.

That level of drama was finally too much for my mother to ignore. Probably in consultation with Saul by phone she gave me an ultimatum: see a psychiatrist or be committed to a mental institution. Not surprisingly, I choose the former. My doctor was a middle-aged Jewish man referred to us by my secret friend Louis Mendelowitz's father, a professor at Stanford University, and luckily for me, the shrink was sympathetic, supportive, and caring. Haltingly, I told him that I hated Palo Alto High School; that I felt trapped between my rejecting mother, whom I loved, and my grandmother, whom I did not; that I missed my father and New York. How my wish to escape to boarding school after my sophomore year had been vetoed by my mother, who, despite our conflicts, did not want me to leave home. How during this, my junior year, we had fought incessantly.

All this took a couple of months of talking. Then one day, as semitropical gardens were blooming around the suburban Victorians and ranch houses, I blurted, "There's something I have to tell you." The doctor nodded, listening intently. Then I sat there. And twiddled my hair, looked at the floor. And sat there. Unable to open my mouth, unable to say the words that I had recently written in my journal, but never said aloud, even to myself, words that could never be taken back. This went on for three weeks. It wasn't a power struggle. He didn't push me. He was just patiently, respectfully waiting for me to spit it out or fail to do so. I sensed this was a turning point in my young life and that honesty was likely in my best interest. Finally, I looked down at the floor and mumbled, "I think I might be a homosexual." The doctor considered while he took this in. My heart beat frantically. It seemed I must be struck dead, that the stucco walls of his house would hate me, crush me. This was in the spring of 1957. The doctor said, "What's so bad about that?"

If you are only as sick as your secrets, as they say in Alcoholics Anonymous, then telling that sweet doctor, and his acceptance, was a giant step toward health. I wish I could say that from then on I suffered no more than the usual ups and downs that young people endure. This is what one sees in gay youth fairly often today. But so many other voices, my own and those all around me, were telling me what ruin this would lead to, how I would be forever a weirdo, outcast, condemned to a life that would be even worse than my high school misery, and, above all, how I would never find anyone to love and love me back.

Like me, many Americans never recover fully from bullying and other torments of their adolescence. The damage is permanent, no matter how much success adulthood brings. Some years ago I dreamed I came upon a brown bear surrounded by a boisterous crowd of street people. I approached the bear obliquely from the back; it was sitting upright and motionless in a hole; only the back of its torso and head were visible. The people were shouting at it and throwing garbage. I realized that they meant in the end to kill it and were only tormenting it from the fun of destroying a robust, beautiful animal who was hopelessly outnumbered.

I woke in terror and threw myself into my girlfriend's arms. "It's you, the bear," she said. "But it's only a dream."

/ / /

The summer after my meltdown I went to Indian Hill, a co-ed music and arts camp in the Berkshires, where I discovered that a lot of the campers were more talented and more dedicated to their instruments than I was. Although I kept at it, my musical education was troubled by a passion I developed for a beautiful black-haired fifteen-year-old named Myra. The Indian Hill campers, arty East Coasters, were sophisticated, and no one passed judgment, at least not publicly, on our relationship.

This was so different from the crushes I'd had on boys. Myra looked back at me tenderly with brown Cleopatra eyes under delicate winged eyebrows, and she let me brush her thick hair. She gave me a gilt-edged old Bible—I still own it. "The sun shall not smite thee by day," she wrote, in her neat schoolgirl hand "nor the moon by night." A Manhattan Jewish princess with a quick brain to match, artistic and sensitive, feminine and graceful, fifteen-year-old Myra held my total attention. This was Sue Wilson all over again in a deeper, more passionate key, the music of an actual, though unconsummated, relationship.

My rival for Myra's attention was a heavy, powerful girl named Leslie, like me the daughter of a shrink, who was whispered to be a lesbian and didn't deny it. (Later I heard she was expelled from Carnegie-Mellon, a common occurrence among lesbians of my generation and class.) I sank into the tar pit of a jealous triangle. My childhood had been a fight for my mother's attention. My insecurity about Myra's affections—though in retrospect, I don't think she cared about Leslie—threw me into a jealous rage, and one night I freaked out in the dining hall, bending silverware in my hands, throwing a plate against the wall, and screaming, "I can't stand it, I can't stand it!"

The camp directors were understandably upset, and I found myself at nearby Austen Riggs, an upscale private mental hospital, being evaluated by a young intern who decided I was not a danger to society and sent me back to camp. The directors also called my father, who had had enough of my outbursts. "Cut the crap," he shouted on the phone. "What the hell are you doing?" My acting out was interfering with his summer, clearly. The upshot was that from his command center in Amagansett my father decided to send me to boarding school to get me away from the situation back in Palo Alto. According to his psychological theories, my mother was the cause of all of my problems. Although I was going into my senior year, he managed through connections—Mr. Powerful always had connections—to get me admitted to the Stockbridge School, a progressive co-ed boarding school close to Indian Hill.

To this day, leaving my mother was the hardest action of my life. She was, and will always be, my first and greatest love. The anger that had built ever since the divorce and crashed on the beach of her bedroom door drained away like waves receding with the tide. I would be alone, bereft. Only sixteen, and so scared. Yet I knew Saul was right; that my situation in Palo Alto was impossible. My mother had already planned that I would go to college at the University of California, Berkeley, to stay close; I could wind up dragging her dog crates around for the rest of my life, caught in her orbit. Or maybe I was more afraid of Saul's anger if I didn't do what he said than I was of leaving my mother. My stiff-necked, secretive, and stoical mother cried when I told her—in a long-distance phone call—that I was not going back to California: "What will I do without my baby?" Her meltdown stunned me, her words piercing me to the core and quivering there. Only as I was leaving could she express her love.

/ / /

Located in a valley beneath rolling Berkshire hills, the Stockbridge School then had something over one hundred students, freshmen through seniors, who were marginals of one kind or another. As the Wikipedia entry tactfully puts it, "Stockbridge School was also used as a sort of 'holding tank' for teenagers who, for one reason or another, were living in an unsympathetic environment at home and whose parents could afford to send them away to school. Much of the revenue used to pay for the school came from this source."[1]

A few were blond rich kids who had been expelled from or flunked out of prep schools. Most were middle-class youngsters who, like me, were high school misfits or whose parents, like mine, had divorced and couldn't cope. Some parents probably just wanted to get on with their lives minus an annoying and needy adolescent. There was a contingent of students from South America whose first names were Arturo and last names were Germanic; the headmaster, Hans Maeder, had been a socialist refugee from the Nazis in 1933, and these were the offspring of other refugees who had gone to South America. He believed in progressive educational principles. Although I saw Stockbridge as a refuge for problem children, I have read that for him the school represented the dream of a fully integrated society and of global education.

For me, Stockbridge was a haven and a respite, a return to the comfort and congeniality of the Downtown Community School in a rural setting. Neither Hans nor his assistant director, Berta Rantz, warmed to me, but they were distant figures. Hans was not as interested in the girls as in the boys—according to current Stockbridge listserv gossip, he was probably gay, although he was married to a woman.

A first-rate Palo Alto education gave me an advantage over the other students, though nobody cared. Academic excellence was not rewarded, but neither was it sneered at. Everyone was accepted and treated with a degree of respect by both students and faculty. If I was a bit of a loner and too masculine (one of the boys observed casually that I had too much yang), so what? One friend was Abbot Lowen, a blue-eyed, dark-skinned girl from Great Neck, whose real name was Abby, or maybe Abigail, but she thought Abbot sounded more exotic. Her room was painted black, and she liked to sit in there cross-legged burning incense and playing the recorder. She was reading the Beats. Another was a sturdy little kid named Gretchen Mehegan, who shared something of my anger and gender ambiguity. Her father was a footloose jazz musician, and her divorced mother lived on Ninth Street in Greenwich Village, an apartment I would often visit in ensuing years.

There was no dating at Stockbridge, although there were some couples. I mooned over two male teachers whom I vaguely guessed were gay. Not having any pressure to date, not being rated by which boy was interested in you or put down because no boys were interested in you—what a relief from the relentless pressure at Paly High! I settled down. There was no more cutting or window smashing. I was still morose and brooding, but there were also some days when the autumn air filled me with pleasure, some nights when I fell asleep without anxiety.

All that truly held my interest was happening in New York City. My friendship with the Bennington graduate and painter Nancy Smith, whom I had met in my father's orbit, grew even stronger. Nancy was taller and ten years older than I, with beautiful, strong hands, expressive eyes, and a sensuous mouth. Not conventionally pretty, she had a determined energy and a raucous sense of humor. Every object—the simple white stoneware dishes, small oil paintings, hand-thrown ceramic ashtrays—in her tiny studio apartment was carefully chosen for the aesthetic pleasure its feel or shape might give. She took me to museums and showed me what to look for in the art. It was the heyday of abstract expressionism, and she tried to explain to her young and not very visual acolyte what was great about Willem de Kooning and Jackson Pollock.

Why did she put up with that feverish, self-absorbed adolescent? Not knowing why, even now, I am grateful for my good fortune and have tried to return it toward generations younger than myself. I couldn't have had a more caring mentor. Nancy was frank, though not happy about, her love for women. She always believed that heterosexuality was morally and aesthetically preferable because of conventional ideas she held about opposites attracting. In this she was a typical tragic homosexual of her time and never escaped ambivalence about herself.

Like my mother, Nancy was an upper-crust rebel. She had gone to the Madeira School before Bennington. These girls' schools had been circumstantially (though not ideologically) agreeable to her lesbianism. But in the New York art world, as in Palo Alto, a woman's status was largely determined by which man wanted her. Bisexuality might be intriguing, but lesbianism got you thrown in the dump. Nancy, an independent woman, was getting nowhere as a painter, and she was bitter about it at the same time she probably wondered whether she was as talented as the male painters who were getting known.

To Nancy I confessed my passion for Myra the Jewish princess, who had recently told me that she couldn't have sex with me because she couldn't do anything that she knew her parents wouldn't approve of. Nancy listened with interest and good humor. It meant everything that I could tell someone I looked up to that I wanted to touch another girl in that way—though what I had learned from fumbling high school boys gave me little idea what that way would be.

At the time Nancy was pursuing her quest for bisexuality, off and on, with a bearded shrink in my father's entourage named Manny Ghent who rode around the city on a motor scooter, which at that time was exotic and daringly European. One spring afternoon in 1958, Manny gave me a thrilling ride on his scooter down the West Side Highway, after which he took me to his Greenwich Village apartment and had intercourse with me.

This for me was a passive event; I just let it happen. It was neither especially painful nor pleasurable. Although he was in his thirties and I was seventeen, it was not forcible rape. I didn't struggle or resist, I was flattered by his interest, guilty and titillated that I was having sex with Nancy's sometime boyfriend, and more glad than not to be rid of my virginity. I had a bowlegged sensation for a day or so afterward, a sense of being physically buffeted that was not unpleasant. What was terrible was not physical. I had been a spectator during this supposedly intimate and personal moment. I had a sense, soon to become numbingly familiar, of looking up at the cracks or leak stains in the ceiling and wondering when it would be over. Nothing like the sensual bliss of brushing Myra's glossy black hair.

My misadventure with Manny Ghent was not something I could tell Nancy about, though back at Stockbridge I boasted to my pal Abbot Lowen that I had lost my virginity, and in Greenwich Village with an older man! But it felt creepy, and as time passed and I became an adult who mentored young people, Manny's seduction seemed reprehensible. As alluring as adolescents can be, and as physically beautiful, I don't think adults should have sex with them—let teenagers have sex with each other. Manny had wanted to fuck me because he could and because my father was the top dog in his world, not because he had cared much about me, and he took advantage of my youth and naiveté in a way that Nancy never did. She waited until I grew up and was able to want her back.

SECTION II

At seventeen I ventured alone to the University of Michigan, where I met my lifelong friend Shirley, did well in classes, and was initiated into lesbian sex by Betty Silver. Gay life was hard to find then, all underground and secret, so Betty's second gift was introducing me to a thrilling and dangerous covert world in New York City of frankly erotic lesbian slow dancing, johns looking to pay lesbians for sexual "freak shows," pot smoking, and an edgy threat of violence. Betty, who had never become my girlfriend, dumped me for an older butch named Robbie, but I soon met Nannette, a former synchronized swimmer turned chorus girl at Club 82, a drag joint on East Fourth Street. She had picked me out, the way Betty had, but this time in a lesbian bar. At 4 AM I'd thread my way through cigar-smoking gangsters parked outside the club to meet her after work. How glamorous she was in theatrical makeup, blue eye shadow for days and inch-long false eyelashes. Nannette had long, orangey hair that had a dry, paper-like texture. A proud femme, she boasted that no man had ever fucked her, and I am quoting. The first time I took her out to dinner in my new men's pants—a couple of gay men owned a clothing store on Eighth Street where you could buy men's clothes—I didn't have enough money to cover the check. I was mortified, but Nannette smiled indulgently and paid the rest.

I have never forgotten the kindness of this exotic dancer or her lithe and muscled body under me. The age difference between us—I was eighteen and probably she was in her thirties—was a turn-on for me. She called me a "baby butch" and I loved it. Sex with this sweet creature compared with sex with men was like the difference between elevator music and a live concert. It was logical to me that she didn't try to lie on me and hump me with a slow gliding motion or tickle my clitoris with her tongue, as she taught me to do to her.

That's what being butch meant in 1959: a masculine girl like me who wore men's clothes, smoked Lucky Strikes, wore her collar up and T-shirt sleeves rolled, and dated femmes like Betty and Nannette. The butch made love to the femme, and the femme, not at all passive, showed her appreciation. All the butches I met in the bars—like the one who was also dating Nannette and threatened to carve up my college kid face with her knife—looked and mostly were tough. Their peroxide DA haircuts were slicked back into the same styles the hoods from the wrong side of the freeway had worn in my high school. Those summer nights I saw and avoided many fights; a butch pushed her rival through the plate-glass window at Pam Pam's, a late-night diner on Sixth Avenue where the queers went after the bars closed, and the ambulance came to take her to St. Vincent's while the Pam Pam workers wiped her blood off the sidewalk. I had passed a butch I knew strung out in a doorway and later heard she died. And there were the broken-down old butches at the end of the bar, drinking themselves into nightly stupors.

"Normal" people called them freaks to their faces, and I knew it hurt, but they had their pride and weren't afraid to fight to defend themselves and their space with their fists or broken bottles. These butches were flashy, stylish, and who could not admire their courage? But their rugged masculinity and tough talk made me seem wimpish. I couldn't fight with my fists, a knife, or even insults. Besides, my part-time job as a waitress at Schrafft's restaurant, working the harried, measly tipping lunch-hour crowd on Wall Street, gave me plenty of incentive to continue my studies. Betty's butch Robbie was a Post Office clerk, the best job that any of the butches had. The worst jobs were working on loading docks or pimping and selling drugs. I had been raised to think that jobs like that weren't for people like me. But I didn't come from wealth, either, and if I was a queer, I wouldn't have a man to support me. I would have to work. What kind of life could I have? Someone who looked like a butch bar dyke—which is to say, someone who looked so obviously gay—could never have a career.

Sometimes in the bars I saw "those ki-ki dykes," as my friends contemptuously called them, meaning you couldn't tell whether they were butch or femme, and they probably "swung both ways." These women dressed in expensive clothes with more sophisticated haircuts, middle- or upper-class women who stuck to themselves in the bar, laughing too loud, smoking filtered cigarettes and clearly slumming. They lived in another galaxy I could see only through a telescope of desire. I had no way to meet them and no idea how to become them. The only adult lesbian I knew was Nancy, and she would have never gone to a lesbian bar.

By the end of the summer, uncertainty about the future was driving me crazy. My little sublet apartment on Barrow Street—the same block as Nancy's, who was out of town for the summer—was crawling with cockroaches and littered with cigarette and marijuana butts. Lesbians passed in and out, got high, had sex. One afternoon a sweet black stripper who was very pregnant seduced me, we both enjoyed it and I thought, there's no way back to Ann Arbor.

Meanwhile, my mother and I had gradually and uneasily reconciled.

Late in August she happened to be passing through New York (for a dog show), and she came by the Barrow Street apartment. She never said what she thought of the unwashed dishes, the broken refrigerator, and the clothes on the floor. What she said was, "You are going back to college," and she and my young Stockbridge friend Gretchen Mehegan rolled up their sleeves to help me clean up, pack my bags, and get on the train to Michigan. Virginia never finished college; her daughter was going to.

The world of the bar dykes was not one I could join without losing my advantages, but Nannette's friends, the femmes and butches who were strippers and waitresses, had left their lipstick marks and their back slaps all over me. I saw those uptown ki-ki dykes through their resentful eyes. They made me taste the smugness of women with money and education and the bitterness of those without. Bar dykes were the first to show me how to be butch, which means that they showed me how to have a style. Postmodernism and consumerism have given style a bad name. It is not necessarily superficial. Adrift in a sea of hostility, drowning in shame, the strong little kid I was had grown into an angry, slump-shouldered lump of teenage flesh, and my secrets made me a loner even with friends. Being butch was the first identity that had ever made sense out of my body's situation, the first rendition of gender that ever rang true, the first look I could ever pull together. Laughable to straight people, of course, and an embarrassment to the uptown dykes, butches in the bar life were fabulous, and they were hot.

/ / /

Back in Ann Arbor, Shirley was shocked at my men's pants and short hair. She barely recognized me, she said. As titillated as she was to hear of my adventures in New York, she made me realize there was no place at all on this college campus in the late 1950s for the butch dyke I had briefly become. I'd have to revert to some version of a co-ed. There was no LGBT student center, no lesbian social network, not even a lesbian friend or acquaintance (Betty had graduated). The police conducted sweeps of the men's rooms of certain academic buildings, including the student union, arresting a number of gay male students and a professor who killed himself. It didn't matter that I'd never had sex in a bathroom and never would, or that I'd had the good fortune not to be swept up in any of the police raids of New York lesbian bars the previous summer. That way was disaster. Resigned, I brought out the hair rollers and lipstick and decided to go into therapy.

At that time, the college health service provided all the talk therapy you wanted, free, and I continued once a week for the next three years until graduation. I liked Dr. Holmes (who as a bonus was black), and when she explained that my homosexuality was just a phase and that I should get back to dating men, I tried to please. In October I met a graduate student, a Hungarian refugee like Laszlo Gluck, the man I still thought had been my father, and we became lovers. "Ivan," I wrote to my mother, a week or so after meeting him, "is just about everything that I always wished a man could be; he's gentle and sensitive and bright without weakness or lack of firmness, he's manly without pushing it down your throat." He had an exotic accent and a dark, *mittel* European face. It was all too perfect. We soon got engaged, much to Dr. Holmes's satisfaction. I wrote asking my mother to publish news of our engagement in the *Palo Alto Times*; I'd show them! My mother, whom I imagined would be pleased, advised caution. One of her favorite admonitions to me was that getting married was no big achievement, and that for every jackass there was some lady jackass who would marry him. She thought I was too young, she said. I had only known Ivan a couple of months.

One morning in April 1960, as we got up, Ivan handed me his shirt and told me to iron it. He explained that since we were engaged I might as well get used to my wifely duties, now. "Hey, we're both students. It's your shirt. You iron it," I said angrily. Except for the two years my parents were married, I had never seen a wife wait on a husband. Saul's fourth wife, Jane, had maids. Mostly my mother had treated me like a little prince; she did all the cooking, shopping, laundry, and whatever cleaning happened; my grandmother, too, had a maid. I had never had to do anyone's scut work and had not had to face what a wife's role involved. Outraged, I got in a big fight with Ivan and walked out. We continued to have sex, but I started to backpedal on the marriage plans I had enjoyed imagining.

Fed up with Ivan, I decided to spend the summer with my mother. She had moved up into the hills behind Stanford University months after I'd left home so she could escape Palo Alto's zoning rules and breed more dogs. This small house and barn on five acres, with a view of the distant bay, was where my mother lived until she collapsed in 1987. (By the time I sold it, the land alone was worth enough to support my mother for the remaining fifteen years of her life.) My grandmother had protested that the cold and damp would be bad for her health, but with typical ruthlessness my mother insisted on the move. Predictably, my grandmother's bronchitis worsened in the harsher climate, and she died in a year. My mother always felt guilty about it, yet she who had been disinherited at last came into enough money to be independent and live out her dream of dog world success.

Only in June in California did I realize I was pregnant. During my freshman year, Saul had insisted I be fitted for a diaphragm by his New York doctor, but I used it fitfully. The contraceptive cream was messy, and you had to think ahead of time, which ruined the "romance." This was before the pill. Confused and unsure what to do, I called Ivan. We had never really made up after the ironing fight, and I told him I was thinking of having an abortion. He wanted to get back together and burst into tears: how could I do this to *him*? I had ruined his life. The heterosexual fantasy bubble burst, leaving a puddle of disgust. Who was the one in trouble, me or him? He was a self-centered weakling, I felt, no help and certainly not a future partner. This thing he had planted inside my body, I wanted to expel it.

I wonder now if I had unconsciously courted the pregnancy out of uncertainty whether my body was normally female or not. Not that my body looked so different from other women's, even though I was taller, stronger, and more athletic than many. But my adult body felt at once alien, inappropriate, and potent. I had had nightmares of growing a beard. Would having a baby make me feel like a real woman? Or was I trying to relive my mother's life, marrying a Hungarian refugee?

Virginia, seeing my confusion, was remorseful. Finally, out came the whole story of my birth. Saul had always urged her to tell me, she said, but she had hesitated, not knowing how to talk about it, not wanting me to feel "less than" other kids. I was stunned of course, angry that I had believed this fraud and suspicious that she had been shielding herself more than me. I was "illegitimate," but was this worse than being a communist? At least I knew my father wasn't a Hungarian after all, and I didn't need Hungarian Ivan in my life. My mother, having a chance to undo her own mother's mistakes, stood behind me, whether I had the baby or not, and I have always been profoundly grateful to her. After a few anxious days I decided that the pregnancy was proof enough of biological normalcy and that I wanted to finish college, which would have been impossible had I kept the baby. But abortion was illegal.

From the first, Saul brusquely assumed I would have an abortion. To him, this was just another day in the life of a harried parent, and he had plans for me to get the doctorate he had wanted. His marriage to Jane had never been an impediment to his dalliances—and Joan Harvey, his girlfriend at the time (who would become his fifth wife)—was an actress on a television soap opera. She knew where the B-list actresses and the girlfriends of mobsters went to get illegal abortions: a doctor in Tijuana, Mexico. My mother drove me to Disneyland, where we took in some rides to kill time and then met a hefty guy with a cigar who was planning to smuggle tequila back to the States in the trunk of his Cadillac.

My mother waited for me near Disneyland while the gangster guy and I drove across the border, our destination a modest house in a dusty neighborhood. The doctor gave me chloroform, but not enough. Still conscious, I screamed with pain, the overhead light blinding me as I whirled down a vortex toward what seemed like death. The nurse put her hand over my mouth and ordered me not to scream; it would attract the cops. Finally, I lost consciousness, and when I woke up they had hustled me into my clothes, and the gangster drove me back across the border.

Back at my mother's house after three days of agonizing cramps, I passed out with a temperature of 103. At Stanford Hospital they discovered that the abortionist had destroyed, but not removed, the fetus. "I hope you realize, young lady, that you brought this on yourself," the doctor lectured, before giving me the D&C that saved my life. His moralizing was perfectly consistent with the shame and disgust with which I had always perceived femaleness and femininity in relation to myself.

The rest of the summer I lay around on my mother's patio, reading and getting a tan, deeply depressed. I had learned I was "illegitimate," failed at heterosexuality, suffered a humiliating illegal abortion, and been kicked out of my elite honors dorm, Martha Cook, that served good food and was close to campus. Women still had a curfew, and toward the end of the previous spring term I had been caught staying out all night. Although I had actually been with Ivan, Deborah Bacon, the terrifying dean of women who was basically an enforcer, called me on the carpet, suggesting that I had been indulging my suspected "immoral tendencies"—I had been seen with another girl inside a telephone booth. We had been simply talking to a mutual friend, but knowing I was guilty in spirit, I didn't try to defend myself—how could I, since other than missing curfew she never said exactly what I was guilty of—and the dean had had me expelled from Martha Cook. I was lucky. Rather than kick me out of school, she had assigned me to a floor in Stockwell Hall that was reserved for misfits and women who were so unpopular they could not get a roommate.[2]

I fell into a pattern that would last the next two years. I just didn't tell my therapist Dr. Holmes about my gender uncertainty or the (disappointingly chaste) lesbian flirtation I had with another camp counselor the next summer. That way I could still appear—even to myself—to be striving for "normalcy." During the school year I dated various men. I got pinned, then a step before engagement, to a blond graduate student in economics for a few days before I backed out. Then there was the handsome Afghan exchange student; a fat philosophy professor from Brooklyn who had a high opinion of himself; a nice African boy who came from a minority tribe in Kenya and with whom I once again became pregnant and had another abortion, this one arranged by my father in New York City through his family doctor. In New York State at that time, you could get a legal abortion if three shrinks would attest that you would be an unfit mother.

The frequent sex I was having with men contrasted ever more sharply with my limited experience of gay intimacy. (In my four years at Michigan I met only Betty and one other lesbian, who was strictly a friend.) With men it was always the same cycle of anticipation (maybe this would work) or resignation (this was expected), and then disappointment. I could not put myself in the picture. There was an unchanging script, and I was an object or an audience, not an actor. My passivity made the whole thing feel shameful, the more so if I felt any pleasure. I knew men wanted "it," so I felt insecure until I had gone to bed with them and used sex to hold them.

/ / /

Since high school I'd been writing sporadically as a way to reflect on my situation and gather the scattered pieces of myself together. The summer of my Tijuana abortion I wrote long and introspective letters—genuine and expressive compared with the more guarded college letters to my mother—to my Martha Cook roommate, Hilary Smith, who had graduated and moved back home to Cambridge.

That I understood the importance of "getting myself together" was reflected in a new focus on the future and an intention to reform, a promise that I took seriously. I began to apply myself to my own construction, which at first meant neatness, cleanliness, and punctuality. "I cut class very little—I take frequent baths," I wrote. "I try not to get too involved with trivia and get a certain amount of work done every day, to make decisions and to think ahead. This is the first year that I have attempted to limit and order myself, and for a first try I'm doing all right, so far. As my dear mother says, I may turn out to be a decent human being yet, although perhaps I shouldn't be overly optimistic on that point."

Before college, my confusion and inner chaos had been reflected in my haphazard bodily hygiene and disorganized personal space. My bedroom in Palo Alto had been a mess. As late as my freshman year in college I was a known slob. Procrastination, cramming for exams, and handing in papers at the last minute were standard. I was a night owl because I could not let go enough to sleep, and when I did, I had violent and frightening nightmares. (Until I accepted my homosexuality at twenty-six, psychic meltdown was always too close.) No doubt my standards of discipline, inherited from a mother whose inability to maintain them made her hate herself, were fairly high. At any rate, there was a wide gap between what I thought I should be and what I was.

Even before the debacle with Ivan, I had begun to take my studies more seriously. That next fall I earned four As and one B+. "I may turn into a scholar yet," I wrote to my mother. My father had sent me to the University of Michigan with a plan. I would get a doctorate in psychology and become a therapist, like him. One Introduction to Psych course whose protagonists were rats running through mazes gave me the perfect excuse to talk my father out of this. He had nothing but contempt for experimental psychology, and he agreed that I could defer my psychology career until graduate school.

While ascending the academic ladder during college and graduate school I struggled every day, sometimes moment by moment, to hide what felt like my real self that no amount of fucking men or wearing lipstick could defeat. The work of monitoring and camouflaging this other self—don't hold your cigarette between your thumb and index finger, that's too masculine—was exhausting alongside the regular work of growing up.

Most young people want to become independent adults. There was a choice for middle-class girls then: career or marriage? (Later on, girls were told they could "have it all," effectively erasing the career-woman option.) Having a career was definitely second best; probably that working gal was ugly and couldn't get a man. Despite my mother's frequently stated opinion that getting married was no accomplishment, I longed abstractly for the marriage-and-family life plan on which the majority built whatever mature selves they could, while I knew or feared that it wasn't going to work for me. What was I going to do about the fact that "women alone stirred my imagination," as Virginia Woolf wrote? What were my alternatives? The failed marriage plans and near-death abortion had shown that becoming a man's dependent and following the '50s life plan I had naively embraced might not pan out.

There was no idea of gay marriage and children then. The children that gays and lesbians had were left over from failed heterosexual relationships. There were no public figures, no Elton John, no Ellen DeGeneres or Martina Navratilova, no Barney Frank, and for intellectual types like me, no Susan Sontag and Annie Leibowitz. Years later, an older lesbian friend expressed the prevailing gay view when she told me, "There are the gay people and the normal people, and it is better for everyone if they keep separate." No gay person expected that separate would be either the same or equal. And if the well-worn tracks couldn't lead you to maturity, where were even the side roads and neglected paths?

In my impoverished emotional life, the world of literature offered pleasure and possibility. One day during my junior year, browsing through an Ann Arbor bookstore, I happened upon John Malcolm Brinnin's biography of Gertrude Stein, *The Third Rose*.[3] From the moment I saw Stein's magisterial photograph on the cover (and uncharacteristically stole the book so the clerk wouldn't suspect that I was gay) I sat down and devoured Brinnin's book, page by page, word by word, and especially photograph by photograph. His book revealed a lesbian world—or so I hoped, for it was never affirmed. Stein had lived with another woman, Alice B. Toklas, a devoted partner who cooked, typed manuscripts, and gardened while Gertrude played the role of salon host and great writer. Around them and their art-filled home was a circle of witty, creative (and wealthy) friends. I was majoring in European history and thinking about graduate school, but if someday I could write, if I could get to France, meaning get away from here—Stein wrote, it isn't what France gives you; it's what it doesn't take away—if I had money, would I be able to find an Alice to love me? Was there a life worth living? Stein became my ego ideal, a masculine Jewish woman who had somehow created a coherent domestic and intellectual life in a Parisian setting of dazzling appeal. I was obsessed with her for many years, and in return she gave me hope.

/ / /

Sophomore year I had taken a lot of English literature courses, including a year with the great Shakespeare scholar G. B. Harrison. I had always loved books and reading, so being an English major seemed a good fit. My proudest moment was earning an A+ from Harrison with my paper on *As You Like It*—all about gender confusion. But a poetry course temporarily ended my writing career. After studying the poet John Donne, whose poems perfectly suited my tumultuous temperament and throttled longings, and Shakespeare's sonnets, we were assigned to write our own sonnet. I could not do it. The puerile free verse I had written in boarding school would not morph into rhyming pentameter. Desperate, I had my roommate Hilary Smith write the sonnet for me. This was the only time I cheated in my twenty years of schooling, and I am ashamed of it still. If writing sonnets was the creative writing requirement, I was a washout.

Admitted into the history honors program, I did well. By senior year, when it came time to pick my honors thesis, I was dating Aron, a Kenyan exchange student. We were at the center of a fun, lively crowd of African men. I enjoyed the dancing and music at their parties and their polite foreign ways. I wrote to my mother, "Aron is good looking and lovable, but not always easy to understand . . . the cultural problems are more difficult than the racial ones. Most Africans have less of a racial complex than Negroes—for one thing you don't have to scrape away a layer of pseudo-humbleness and polite hostility. They are anything but humble and if hostile, not polite about it." I wasn't planning to alter my life plans for Aron. *"Ne t'inquiet pas,"* I wrote to my mother, showing off my proficiency in French. "I'm not getting married. . . . I hope you're not anxious for grandchildren, because it looks like it's going to take a while."

Instead, I altered my intellectual plans. Up to this point, my studies had seemed abstract. The closest connection to my own life had come in John Donne's feverish love poems that expressed somehow my doomed lesbian desire. But now my personal life began to guide my intellectual interests, and I decided to pursue a merger of European and African history after I found primary sources on the Belgian occupation of the Congo in the University of Michigan library. But as winter dragged on I kept doing more and more research, unable to start writing. The task seemed overwhelming. I had written mostly ten-page papers up to this point, and the thesis was supposed to be at least fifty. How to organize so much material? How to pace myself? Could I do anything worthwhile?

Choked up with anxiety, I turned to my shrink, Dr. Holmes, for help, and she prescribed Valium, which calmed my sweaty hands and palpitating heart. During spring break, I holed up with my friend Marilyn Berman, who was working on her own thesis on aphasia (she would become a speech therapist). I sat down at my typewriter, surrounded by notes. Even with the Valium my hands shook so violently that my fingers kept slipping off the keys. This was an extreme test of courage, like telling the Palo Alto shrink my secret, or leaving my mother, or having sex with Betty Silver. In the *bildungsroman* of any young scholar there are sphinxes and dragons she must slay or outwit to continue on the path, and this Congo Reform Society thesis was one of mine. As I finally got going I wrote proudly to my mother that I was engrossed in my honors thesis, working diligently, and thinking about going for a doctorate in anthropology.

With the start I got over spring break I was able to finish and graduate with honors. Saul, I wrote to my mother, "as excited as a ten-year-old with his first baseball mitt," presented me with me a secondhand Volkswagen with only ten thousand miles on it and treated me to my first trip to Europe as a graduation present. A Michigan friend, Faith Weinstein, had bought an Austin-Healey sports car with an inheritance, but the car was in England, and she was afraid to drive in Europe, so I agreed to go along. (I could drive anything, was my attitude.)

We went to England, where African men tried to pick us up in Trafalgar Square; Scotland, where I nearly froze to death; and then France. This was more like it! However inadequate my academic French, we bumbled along, wide-eyed American innocents. My one indelible memory, besides the zippy Austin-Healey, was our visit to a lesbian bar in the Riviera town of Ramatuelle in the hills above Saint-Tropez. Faith was just slumming, but the sleek and fashionably dressed dykes meant so much to me. When these women line-danced their way past our table, it was as if they'd pinned a badge labeled FRANCE over my heart. I knew I would come back one day.

— CHAPTER 6 —

ANTHROPOLOGY OF THE CLOSET

My graduate school was already picked out: the University of Chicago, where my mother had gone, where she had met Saul, and where she had not been able to graduate because of her politics. But that's not officially or even consciously why I went there. I had decided to study anthropology, which, unlike history, was not exclusively pursued in libraries. My subject was to be Africa.

The African interest sprang partly from the African men I had hung around with at Michigan but also probably from my fascination with two movies that my mother and I had loved: *King Solomon's Mines* and *The African Queen*. Apart from the picturesque African scenery and the compelling "natives," especially the gorgeous and exotic Batutsi in *Mines*, I had been swept up in both heterosexual love stories, featuring Deborah Kerr and Katharine Hepburn, respectively, two fair-haired beauties beloved by compelling, though difficult, men with whom I identified.

Anthropology ran on my father's side of the family. Both Elman Service, from whom I took my Introduction to Anthropology, and Johnny Murra were Saul's anthropology buddies from their Spanish Civil War days, and Johnny urged me to go into the field. Jane Pearce's father had founded the anthropology program at the University of Texas, and as a young woman she had dated the anthropologist Wally Goldschmidt. When it came time to choose from the three graduate schools that had accepted me, Jane called up Carl Withers, who under the name James West had written an excellent ethnographic study of a Midwestern town, *Plainville, U.S.A.*[1]

Over tea in his beautiful old Greenwich Village townhouse I told Withers I'd been accepted to Yale and Chicago with partial scholarships (ironically, the Chicago money came from a fund for descendants of World War I veterans, which I got through my grandfather Bash), and Northwestern (with a full scholarship from the Defense Department). Which should I accept? Saul had already said he would help support me through graduate school, so I had options.

Withers got on the phone with his pal, the anthropologist Hortense Powdermaker, and they chewed it over while I sat there wondering whether I would ever live in a house with beautiful books and wood paneling and have distinguished friends like these people. Fairly quickly they agreed: "Yale is too starchy; you won't like it. Northwestern is second-rate. Go to Chicago. David Schneider has some interesting students." Actually, I think Withers added, "And he likes weirdoes," because I decided to take his advice.

It was good advice. I was beyond lucky to attract Schneider's intellectual and moral support, without which I most likely would not have succeeded in graduate school. Father-mentors were very necessary to professional women of my generation. There was not one woman professor in the Chicago Anthropology Department then. My "role models" were all men, and most would not go out of their way to help female students develop as intellectuals and professional academics, mostly because they believed, despite the presence of some distinguished exceptions, we would not become professional anthropologists. Carl Withers and Hortense Powdermaker had not told me that Schneider was one of the few willing to mentor women students when they urged me to go to Chicago, but probably they knew it. Although Schneider was not exempt from sexist attitudes in those days before second wave feminism, most of his female students got much more help than aggravation.

On the face of it, David Schneider seemed an unlikely person to harbor radical ideas. He had himself successfully concluded non-Western fieldwork. There was certainly no outward indication that he would be sympathetic to "weirdoes." The chair of an elite and conservative graduate department, long married to the same woman, father of two sons, he lived a conventional bourgeois life in a Chicago townhouse filled with Danish modern furniture. But the profoundly unruly and agnostic side of him was captured by a mutual friend's comment that if you could open David up, you'd find an alien inside.

This combination of insiderhood with an iconoclastic temperament proved a blessing for those of his students like me who were marginal and offbeat, for in addition to the white men whom everyone thought would succeed, Schneider was attracted to closeted gays, women, and other such students who could not easily attract the support of the powerful.

One of my worst moments in graduate school came when Schneider reported to me on the year-end departmental review of my progress. The professors relayed to me through Schneider that my wearing pants and riding on the back of a (male) friend's motorcycle manifested a lack of commitment to the anthropological vocation. I was hurt and angry at this personal attack, and it seemed to point, covertly, at my shameful secret. Why weren't they focusing on my work? Julian Pitt-Rivers, another adviser of whom I was fond, warned me that, after all, it was important to be attractive and feminine, and he thought the department had a point. Why did professional women have to try to be like men? (Then again, my first mentor, Johnny Murra, had warned me against flirting lest I be dismissed as a bimbo. As Betty Friedan pointed out, you couldn't win.) In the Schneiders' living room, I was told that wearing dresses was neither here nor there in the ultimate scale of value and that David and his warm and wonderful wife, Ady, rather enjoyed my unconventionality. (They did not know I was gay, though perhaps Ady suspected.[2])

I was unhappy at Chicago, especially during my first year when I lived in the Woodlawn neighborhood surrounded by angry slums. I often found the antenna ripped from my car, the air let out of a tire. The streets were never plowed. The weather, below zero for weeks at a time, was even worse than Ann Arbor's.

Terribly lonely, I got involved with another Kenyan that I met in my student boardinghouse, John, who was studying political science at

Roosevelt University in downtown Chicago. He was engaged to a Kikuyu woman back home (and after he returned to Kenya, it developed that he also had an African American girlfriend at Roosevelt). I wrote to my mother that without a relationship it was almost impossible to survive the anomie of graduate school. At first I found little refuge in my studies, which I described to my mother as "the least satisfactory part of my life." I was bored and found it difficult to study.

To my friend Hilary, I was more specific:

I spent this evening (it is now two in the morning) struggling to read some extremely dry and uninteresting archeological syntheses. Amazing how boring this intrinsically romantic subject can become in the loving hands of the "scientists."

When I attended the annual hamentashen-versus-latke debate, a spoof on academic pedantry, I wasn't Jewish enough to join in the fun. In classes I felt silenced by the bravura brilliance of my classmates, many of whom had majored in anthropology at Harvard and Yale and were far more advanced than I. Instead, I lost myself in my relationship with John, who was handsome, dynamic, sociable, taller than me, and mean, just what I'd always wanted in a man. He took me to some very interesting venues in African American Chicago, which prompted me to reflect on the graduate school experience, as I wrote to Hilary:

[Hyde Park] is truly interesting though hardly aesthetically pleasing. A large, poor, hostile and quasi-criminal Negro population surrounds it. Next weekend John and I are going to a large dance being held in honor of the "Mayor of Bronzeville," who happens to be a female this year. "Bronzeville" is a Negro euphemism for the Black Belt, and every four years the Negroes elect their own mayor, who has largely honorary functions. God knows they get little enough satisfaction from Chicago's mayor, Boss Daley. This city is so incredibly corrupt that I still can't believe it, much less describe it. In the midst of this morass of human misery and privation sits the smug U of C, openly discriminating (it is the biggest slum landlord in the area) and its ulcer-ridden faculty, grimly turning out badly written joyless little academic exercises of minor interest.

Although I didn't know it then, my mother had had a very similar perspective thirty years previously when her mink-coated appearance in court brought down her father's wrath. *My* father's unconditional support—as long as I kept at my studies—was a big plus. In any case, at that point I had none of the fervent political commitment of my mother's Depression-era college years, subscribing only to the diffuse liberalism of the Democratic Party. My mother had been for Adlai Stevenson (who was supposed to be a distant cousin from the Illinois branch of the family) and I was for John Kennedy, though never in any activist way. I supported civil rights for "Negroes" but did not, like some of my contemporaries, including my college roommate Shirley, sit in at lunch counters or register the disenfranchised to vote. I was too self-conscious, too estranged, and, despite my initial problems with graduate school, too careerist to risk open activism. I had already chosen higher education over the strongest passion in my life, my love for women, because the two seemed incompatible. And inside my head were the voices of a father who had wanted to study physics and a mother whose ambition to be a biologist had been thwarted by General Bash.

"I more or less got through the school year by the force of my own dead weight," I wrote to my mother, "and I still can't say that the academic life thrills me." But as always, I carried on and passed my four field prelims, which tested one's knowledge of cultural, physical, linguistic, and archeological anthropology, and was allowed to continue on toward my master's degree. It was at this point that David Schneider agreed to sponsor me, giving me a summer job coding data on what we called "the kinship project," where I began to know a group of young people who were to varying degrees Schneider's students.[3]

These students became my dearest friends, dinner companions, and card-playing buddies. Now I became totally involved in the hermetic world of the Anthropology Department. Although I had met outsiders through my relationship with John, I never knew any Chicago students outside the department, and I doubt that the others knew many, or any, either. We went to departmental parties, awkwardly clutching our drinks and trying to catch the attention of the professors or, to a lesser extent, their wives; we saw one another in classes and events—for example, when distinguished speakers came in. Some of us got high together on liquor, marijuana, amphetamines, and peyote, and we all complained about our meager fellowships.

John had graduated and gone back to Africa at the end of the summer

With my friend and fellow graduate student Ben Apfelbaum.
Chicago, around 1964.

of 1963. I was obsessed with his handsome milk chocolate face, self-confident strut, and quick intelligence. He was hot-tempered, and we fought and argued a lot over politics, cultural differences, and the fact that I wanted more of him than he wanted to give. We had talked about marriage, though he was wary of commitment. He suggested I come to Africa and we could perhaps marry there. My mother advised caution, and I agreed with her. What would I do in Africa apart from being his maybe wife? Yet watching him actually board the plane felt traumatic. Afterward, at intervals, two letters came from Kenya and then silence.

If this was what heterosexuality meant for me, I didn't want it. I had felt feminine in relation to him; how was it different from submission? Though from his perspective I fought his dominance tooth and nail, I felt more womanish when I lost. If this was real heterosexuality, enthralled by a brilliant and forceful man who was cruel and dismissive toward me and cheated with other women, what did this say about that part of me that was capable of loving a man? Too much like how Saul had treated my mother and still treated his fourth wife, Jane Pearce. More than a little it seemed that John had played the father part in my inner dream world, and that the pain of his leaving reprised the desertions by my fathers. All right, I thought, after some months had passed, you've done it. You gave it your best shot.

This was the context when Cal Cottrell, one of Schneider's other graduate students, asked me out. Cal had handled the statistical parts of the kinship project; he was intellectually immersed in anthropology, sociology, and the psychology of Otto Fenichel, an Austrian doctor who was influential at the time. I remember Cal as a dark and brooding twenty-something with close-cropped brown hair, unusually well built for an academic, his biceps bulging out of tight T-shirts, always with a drink in his hand (the liquor that, so I heard, eventually killed him), the ice sloshing and clinking to emphasize obscure points about anthropology and psychology. He had a twin I never met and came from the Midwest.

After going to the Loop for a cheap steak dinner, we came back to my Hyde Park apartment and sat on a Salvation Army couch, the first couch I had ever owned. While we talked departmental gossip I waited nervously for him to make a move toward me, trying to think how I would fend it off without spoiling our budding friendship. The move didn't come, and after a few drinks he confessed to me that he thought he was homosexual. His gaydar was obviously working overtime; he must have been extremely confident to reveal his secret to a fellow graduate student who could potentially destroy his career. Freed by my own drinks, I answered that I thought I was, too. This was a life-changing moment. We settled back on the couch to talk it over. It was probably the first time in my life that I was completely comfortable and relaxed with a man. He was the only person in the department, aside from Harriet Whitehead, with whom I was later intimate, that I ever told my secret during those six years. Cal opened the door to my career in queer anthropology.

Despite Cal's conviction, stoked by his immersion in Fenichel, that homosexuality was a personality defect that one ought to try to change, he was just embarking on his first gay relationship with a slightly older man named Bill who worked for the phone company. Bill was fully engaged in the middle-class closeted gay and lesbian life of mid-1960s Chicago, to which he introduced Cal and me. Afraid of my attraction to gay bars, I had shunned them since the summer of 1959.

Bill lived two completely separate lives. He was masculine and passed as straight at work with no difficulty. By night and on weekends, his friends called him "Mary" and "Miss Butch Thing," and he went to gay parties and bars. Through Bill and Cal I went to a gay and lesbian bar on the lakefront near the Loop and began to see how one could manage a life like this. At the bar, which was clean and never raided, men and women danced together while men cruised other men at the bar and women tried to meet one another at the tables. I didn't find a lover, but I did begin to have nodding acquaintances with other lesbians, who, like me, could pass if they had to.

Through John, I had come to know a biracial circle of Woodlawn residents, among whom were several black women that I found attractive and with whom I had dalliances. They in turn introduced me to others, and this gave me the idea to write my master's thesis on black single mothers, a hot topic in social science then as now. Why were poor black families centered on women? Why were women so independent in the urban ghetto? In the anthropological literature on the Caribbean these families in which women were central and men were peripheral were called "matrifocal" and, in the conformist atmosphere of the postwar period, seen as aberrant. The U.S. Department of Labor's *The Negro Family: The Case for National Action*, known widely as the Moynihan Report, blaming black mothers for urban poverty had just come out.[4] I knew there was something wrong with these analyses, although my own master's thesis, "Men, Women and Status in the Negro Family," pointed toward the complicity of black mothers in creating sons who would grow up to be the very men whose reluctance to commit to relationships and family life they complained of. At any rate, the thesis proved satisfactory enough for me to be admitted to the doctoral program.

Then I had one last fling with the romance—though not the reality—of getting married. It must be nearly impossible for young queers today to understand the absolute dominance of the heterosexual life script at that time, how difficult it was to dissent—not only publicly, but even in one's own mind. In fact, most gays and lesbians did not dissent. Like me, they just gave up trying to achieve the norm, or if they could marry, they relegated their truer desires to fantasy, restrooms (men), or secretive relationships (women).

Martin Silverman, a brilliant up-and-coming star in the department, was also Schneider's student. He had majored in anthropology at Harvard and seemed to know every ethnographic study, from the Andaman Islanders to the Zulus. He was intellectually confident; unlike me, he never hesitated to voice an informed opinion about matrilocality or the affiliation-versus-descent controversy in kinship studies, then the dominant interest in the department. He was pale, plain, bespectacled, intense, witty, the young Jewish scholar who never made a political misstep.

Martin had long planned to do his fieldwork in Fiji. In the weeks before he was to leave, we experienced a strange phenomenon of attraction probably not unlike that of the soldier and his girlfriend just before he ships out. He asked me to marry him, and on impulse, I agreed. He left—we had barely kissed, much less had sex or met each other's parents.

This was the perfect situation. I was engaged to a literate man to whom I could write long letters and who returned them in kind; I was able to show off his ring in the department and boast that this prodigy was my fiancé without actually having him present. I reoriented my studies once again, studying Fijian grammar and developing a plan to research the Fijians' elaborate social hierarchies.

But once again, my stronger impulses prevailed. It was not many months into Martin's absence that I fell in love with Harriet, another anthropology graduate student referred to locally as "the steel trap mind," who was expected to do great things. Harriet, like her close friend Cal, was a twin. Coming from the South, Harriet spoke with a drawl that reminded me of Peggy and Tex, my favorite counselors from Belgian Village Camp. She was small and slight, with light-blue eyes and a disposition that was both sly and shy. Harriet was one of those women who had avoided any kind of intimacy in favor of her studies so that, as callow as I was, I was more experienced than she. From the moment I sensed her interest, I began wooing her, trying to "bring her out," as we described introducing a supposedly straight person to a gay relationship. It didn't take long. The bigger difficulty was hiding our intense and tumultuous relationship and our growing involvement in Chicago gay life via Cal and his boyfriend Bill from our straight friends, such as Bobby Paul and Sherry Ortner, whom we saw almost daily. As to my fiancé, Martin Silverman, he was in Fiji, and I thought vaguely that I'd deal with the complications when he came back. Possibly Harriet's belief that I would eventually marry him made it easier for her to love me. But when the day of his return came and he held out his arms to me, I realized within hours that in pursuit of a fairy-tale I'd made fools of us both. I broke off with him the night he returned with no explanation— as a closeted homosexual, I couldn't tell him the truth. I knew then how unfair that was, but I had no choice.

/ / /

Quite unexpectedly, the inspiration for my life's work had already appeared on the cramped stage of a gay bar. I trace my love of theater and spectacle to the Gilbert and Sullivan operettas that were favorites of my mother's when we lived in New York. There was a small repertory company in our Upper East Side neighborhood, and over several years we saw everything, from the more obscure *Iolanthe* and *Princess Ida* to the more popular *Pirates of Penzance*. The costumes, makeup, lights, music, and, especially, words—Gilbert's witty rhyming "patter songs"—delighted us both. Going to these operettas was the one pleasure, besides dog training and movies, that my mother and I shared during those years of her despair.

But probably this love goes back further into both the delights and terrors of childhood. When I was five or six, my mother took me to see a small circus on the grounds of Bellevue Hospital near where we lived on 33rd Street. I remember little about it except for the clown. This medieval figure, with his white makeup, red nose, fright wig, and floppy shoes, panicked me. Was this a man or a woman? Was there a recognizable adult under those mismatched, loose, hanging clothes? Should I accept the candy he was holding out in his dirty white glove, or should I run for my life? I recall crying and clinging to my mother, demanding to leave. Perhaps all great loves spring from trauma. Part of my terror was fascination, awe of this aberrant and memorable character.

When I first saw Skip Arnold perform in a Chicago gay bar in 1965, I sensed he would change my life. Skip, who worked live, using his own voice and singing with a small band, appeared to be a huge woman figure in makeup, gown, wig, and high heels. The audience of gay men laughed, shouted, clapped at Skip's smutty, witty political patter. It was interactive, live performance:

> I'd like to tell you a fairy tale from the book of fairy tales, as told by an old fairy. An old blue-haired fairy (pats wig—audience laughs) I really look good tonight, though. I think I look gorgeous . . . with these bangs and this blue hair. I look like a knocked-up pouter pigeon . . . or robin redbreast. Oh well (clears throat in low voice) maybe it's what you're smokin' out there, my God . . . Mexico. We'll just sit here and hold our breath and we'll all go together. With our luck, it'd be the same paddy wagon.[5]

I had fleetingly seen drag queens and even lesbians dressed like men who worked as waiters at Club 82 in New York's East Village, where my former girlfriend Nannette had worked as a dancer, that summer of 1959. But this drag queen, Skip Arnold, was something special: a clown. This impression was strengthened when I saw him between shows. Up close, I could see the thick whiteness of his makeup and how over-the-top were his lipstick and false eyelashes. He was big, magical, and scary. Perfectly comfortable wigless with his feminine stage "face," Skip was holding forth to adoring men who were buying him drinks. A few weeks later, heart in my throat, I squeezed in next to him between shows and introduced myself as an anthropology graduate student. "I majored in anthropology in college," he drawled, with a flat Plains accent. "*Love* the subject." What had I expected? Not this. Who was this guy?

Back home my head raced around with the power of what I had seen: Skip looking down from the stage at his rapt audience, who were giving back an energy that ricocheted around the performance space and through our bodies. One of my friends was the ethnomusicologist Charley Keil. He was writing his dissertation on blues singers and understanding their audiences through their music and performance. Charley saw these musicians as symbolic leaders of the black urban community.[6]

His example, along with Schneider's work on American kinship, was fundamental for me. Both were working in American culture, and Keil was specifically analyzing culture through performance.

The academic fields of anthropology and sociology had different histories. In broad outline, sociology was developed by English and German intellectuals who were trying to understand the mechanics of European societies, while anthropology came out of nineteenth-century colonialism, the study, at first by missionaries, of non-Western, so-called primitive peoples. Although there were notable exceptions, by the 1960s anthropology and sociology departments had developed fairly rigid divisions of labor, and anthropological work on America and Europe was frowned on and rarely done.

At that point, I was still planning to follow Martin to Fiji, so I told myself I would write a course paper about the Chicago drag queens. When I told Skip that I wanted to tell the performers' story, he offered to help me. He would introduce me to performers, he said, and help me get interviews.

Then Martin and I broke up. Fiji was obviously part of a failed fantasy, and when I showed David Schneider some field notes about the female impersonators, he encouraged me to make them the subject of my doctoral dissertation. The drag queens excited me so much more than Africa or Fiji ever had. And yet, how dangerous! People would suspect I was gay. At least these were *men* I was thinking of working with, and not lesbians, with whom I would not have dared associate professionally.

Gay people were then looked on within social science as the object solely of psychological, medical, or even criminological study. Our supposedly bizarre behavior was presumed to arise from physical or psychological abnormalities. To the degree that *Mother Camp: Female Impersonators in America*, the book that resulted from my thesis, was the foundation document of gay and lesbian studies in social science, my mentor David Schneider was behind the paradigm shift that made this field possible. What he imparted to me, more in his office or his home than in the classroom, was that female impersonators (about whom he knew nothing more than what I told him) were a group of human beings and so necessarily had a culture worth studying. The insight that gays were not just a category of sick isolates but a group, and so had culture, was a breathtaking leap whose daring is hard to recapture now, when the term "gay community" is so familiar, but Schneider made it without any fuss. He helped me to develop the intellectual tools to do the work, and just as important, he was prepared to back me up with his departmental clout.

Schneider and I were both naive. Although frightened of being associated with homosexuality, I was young and energetic and plunged into the moment, with no concept of how profoundly this choice would shape my career and my life. Schneider was confident in his power as chair of the department, and he kept his promise to back me, right to the end of his life. But he had no experience with the virulence and pervasiveness of homophobia and did not even realize I was a lesbian. How could he understand the danger I was putting myself in? We both relied on the convention that academic work and personal life were, and were to be kept, completely separate, which was dominant in all scientific fields at the time. No one talked publicly or wrote about "private" reasons that they chose a field of study or their "private" experience of doing fieldwork. So no one, I hoped, could publicly accuse me of being a lesbian because I chose to study male homosexuals.[7] Had either of us foreseen how much writing about female impersonators would hurt my career, I wonder whether I would have charged ahead. In retrospect, though, this dangerous decision was the gateway to my true life's work in writing and teaching.

The same Maginot Line between public and private experience also meant that I had no idea how to do fieldwork. We had one Methods course in graduate school taught by a happy-go-lucky sociologist, a time waster that the department had developed because most anthro graduate students could not pass a statistics course. You could get some idea of what anthropologists did with "their" people by reading the ethnographies that described these cultures but not *how* they did it in a practical sense or how they dealt with fear, loneliness, and the daily frustrations of trying to survive in difficult and alien circumstances. I got the best and only advice from Schneider: never go to bed without writing up your field notes and always make a carbon copy to mail to your adviser.

And so I set off.[8] At that time there were five or six different venues for drag in Chicago, all of them in gay men's bars. These men accepted my presence because they assumed, correctly, that I was a lesbian (if they asked I told them) and because of my friendship with Skip. From

With David Schneider and his standard poodle George. Santa Cruz, California, around 1990.

the beginning, my fieldwork involved hanging around gay bars and drag queens and watching drag shows. Fairly soon I was able to do taped interviews with performers and found that I enjoyed this work. I had a gift for listening, it turned out.

From the outset I rejected the then dominant stigmatizing psychological paradigm ("The queers are sick. How can we cure them?"). My perspective had been formed by the pioneering work of the Chicago sociologists who had sympathetically written about all kinds of "deviants," such as pickpockets and pimps, and above all by Erving Goffman's amazing book *Stigma*, a theoretical approach to understanding how and why socially disfavored groups come to have "spoiled identities" and how they manage their situations.

So my questions to female impersonators were never "Why are you like this?" which they would have resented, but always "How did you learn to do female impersonation?" and "How do you understand your performances?" As I was getting deeper and deeper into the gay male community, Skip moved to a different gig in Kansas City. I couldn't imagine continuing without his support, and so I made two trips there, where he got me in backstage. There is no substitute for direct observation. I saw and heard many things that no one told me in an interview, like how they "tuck" their genitals back and how tiny and dirty their dressing rooms were. I met their boyfriends, saw them get high and get harassed, and learned how much safer Kansas City was for gays because of Mafia protection for the bars.

Although the Kansas City scene couldn't have been queerer, it was as male-dominated as a New Guinea men's house. I let them know I was gay, of course, and that helped me gain trust. But I was still a "fish," as they said, and to a large extent out of water. They never forgot it, and neither did I. My worst moment came during one of my stays in Kansas City. Skip took me to a party at which the buffet meal featured a foot-long pâté in the shape of a cock and balls. Suddenly I couldn't stand one more prick, dick, or phallus. I was lonely, doubting my ability to pull off the fieldwork, the thesis, an academic career, and my life. Outwardly cool (I hoped), I really felt totally out of my depth and excused myself from the party. In tears I drove around Kansas City in the Plymouth Valiant that was a hand-me-down from my mother, with the radio blaring Motown, until I recovered enough poise to return to my rented room.

Finally, in 1968, I had finished writing "The Drag Queens: A Study in Urban Anthropology." My thesis committee, composed of the ultra-distinguished anthropologists David Schneider, Julian Pitt-Rivers, and Clifford Geertz, had suggested minor revisions and signed off on them. David and Ady had me over to their house to prepare me for my thesis defense, which could have gone badly, since several professors found my topic more of a dirty joke and also illegitimate because it was not about "primitives." I had to play the game, David and Ady said, urging me to wear a dress to my thesis defense in my own calculated interest. I did, and when the hearing date arrived, Schneider was there with his sleeves rolled up to take on the professors who said my thesis wasn't

My onetime drag appearance during the ceremonial Invasion of the Pines.
Cherry Grove, New York, 1988.

really anthropology. I think I was the first in my class to finish, and certainly one of the few women to do so; as the graduate of a prestigious anthropology program, with a powerful mentor, my future should have been bright.

After my successful defense, the august professors, as was the custom, took me out to the Quadrangle Club for lunch. It was me and my dress among thirty or forty men in suits. The head of the department asked me why it was that, although the department was admitting lots of women to the program, so few were finishing their degrees. The answer was sitting there at lunch.

/ / /

In treating drag queens and homosexuals from a cultural perspective, and in highlighting both the condemnation from which they suffered, greatly, and the adulation they received from their audiences, I was saying that gays were a group like any other, a proper subject for anthropology. I used the language of symbolic anthropology and social deviance that I had learned at David Schneider's knee, and I poured into it every insight and every ounce of anger I'd experienced while trying to be a girl for twenty-five years, living the double life of a young closeted gay person, turning away, not daring to respond to the daily insults and suspicions.

Drag was the milieu of that same gender dysphoria that had tormented me, where a kindred pain was spun into connection, laughter, and creative gold. After all, I, too, had practiced female impersonation of a different kind, most intensely during my high school and college years. Since writing Mother Camp, I have always loved drag, which I recognized as a theatrical performance related to my inner life and experience.

I saw hardly any male impersonators—who were then simply called drag butches—with the exception of the waiters at Club 82 in New York and the great Stormé DeLarverie, who performed with the racially inclusive Jewel Box Revue. The Jewel Box advertised as "Twenty-Five Men and a Girl," the punch line being that among the drag queen chorus the one performer who looked like a man revealed herself to be the girl. At the time I speculated that lesbians doing drag were scarce, ironically, because drag performance was much more accessible to men than to women, and I was proved right by the later emergence of the raucous lesbian drag theater, strongly influenced by female impersonation, that began in New York City at the WOW Café in 1981 and a successor group, the Five Lesbian Brothers.[9] By the 1990s, "drag king" performers and revues had appeared, while female impersonation had itself become much more varied and sophisticated and even mainstream.

By temperament and training I am a scholar, and my only performances have been as a teacher in front of a class. I have only done drag once in my life, in the gay community of Cherry Grove. To me, passing as a man in everyday life, out of a gay context, was quite a different thing that I never attempted, through a failure of nerve or feminist conviction, or both, although countless times I have been mistaken for a man: "Come right this way, sir." Until the past few years, I would correct that attribution, leading to flustered apologies that never failed to annoy me. In my old age I mostly don't bother, although the other day, at the geriatric health center I frequent, a woman politely confronted me with, "Do you know you just used the women's bathroom?" There was no easy way out, so I replied, "Yes. I'm a woman." As she started the usual apologies, I added, "and I can read."

CHAPTER 7

LESBIAN FEMINIST NEW YORK

Little by little this idea of being Gertrude began to grow
inside my head. It wasn't yet about living in Paris or
about writing, but about being accepted as an equal by
men within a very small select circle, and of living in a
happy domesticated couple with heaps of good food. So
naturally, the big thing was to find an Alice.

—ESTHER NEWTON, *Alice Hunting*, unpublished manuscript

By the summer of 1966, the stormy affair with Harriet Whitehead, my
fellow anthropology graduate student, had blown over, and I had moved
out of Hyde Park to the Near North Side, to be farther from the university and closer to what I thought of then as the gay community (actually
the white gay community). No blame attaches to Harriet or to me for
the breakup; between us, we might have had the emotional maturity of
one young adult.

Although now fairly neat and usually punctual, I was still controlling,
anxious, inflexible, and given to fierce eruptions of temper. In those
days, young queers reached adulthood in a stunted condition. While the
majority of young women and men were growing, one supposes, through

dating, love affairs, and parenting, we were like little hamsters racing around the same wheel of fear and uncertainty. The most important discovery of my hetero years was that it didn't work for me, but what *would* work?

One factor among many in our breakup had been Harriet's desire to touch me sexually, which no woman before had asked. I had no conscious desire for this reciprocity—quite the contrary, as I still thought of myself as a stone butch, meaning "untouchable." The word "touch" is apt because hands are often central to lesbian eroticism. Hands in our world are not just penis substitutes. For many gay women they are also erotic organs, all the more attractive the more competent they are at playing violin or smacking a volleyball. A future figurative lesbian erotic art would feature hands more than fields of flowers or vaginal dinner plates. But I digress.

Making love to a woman was still precious to me, transgressive and thrilling. Harriet had been my first homosexual relationship (as opposed to frustrated crushes and sexual adventures), and I still could not believe that a woman would want me. (Even the passage of decades and many lovers has not completely demystified the magic of an appealing woman's come-hither glance.) Despite my struggle to go straight, it was clear by age twenty-six that I'd rather kiss a woman who attracted me than be fucked by any man. But kissing wasn't the end of it. I took pleasure in my own sexual excitement as I touched women's breasts and genitals, as I humped them enthusiastically and went down on them, as Nannette the exotic dancer had so helpfully taught me. I had never had an orgasm with a man, either, always experiencing the failure of a femininity whose moments of success had also creeped me out.

My first mature love was the painter, Nancy Rae Smith, who had been fresh out of Bennington College when she had taken me, then thirteen, under her wing. When I came to New York every summer and at Christmas during my California exile, hers was the first phone number I would call. She would invite me downtown, and as I climbed her worn wooden stairs in Greenwich Village, my heart would thrum happily. Her door would fly open, and she would open her arms to me for a big hug. Literally big, for she was several inches taller than me with long arms and hands, big feet. She had WASP-straight brown hair that she mostly wore down her back, tied at the nape with a plain brooch, and a long, plain, expressive face. I remember her in the white chinos and Woolrich navy shirt she wears in one of my favorite photos. Or she would wear a loose cotton shirt of a kind I had never seen before, a deep and foreign blue, with several big pockets, which she explained was a French work-man's shirt. She knew about so many intriguing things. Often she had oil paint under her nails and on her long sensitive fingers, which always cradled a beer or something stronger.

When I was nineteen, during the summer of 1959 when Betty Silver introduced me to New York bar life, I told Nancy all about it, and to my utter shock she made a pass at me. Likely she was drunk, though I was clueless. Terrified, I fled. To me at that time, lesbian meant butch-femme. Nancy was not in any obvious sense femme to my butch; if any-thing, she was androgynous. Most centrally, she was a maternal figure, and the whole thing was too complicated and scary.

Over my college years, our rift was mended with nothing more said of it. Around 1960, Nancy fell in love with Patsy, a composer and musician. Patsy, like Nancy, was from a WASPy and affluent family. Both had gone to expensive private women's colleges, and both were arty. They moved into an apartment in Brooklyn Heights, where a visit once in 1966 left a profound impression on me. Like most young lesbians of my genera-tion I had only inferred from books that lesbian homes must exist. For the lonely child of a suicidally depressed mother, the home—an imag-ined place of safety, comfort, and pleasure—was as alluring as travel and adventure were to those whose homes had been too confining. As Nancy and Patsy discussed their planned summer vacation in Rhode Island and the trips they would take in their kayak, I listened in envious wonder. The lesbians I had known in the bars counted themselves lucky to take a day trip to the "gay" beach at Riis Park, where they might float on an inner tube. I remember no details of their apartment, only that it was full of light, showing off subtle colors and beautiful objects, includ-ing a grand piano. This was a grownup life I wanted to aspire to. I found Patsy, who was slim and athletic-looking, with blue-green eyes and a spray of freckles across her nose, very attractive (which would later lead to some of the more painful episodes of my young life).

By the summer of 1966, Nancy and Patsy were breaking up for rea-sons that were never explained to me, although Nancy once told me that Patsy was "boring," meaning, perhaps, that Nancy found her more

Greenwich, Connecticut, than Greenwich Village. It is a measure of how restricted and private middle-class lesbians were then that eventually Nancy had relationships with Patsy and with me and with a woman named Elizabeth; I had relationships with both Nancy and Patsy, and Elizabeth had relationships with both Nancy and Patsy; in other words, we exhausted all but one of the theoretical possibilities. These women never went to bars, never participated in any lesbian "scene."

Meanwhile, Nancy had had one too many rebuffs in the New York art world. You had to be a man or the girlfriend of a painter to have a chance, she said, a situation with which I was familiar in academia. She had reluctantly turned away from her painting career and moved to Boston, where she had started graduate school in art education. That summer of 1966 she was attending a summer program at the Bank Street College of Education and staying in a Village apartment that had three windows on the street and was radiant with sunlight.

I remember nothing about our conversation; likely it was about my drag queen thesis and her studies. Nancy was excited by ideas, and while we talked I could feel the tension rising between us until finally she held out her long arms to enfold me. Butch-femme didn't apply; she was more powerful, ten years older, so sophisticated, my protector and my friend. Gone also was the terror that had gripped me at her approach seven years earlier. I never felt exploited or manipulated, before or after. Now I was ready, I wanted this although I hadn't expected it, and I opened myself to her, followed her lead. With her I didn't feel feminine. I felt like a cherished love object just as I was—or, even better, just as she saw what I could be. Nancy was the first lover that I ever trusted. She had taken in my teenage self, acne, misery, and all, given me friendship and her time, listened to my sophomoric certainties and pains with patience and humor, and opened me up to the ways of the world: Chet Baker! Rhode Island summer rentals! Kayaks! Having her as a lover was more akin to the ancient Athenian experience, though I knew nothing about Sappho and Plato's teacher-student homoeroticism (which had not been mentioned in my college philosophy class).

The apartment had no air conditioning, and I twisted in the sweaty sheets, flying higher and higher in her knowledgeable hands. Always before I had put on the brakes when facing this open road, sometimes on purpose but many times just grinding, without willing it, to a halt.

Nancy Rae Smith, around 1967.

Nancy was attuned to me; each time my brakes came on she would step easy on the gas. Eventually my body was no longer a car I could steer or brake but a rocket that exploded, the debris orbiting the earth a couple of times and floating back to the ocean. I lay there in shuddering spasms, rigid with fear, gasping for breath. "What is this?" I whispered. Nancy held me in her arms. She laughed, explaining that *this* was an orgasm. Wow! I was always afraid of death, even of sleep; this letting go was new territory. Once you've seen the promised land, you may not be able to get back, but you know it's there.

"Motorcycle lover," 1967. Photograph by Nancy Rae Smith.

We became lovers. Not just because of the orgasm; I truly adored her and gave her as much commitment as I then had to give. There was nothing left for me in Chicago, and it was not hard to leave. I would have moved with her to Boston or to another galaxy, but Nancy wisely suggested that, as I already knew New York, I should move there and we would commute. I had finished my fieldwork with drag queens and was writing my dissertation, so I could be anywhere, and at the end of the summer of 1967 I packed all my belongings in a U-Haul trailer and drove back to the city of my birth.

I was twenty-six. The next two years, from the time I moved back to New York until I met Louise Fishman at Frederica Leser's Christmas party in 1969, were chaotic and eventful. My roommate in a two-bedroom apartment on the Upper West Side of Manhattan was Roz, a straight woman my age, someone I'd had a crush on when we were both counselors at a Zionist summer camp, after my junior year of college.

The arrangement worked out pretty well, as I was frequently away on weekends visiting Nancy in Boston.

Nancy and I lasted for about nine months. She picked out flattering shirts and pants for me, she took photos of me that captured a romantic beauty I hadn't known I had, and she gave me presents: a gold ring of an arty design that I didn't really like because my style was more tailored, paintings and photographs, records of medieval recorder music. How I needed to be cherished. I wanted it to work with Nancy, but I was immature and naive. What our fights were about I don't recall, but they intensified in tenor and ferocity, and toward the end I began to understand that the more she drank, the worse the fights. The last screaming fight, the "it's over" fight, took place in my New York apartment awash with her wine bottles. We were both devastated.

Later, Nancy began to descend into alcoholic despair. All progressives were distraught by the reversals of the 1970s: Nixon, the wars dragging on. Nancy got her doctorate and was hired as an art educator at Boston University, and then tangled with John Silber, the university's right-wing president, who had her fired. After that, she told me, "They won't give me any space for my ideals—they don't even credit me with having any. What's the use, the bastards! There's no way to live, nothing left to live for."

Nancy was a martyr to sexism, homophobia, and alcohol. Her painting career was derailed in the male-dominated art scene, and she couldn't fit into its heterosexual framework, though she tried. For the rest of her life she never had another male lover, but she couldn't accept herself because she bought into bohemia's dismissal of lesbianism as too limiting. After her academic career she founded a progressive school in the Boston area in order to teach art to kids and spent the last years of her life pining over a straight woman colleague who did not fully return her love. As I became more and more committed to feminism and then to gay liberation, she disapproved, and from the 1970s on, we saw each other less frequently.

Her physical decline was shocking. The last time I saw her, though only in her fifties, she had difficulty walking up a slight incline, thanks to what she called "the hooch." Once she explained to me how much she loved drinking, how it was like sucking on a nourishing breast. During the same years of her life that she wasted longing for the straight woman she had found a therapist who convinced her that under his care she would be able to continue drinking, in moderation. Hepatitis did not get her to stop. Cirrhosis did not get her to stop. Her liver and kidneys were giving out, and she got an infection. Faced with having to live on dialysis and stop drinking, she elected to die. This was in the 1980s.

I was right to dread going to her memorial, which was well attended. The private-school teachers and employees spoke only of her passion for education. Although her three most important exes, Patsy, Elizabeth, and I, were all there, we were not invited to speak, and nothing was said of her personal life. She was pictured by these well-meaning school teachers as solely dedicated to art education and children's well-being. Left out was the raunchy, bohemian drunken WASP who loved women and was passionately loved back. I understood that gays in education could not easily come out during their lifetimes, but now she was dead. But when I complained to Patsy, she said that Nancy would not have wanted her lesbianism mentioned, and the fact that she was likely right only made me feel worse.

When I first went to Al-Anon decades later, I couldn't identify with all the partners of drunks who claimed to be doormats. Later I understood that there's another kind of co-dependent: the rescuer. To rescue my mother from her disinheritance, her violent husband, her depression, and her drinking . . . that was the life project that propelled me toward her avatars whom I also held responsible for entertaining me and making me laugh, as my mother had.

/ / /

Like most women, I was preoccupied by romantic intimacy, but three of the most important things that happened during those early years back in New York, in retrospect, were not romantic. I strengthened my friendship with my college roommate, Shirley Walton; my dissertation got finished and published as a book; and I became a feminist.

One of the benefits of moving back to New York was that two of my former college roommates, Hilary Smith and Shirley Walton, were then sharing an apartment on Veranda Place in Brooklyn. We began to see one another regularly. As in college, I was especially close to Shirley, and our chosen sisterhood came to sustain both our lives.

In the summer of 1965, we had traveled together to Mexico for a few weeks. The trip was not all roses; we drove down through states where we feared my Volkswagen Beetle might be run off the road or the cops might use our Illinois plates as an excuse to arrest us. It was the mid-'60s and the civil rights battles were still fresh. In Mexico, I got *tourista* and felt sorry for myself, which annoyed Shirley, and I blamed her short skirts partly for our unwanted attentions from Mexican men. When we took a trip into the hinterlands to buy some Mexican blankets, we were menaced by scary villagers and fled for our safety. But it was an adventure, and in the long run it strengthened our bond.

Shirley and I both wound up living most of our adult lives in New York City, and we both became dedicated feminists, even writing a book together, *Womenfriends*, about the strains on our friendship during the tumultuous years of early second wave feminism.[1] I often took her advice, laughed at her wacky sense of humor; we shared popcorn and Raisinettes at many movies. I admired her intelligence and enjoyed her cooking. But most of all, I loved what her husband, Stan Fischler, called her "no bullshit" attitude. Outwardly conventional from her thirties on, Shirley never said the expected or trite. Intuitive and astute, she could spot a phony or a toupee immediately and never hesitated to say so. Through her and our friendship I learned so many life lessons and had such a good time.

Shirley dreamed of writing the great American novel, but mostly what she turned out were articles and books about men's professional hockey in partnership with her husband. When we met as freshmen, I played the nerd with good grades, and Shirley, the bad girl with a taste for black men and drugs. But in our late twenties, the roles reversed: I became a gay liberationist while she married Stan, a Jewish newspaper journalist who later became a well-known hockey writer and television personality. Yet she still thought of herself as a badass *playing* the role of housewife and mother, and although I no longer wanted to be "normal," she saw me as conformist and careerist in my professional life. Despite a couple of painful ruptures, we always managed to forgive, if not forget, and adhere somewhere in the middle of shitkicker and the "bubblehead" she feared being taken for. We were, in fact, both rebels and conformists in our respective spheres.

Shirley was a complicated woman, full of ambivalence and contradictions, but she was fiercely loyal to those she loved: her husband; sons Ben and Simon; and, later, five grandchildren, whom she adored. Surrounded and sometimes aggravated by the men in her family, she valued her close female friends, some of whom, like me, dated back to her University of Michigan years, welcoming them to share the stability and warmth of her home. I can't count the Passovers I shared with the Fischlers or the vacation days I spent at their house in the Catskills.

Even as our lives diverged, we shared intimate secrets and turned to each other for practical, emotional, and, occasionally, monetary help. If my car broke down in New Jersey, Shirley would come get me. When she was stuck in an abusive relationship in college, and another in New York with an older man, I was the one she called to help her escape. She got a loan from me to finance her younger son's bar mitzvah.

We kept few secrets from each other and told each other things no one else knew. For example, in my fifties I had my first "senior moment." Back then, if you wanted your word processing program to change fonts—I had acquired my first computer a few years before—you had to tell the machine what to do by typing codes, like this: <italics>. While working on the manuscript of my book about Cherry Grove, the word "italic" suddenly would not come to me, and I feared it might be early Alzheimer's. Utterly panicked, I phoned Shirley (and no one else, not even the girlfriend in the next room). "Well, let's see," she said calmly and administered a memory test from the Harvard health newsletter. I passed, and we joked about it.

Around 1990, Shirley joined me for a cross-country road trip in an Isuzu Trooper, with my two standard poodles riding in the back (she, too, was a dog lover). We shared the driving, but only after Ms. Leadfoot laughingly promised she wouldn't indulge in her habit of speeding. The Blue Ridge Mountains in the fall were at their most colorful, the vistas magical. I never dreamed that it would be our last road trip.

/ / /

My other friends in those years were mostly young people my age who were connected with my father's growing circle of therapists and analysands. We had all been radicalized by the Civil Rights Movement and

With Shirley Walton Fischler. City Island, New York, around 1976.

the endless war in Vietnam, events that had somewhat passed me and my friends by in the early and middle 1960s, cloistered as we were in graduate school. These New York friends were looking for revolutionary change and thought they were finding it in my father's Marxist therapeutic community, which had already become cultish—for example, while the therapists lived in their own apartments, the analysands lived with roommates whom the therapists picked out for them.

In the summer of 1968, I rented a small house in Amagansett in Suffolk County on the end of Long Island. For years I had visited my father and stepmother's house on Gardner's Bay, and before Shirley's marriage we had hung around a gay bar out there called End of the World, a tonier place than the bars I had known in 1959, so that affluent straight couples felt safe enough to come to ogle the dancing queers, a humiliation I've never forgotten.

Without Shirley, I quickly felt lonely and drove to the Catskills to visit her new cabin on Traver Hollow Road. One day I decided to look up Nancy's ex, Patsy, who had rented a house for the summer in Byrdcliffe, in the hills north of Woodstock. The house overlooked the valley, and like the apartment in Brooklyn Heights where Nancy and Patsy had once lived, it was full of beautiful old furniture, prints, and all kinds of music. Patsy introduced me to Joni Mitchell—I still associate "Sisotowbell Lane," a beautiful ode to domestic bliss, with our affair, and she explained why the Beatles and Paul Simon were so musically great. Her students played chamber music and piano sonatas, and Patsy and I played recorder duets. To the sounds of music we fell into her bed, all the more exciting, I am sorry to say, as we both knew Nancy would be upset.

Patsy, I'm sure, has never identified as butch, it would be too déclassé. She was the daughter of a wealthy banker and never had to have a salaried job. But her slim, athletic body, the crisp way she held herself, and her frontal rather than seductive approach to sex made her the first more masculine woman I had ever been intimate with. Back in the bars in 1959, I had occasionally, with surprised alarm, felt attraction to other butches. That world was, within its outlaw status, conventional, with compulsory lesbian genders and butches to be attracted to femmes only. Getting it on with other butches would have been beyond queer.

But I was besotted with Patsy. Back in New York I thought of nothing but our week in Byrdclyffe. I assumed she was my true love and that we would establish an enchanted musical life together. She didn't even call me. When finally I swallowed my pride and phoned her, she was blandly noncommittal, which depressed me more than if she had been downright rejecting. For Patsy, this was just a spicy episode, but I carried a torch for years afterward. We would have two more fiery and, for me, thrilling encounters, after which, each time, she dropped me with no explanation.

In a way this was part of my class problem. Later I wrote, *"Whenever I see Patsy, I leave feeling like shit. I imagine I have bad breath, body odor, wrong fitting clothing, etc. What is it? Despite myself, I will always feel less than her, smaller, or bigger, more grotesque. As she said to me once, smugly, after I had complained about Yale, where I had once taught a course, 'that shows how little you know about Yale.'"* In her presence I was once again not quite white, not really a WASP, the illegitimate child of the failed debutant. I responded to these privileged women aesthetically, emotionally, and erotically and with a fierce anxiety that I tried to quell by devouring them.

I have thought a lot about these episodes with Patsy and the intensity of my involvement. Years later, in one of the fancy sublets she was always getting from well-connected friends, Patsy casually confessed to me, "I only contacted you when I needed an ego boost." The torch I'd been carrying for so many years flickered out—a blackened stump. I was ashamed. How had I wasted so much longing on an unrequited and undeserved crush, to the detriment of the women who actually loved me? The experience led me to reflect, not for the first or last time, on the phantasmagoric nature of romantic love.

/ / /

In retrospect, my tentative interest in the counterculture came to a halt in the summer of 1969, when a group of us rented a house on Zena Road outside Woodstock. The experiment was unsuccessful. Group or communal living during the '60s was as ideologically desirable as it was personally intolerable. I had put myself together as a functioning adult in college with difficulty, and it turned out that I needed plenty of private space to stay sane. Or maybe it was as Shirley said: that as a spoiled only child with my own room, I needed to have everything my own way. (She had had to share with three siblings.)

Restless and unhappy on Zena Road, I packed up my suitcase and dog to head back to New York. On the way I decided to stop to see the Woodstock Festival in Bethel, New York. As I crept along in the rain and mud, surrounded by longhaired kids laughing, tripping, or miserably trailing damp sleeping bags, I felt my otherness so acutely. Alone except for my dog in this groupiest of heterosexual scenes, I became terrified that I would get stuck in traffic or muck and not be able to get out. I turned my car around and sped away. My kind of alienated perspective never appears in accounts of the Woodstock experience; it was their world, we just tried to survive in it.

/ / /

My mentor, David Schneider, never stopped believing in the importance of my work. He got me a contract in an anthropology series he was editing, and I revised it for the book that became *Mother Camp: Female Impersonators in America*.[2] This should have been my ticket into the permanent professoriate, because a published book was required for tenure. Although it was hardly reviewed and attracted no notice at the time, *Mother Camp* became the basis of my reputation in LGBT studies and eventually proved to be a radical breakthrough.[3] My approach was an alternative and a reproach to stigmatizing discourse of the shrinks that shaped public opinion about homosexuality until 1973. Clearly, I had broken away from my father's domination.

/ / /

After I had moved back to New York, Shirley and I formed a proto-feminist women's support group along with the anthropologist Jill Feeley, whom I had met through Nancy Smith, and a couple of other women whom neither Shirley nor I could recall. Unfortunately, the group broke up as each member found a lover. Shirley accused me of being the first one to defect. It was the failure of the "girls' night out" that, by her account, decided Shirley to marry in February 1968.

Later that year, I was watching the Miss America pageant on television when suddenly from the balcony a banner appeared with two words: "Women's Liberation." I don't recall seeing footage of the protests outside the hall, or the picture of the woman marked up like cuts of beef, or the crowning of a live sheep as Miss America. What I remember is my astonishment that women were protesting womanhood. There were other women out there, even women with long hair, feminine women, who were fed up with being good girls. As I saw it, they were joining me. I was no longer alone with my anger.

My mother, influenced so strongly by her grandmother, the journalist Lucia Gilbert, had always been a feminist. She believed in equal rights; she never tried to force me to conform to the gender codes, certainly not to date or get married. Her bitter life experiences had stripped away all romanticism from paternal authority and from heterosexual relationships. "Hoover's Greatest Erection," she would say sarcastically as we passed the Hoover Tower on the Stanford campus. Not for a moment did she believe that men were smarter or better, and she frequently complained about the all-male board of directors of the prestigious Westminster Kennel Club. My father, too, supported feminism, in theory; women's equality, along with racial equality, were central to the platform in the Communist Party. As long as the women in his life deferred to Saul and served his needs, he supported their aspirations as he had supported mine. So I already shared many of the ideas that became part of second wave feminism. What my ideas did not have was coherence or support from like-minded companions: a political movement. At that time, I knew nothing about nineteenth-century feminism.

Over the next year I started looking for this Women's Liberation, despite my doubts that a lesbian would ever be accepted. It is possible that I found feminist groups through the poet and activist Martha Shelley, whom I knew because she was in therapy with one of my father's crowd. The day after Valentine's Day 1969, a group called the Women's International Terrorist Conspiracy from Hell (WITCH)

> swooped down on Bridal Fairs held simultaneously in New York City and San Francisco. "Confront the Whoremakers" they told prospective brides and their mothers. WITCH leaflets said "marriage is a dehumanizing institution—legal whoredom for women. . . . A woman is taught from infancy that her only real goal in life is to fulfill the

role of wife and mother of male heirs. She is allowed an identity only as an appendage to a man. . . . The wedding ceremony is the symbolic ritual of our legal transference from father's property to husband's property." At the shows WITCHes chanted, "Here come the slaves. Off to their graves."[4]

The cheekiness of it, the radically unfeminine viewpoint, the media savvy, the theatricality, I loved everything. In September 1969, I went with Martha and some feminist women I barely knew to the second Miss America protest in Atlantic City. I wasn't much of a demonstrator, more of a spectator and supporter. In radical feminist Jo Freeman's photos, there is a figure that could be me, standing slightly outside of the circle of younger feminists seated on the boardwalk. Martha is in at least two of the photos: in one carrying a poster with the likeness of a nineteenth-century feminist and the words, "But My Dear, I Am Already liberated," and another with a portrait of the suffragist and abolitionist Lucy Stone.

Besides Martha, one person present stuck in my long-term memory: the radical black lawyer Flo Kennedy, a tower of a woman who was there as a kind of mentor and to intervene if protesters were arrested. She was so strategic about achieving visibility and impact; so firmly undeferential to the police; and such a steadying force for the energetic, young, middle-class, white feminists that I thought, Now here's a woman I can respect.

But the white feminists impressed me, too. The Miss America protest was, for me, what the French call a *coup de foudre*, a falling in love like a thunderbolt. In a skit the protestors performed right there on the boardwalk I saw what my life would have been had I, at nineteen, married Ivan and had a baby. First, the years of cleaning, cooking, and tedium. Then the wife character tries to get a job while harried by signs that read, "Boring Job: Woman Wanted," "Low Pay: Woman Wanted." Then she meets the "Revlon Lady" (a sponsor of the pageant), who tells her that life will be better if she puts on a mask. "Get a whole new face, a whole new look," "Buy! Buy! Buy!" So the wife buys, puts on a dress, puts on a mask—and nothing changes. She's mopping the boardwalk. Then finally—a typing job. As she types, the other performers, "Revlon lady," "husband," "sign carriers" beat her till she has collapsed, defeated, on the boardwalk.[5]

Here was the future I had, with whatever regrets, rejected: marriage, scrubbing floors, being a secretary. These women were saying I had been right. What they stood for, what they were enacting, was true. Palo Alto was over. The '50s were over. No more nice girls!

So-called consciousness-raising groups were springing up in many urban areas and on college campuses. Young women who had been politicized in student antiwar movements, where they had gained experience as organizers, usually formed these small groups, whose purpose was to transform women's individual self-hatred and acquiescence into united action to change "capitalist patriarchy." I later understood that we were the "second wave" of a movement that had begun in the nineteenth century and that our antiauthoritarian organizing principles had anarchist roots, but Americans' ignorance of history means that every generation must reinvent the wheel.

The slogan that feminists lived by in those early days was "The Personal Is Political." What we meant was that those experiences that we had thought private, from hating our body hair to being raped or being discouraged in school, were shared with other women and the result of systematic male domination that we could expose and fight against as a group. More and more women would join us as they saw the light of sisterhood.

My group, called Upper West Side WITCH, met once a week and consisted of fifteen or so young women. For a couple of years, these women became my sisters in feminism; they provided an alternative perspective not only on the future I had rejected but also on the future on which I had embarked: academia. The grotesque Vietnam War had delegitimized liberals in our eyes. Academics were liberals: feh! The career ladder: tenure and full professorhood were dry, dull, conformist, co-opted, something I had already suspected. Every WITCH meeting gave birth to new ideas, more solidarity.

How to convey the excitement? Often we were out demonstrating. One night we disrupted a local meeting of indignant Republicans. We went to high schools to tell students that the war was racist and that white men were oppressing all women. We sweated in packed halls where hundreds of spellbound women would watch the new feminist theater groups such as It's All Right to Be Woman, and we went to concerts where Holly Near would sing the praises of sisterhood. We went to Washington, DC, to protest the war. As it dragged on, several of the women had friends who joined the Weather Underground, but the feeling in my group was that the Weathermen were going off the rails.

My biggest hesitation about feminism was the fear that straight feminists would reject me. With the exception of my psychiatrist in Palo Alto, twelve years previously, I still had never confessed my homosexuality to any straight person other than Shirley. Not one. Even though I have met gay people that I wouldn't trust to wipe my glasses and, more recently, delightful gay-friendly straight people, there are many situations where, as a result of my years in the closet and loyalty toward my fellow outcasts, I see the world as "us" and "them." A dance floor, a movie theater, a beach—they are all either gay or straight to me. I thought a feminist group would be straight, and in the beginning that seemed true.

After several months of silence when the weekly topic would touch on boyfriends ("Women's work is unpaid labor. How do we get him to share it?"), I blurted out that I was bisexual. Although I had never thought of myself that way, it was the most I could dare. They volleyed back reassurance: "feminism is about ALL women," and the like. I did not then know it, but this response disguised fears of some others in the group that they might be lesbians, too. Some months later, during one of our visits to a high school to discuss the movement, my sisters planned how they would bring up the topic of lesbianism, which they understood as important, if not central, to feminism. "Don't let Esther say anything," they said. "She's too vulnerable. One of us has to deal with it." This taught me a lesson I would never forget in how to evaluate the trustworthiness and savvy of straight allies. From then on, I had confidence in the sisters' political judgment and their sincere acceptance of me personally and of lesbianism.

We saw ourselves as leading a revolution that would change the world. When the second wave began, abortion was illegal; women could not get credit cards or mortgages in their own names; and husbands could not be arrested for raping their wives. So there has been great progress, at least in our country, although feminism does not get the credit it deserves. But there has been no revolution against the patriarchy, much less the military-industrial state. The rich are richer than ever, and capitalist ideologues and advertisers have partly succeeded in transforming feminism into a career path for affluent white women ("Lean In"). Instead of a left-wing feminist revolt, we got Reagan and the Bushes and now, the worst of the worst, Trump.

Still, feminism was and is revolutionary for me personally. Since childhood I had resented my second-class status, and feminism legitimized my anger. Up to that point, my whole life had tended toward my becoming, like Gertrude Stein or Marguerite Yourcenar, an exceptional woman, a woman fitting into a male world with masculine values and ideals. Most women were feminine; I was not. Most women wanted to get married and have children. Most women had menial jobs or were homemakers; I was going to be a college professor. The feminist paradigm interrupted all that. My exceptionalism, I saw, was situated within the same gender matrix that constrained all other women. Now when I thought about how I'd been reprimanded for wearing pants too often in graduate school yet told not to be a flirt, I saw that dilemma in a political context. From this point on, feminism would affect not only my choices of partners and friends, but also my career path, with all of its ups and downs. No longer did I shun women at parties. Suddenly women were more interesting than men, more politically savvy and involved.

/ / /

The Stonewall riots in June 1969 did not have as big an impact on me, at first, as the Miss America protest that September. I had just finished my first year as an assistant professor of anthropology at Queens College in the City University of New York (CUNY) system. My salary was about $9,000 a year, which meant an end to student poverty. In graduate school I had my own apartment and a secondhand car only because my father sent me $100 a month to supplement my departmental support. I had lived from dollar to dollar during my first years back in New York, too. Not only was I trained for nothing else but an academic career, but having a salary was wonderful—buying furniture that didn't come from the Salvation Army; getting a television set. I wanted to keep my job. Especially because I had written my dissertation on a gay topic, I could not be publicly associated with gay protest; it would have ripped off the mask of objectivity on which I had depended, and there was no question in my mind that if my colleagues at Queens College found out I was gay, I would be fired. But the Stonewall riots thrilled me, and I wasn't completely surprised, because the gay community of the mid-'60s had been bubbling with furious energy.

Many people in Gay Liberation were looking for radical personal and political change. The circumscribed middle-class lesbian networks, too, were exploding outward. So despite my overwhelming fear, I attended one of the first Gay Liberation Front (GLF) meetings at Washington Square Church. The men took up a lot of space, and it wasn't long before the lesbians, already influenced by Women's Liberation, suggested meeting separately.[6] These meetings were like what were then called "encounter groups," with a lot of emotional back and forth and hand-holding. I hated the "trust" exercise that involved purposely falling inside a circle and letting the others catch you. I could never have built trust with strangers in that way and I refused. Lois Hart, the de facto leader of the group, and her girlfriend wanted to try open relationships— much to my shock—since I was looking for a life partner. This mixture of counterculture and lesbian politics did not work for me or others, as the group was short-lived.

/ / /

My first day of teaching I slammed my fingers in the car door and went to class with my hand wrapped in bloody Kleenex. It was the fall of 1967, and because I had not yet finished my dissertation, the Anthropology Department of Queens College hired me to teach one class each semester until the following year, when I would start full time. There was no question then that all PhDs from a prestigious department such as Chicago's would get jobs, probably good jobs. I wanted to stay in New York, so Queens College suited me fine, and I was promised an appointment at the Graduate Center, as well.

There was one teeny problem: my total lack of teaching experience. Academia was so flush with federal money in those Cold War years that Chicago could support many of their students with no-strings fellowships, which was my case after I passed my prelims. In retrospect it seems crazy to spend six years preparing for a career for which one might have no talent or liking.

For weeks before the first day of class I lay awake at night, tossing and turning. What would I say? How to prepare? What would I wear? I had not had a female teacher since junior year in high school, so what to wear was not obvious, even if I had not felt like an imposter in feminine clothing. I probably wore the same Lord & Taylor suit—it seems to me it was orange—that I wore later to my dissertation defense, and black pumps with stockings. There was no unisex then; male professors wore suits and ties, females wore dresses, period. So I was bundled into this getup, topped off with lipstick, driving my secondhand Plymouth Valiant from the Upper West Side to Kissena Boulevard in Queens, about a thirty-minute commute, literally shaking with fear the whole way. And in front of the Departmental Offices, I had this accident getting out of the car. "You should go home," the secretary said. "We'll understand." Had I taken her advice I think I could never have gone back. It had taken every ounce of courage and determination to get that far. It was a case of get back on that horse or forget about the Derby. I had no idea whether I wanted to be a teacher or not, but as always, I knew I didn't want to be a secretary, waitress, or wife.

The most useful advice somebody gave me was, "No matter what, you know more about anthropology than they do." That first day I apologized to my students for the bloody Kleenex around my hand, and they seemed forgiving, so it broke the ice, and I went on from there. I can't recall what I was teaching. It could have been urban anthropology (there was no such thing as LGBT or even women's studies), but it was a small group of upperclassmen, and they were good students. After a month or so I knew I could do this, though it took a couple of years before I loved it and longer than that before I was truly confident. Lecturing to a hundred students the next year—Introduction to Anthropology—was scary all over again, so I was lucky not to start there. Intro filled a requirement, so we got pre-dental students who would read the newspaper in the back row, and sorority girls. I didn't have the authority or skills yet to snap them to attention.

So almost from the beginning I found I liked teaching. But academic life at Queens College was another matter. There was no mentoring program for new faculty. It was all sink or swim. Nobody taught me the ropes, and pretty quickly I got tangled up in them. The department chair was a quiet, rather sugary woman named Sydel Silverman, and I never felt comfortable with her. She was so girly, and I could never tell what she was thinking. Another colleague was the Australian anthropologist Mervyn Meggitt, who had not liked me or thought I was a real anthropologist when he had been teaching at Chicago. His specialty was New Guinea, then the hottest place for young anthropologists to go to study "primitives," and Meggitt didn't think that drag queens were exotic enough to validate one's anthropological manhood. Even Margaret Mead once told me that I would never be a "real anthropologist" until I did foreign fieldwork, and to this day anthropology is dominated by the romance of the pith helmet, now called "transnationalism."

My closest friend was the tough guy Ed Hansen, an assistant professor with a doctorate from the University of Michigan, another top department. But when Ed went out drinking with Meggitt and the other guys in the department, I was never invited. There was Miriam Slater, a senior woman in the department who was also vaguely and distantly nice to me. Some gossip had it that she was a closeted lesbian, and possibly she didn't want to get too close. There was Edgar Gregerson, who was pleasant in a low-key sort of way because he, too, was a closeted gay man, and although that was never said, he showed an interest in my work.

These were tumultuous years for Queens College. In the spring of 1968, my first year of full-time teaching, the student protests at nearby Columbia University erupted. The following spring, a large group of students blockaded the administration building at Queens College. I never joined these protests as some faculty did; I felt too vulnerable. But I was with them in spirit. I was coming to see the academic establishment that had ruled my life for so many years as part of the patriarchal war machine and feeling even more alienated than I had in graduate school. I would linger in my Lord & Taylor suit on the periphery, filled with excitement.

The demonstration I remember most vividly was one by black students seeking open admissions to the CUNY system. The students marched to the library and dumped the contents of some card catalogues on the floor (this was well before catalogues were digitized). No action could have outraged and frightened the faculty more. At the ensuing all-campus faculty meeting I sat at the back of the auditorium, conflicted and confused. On the one hand, I, too, was viscerally threatened by the black students' assault on the library, an institution that was at the heart of my young life's work. I also had doubts about open admissions. While committed to the idea of an integrated society, I wondered how much institutional support there would be for an influx of poorly prepared students.

On the other hand, the freaked-out speeches of some senior faculty that day repelled me. Many of these professors were European refugees, a group that theoretically I respected. But by comparing the black students to Nazi storm troopers they lost credibility, and their hysteria lacked any compassion for the plight of minority students on a largely white campus. "Crack down on them, restore order, call the police!" was the cry. Then and throughout my career, I have always opposed police intervention against my students. Not only do I lean more toward the students' politics than toward those of the administration, but I saw myself as the captain of my classroom, and I hope that I, like those brave colleagues during the Virginia Tech shootings, would have stood between my students and danger, even mortal danger. It wouldn't have been the worst way to die.

For reasons that were attributed to obscure bureaucratic rules, I came up for tenure at the end of my second year of full-time teaching. I have never heard of this before or since, and I wonder if my enemies were so eager to be rid of me. Though completely closeted and trying to keep my head down, I wasn't politically savvy. I didn't understand how the department worked: who had power and whom I would have to please if I could have done so. Nobody had told me what I needed to do to get tenure, except publish my dissertation, which had been accepted by Prentice Hall. Feminism was giving shape and voice to an inchoate anger that had been with me always. No doubt, my department sensed my difference. At any rate, the committee voted three to two to grant me tenure. At Queens it was known that the administration denied recommendations from split committees, so I was fired in effect by the two faculty who, as Department Chair Sydel Silverman explained to me, questioned whether I was sufficiently "committed to anthropology," the same question that the Chicago faculty had raised because I wore pants too often.

I hadn't seen this coming. Whatever my bad attitude, I had worked my tail off and had a book in the works. I had a doctorate from the top department in the country. How could they fire me? Getting fired in academia is worse, I imagine, than in the business world. There it's all about profits, efficiency, and power games. But how do you measure success in scholarship and teaching? In between the privileged stars and the duds who miss classes and never publish is the majority in the middle, whose tenure can go either way, depending. Depending on who likes you and who doesn't, depending on budget cuts masquerading as quality standards, and depending on who is in power, you can wind up with iffy letters of recommendation or emphasis put on a couple of bad student evaluations. Over a lifetime in academia and participation on many tenure committees, I have come to see our promotion system, which is nominally about meeting objective criteria, as corrupt, and to prefer the French system, public and unionized, where if you publish X number of essays and pass certain standardized tests, you are automatically promoted.

In academia, when you don't get tenure, you get a further employed year to look for another job, a sort of lead parachute. The price you pay for the privilege is a year in social Siberia. My last year at Queens College was pure misery. All of my colleagues were embarrassed, and they tried to pretend I wasn't there, with the exception of Bob Glass, a sweet, very straight-arrow-looking man, always in impeccable suits, whom I presume voted for my tenure and about whom there were whispers that he was passing for white. My only friend was a geographer named Andy, who had also been fired. We passed the time churning in our bitterness. Andy was discouraged and talking about some other career, but I wasn't trained for anything else. I got several job interviews at the Annual Meetings of the American Anthropological Association in San Diego that fall, where I was horribly anxious. Running to one interview, I got my period and stained my dress and was rescued by Ellen Lewin, a young anthropology graduate student who would become a lifelong friend. I remember I had such bad cramps and was so wired that when the others went to the San Diego Zoo, I stayed in my hotel room curled in a ball.

None of the interviews panned out—one was at a mental hospital, where, to my embarrassment, I was afraid of the screaming patients— except at the College at Purchase, a new unit of the State University of New York (SUNY) system in Westchester County, commuting distance from my Upper West Side apartment. Part of Governor Nelson Rockefeller's expansion of the SUNY system, Purchase, I've always thought, was conceived as a home for the art collection of Roy Neuberger, Rockefeller's Wall Street pal. To justify the Neuberger Museum, Rockefeller established schools of dance, music, theater, art and design, and film. To support the arts, there would be several large auditoriums. And—oh, yes—there would also be a liberal arts program.

Even though it seemed to my colleagues and me that the liberal arts program was an afterthought, we had high hopes for it, despite the all-brick campus, designed as a unit by renowned architects of the day—Philip Johnson did the Neuberger Museum—that must have looked good to them on paper but depressed and frustrated its occupants. Almost instantly graffiti marred the underground tunnels connecting every building that, campus legend had it, were meant to facilitate the movement of tanks onto the campus should protests erupt. There was an immense and barren brick plaza over which, in winter, arctic-strength winds battered dwarfed and scurrying students, faculty, and staff.

Inspired by the reform impulses of the 1960s and with such sister schools as the University of California, Santa Cruz, Purchase had no departments; all of our work would be interdisciplinary, including with the arts. For someone who had just been rejected by a department that was rigidly hierarchical and opaque, "no departments" sounded great. There would also be small classes and written evaluations instead of grades. Queens College had been largely a factory for sorting student sheep from goats, so no grades sounded good to me, too. I liked most of my new colleagues right away, especially Mary Edwards, a pugnacious Irish American political scientist and feminist product of a Catholic education, whose wit and originality were tonic. Her trim, almost petite appearance belied the determined toughness of a Navy Seal and the ideology of a union firebrand.

Nothing and no one intimidated Mary. Although her projects were rarely supported by the administration, and often opposed, she got a lot of them done. That included starting a women's studies program with me and a few other young feminist faculty; establishing a Children's Center for our employees; organizing the faculty labor union; and, as presiding officer of the faculty, fighting the administration to a standstill over proposed job cuts.

Mary was dedicated to sex with men, and she never understood what lesbianism or gender dysphoria was about. (Once when I tried to explain gender studies to her, she said, "Well, if everyone undresses, isn't it obvious?") Yet we loved and respected each other and stood together on most political issues. If Mary agreed with you, there was no better ally. If she disagreed, she would oppose you, friend or foe. Her early death from lymphoma was tragic and a gut punch for me personally.

Almost all of the faculty were young and progressive and dedicated to teaching. Quite a few, like me, had been fired from other, stodgier institutions but, like me, came from elite graduate schools. None of us foresaw the political and budgetary disappointments that the 1970s and '80s would bring. We were too inexperienced to understand that without departments, the faculty would have no power, and we would be at the mercy of administrators, who mostly turned out to be as selfishly ambitious as they were inept. In any case, I had no other choice. Though I started the job with gratitude and a degree of hope, it never occurred to me that thirty-five years later I would still be teaching there, bitter and burned-out.

/ / /

As the fall of 1969 came on, I was unhappily single. Intimacy had come to me so late, I desperately wanted feminine companionship. Over Thanksgiving I went to Cambridge to visit Nancy, with whom I was becoming friendly once more. We took our dog Charlie to a dog park, where a young Weimaraner ran into me and broke my knee. Nancy drove me back to New York with a full leg plaster cast but couldn't stay, and as it was difficult to get around with the crutches—though I did go to work—I called Patsy and asked her if she could help. I was still obsessed with her. Patsy was then staying in the spacious apartment that belonged to some affluent friend of hers in Washington Heights, which in 1969 was still the sort of neighborhood that a Smith College alum would consider suitable. (Ironically, Patsy's borrowed apartment was around the corner from the one that Amber Hollibaugh and I would buy in 1981, by which time the neighborhood was almost entirely Dominican.) Once again, Patsy and I fell into bed, cast and all, and once again I experienced a blissed-out dopamine rush. I have never been more ecstatic than when Patsy was pushing me along the streets of Washington Heights in a wheelchair. But as soon as the cast came off and I could get around more easily with a cane, she dropped me off at my apartment and didn't bother to call back. Obviously, I didn't fit into Patsy's life plans, and I was left feeling like a pet rejected for its fleas.

Yet Patsy's dismissal turned out lucky for me. If I hadn't been single, I wouldn't have met the painter Louise Fishman, who was to become my lover and lifelong intimate. Through Nancy I had met a Bennington contemporary of hers, Frederica Leser, another one of those independently wealthy, genteel lesbians. (Thea Spyer and Edie Windsor were two of the brightest stars of this network, along with the archeologist Iris Love.) Frederica worked at the Museum of Natural History and owned an entire townhouse on 11th Street in Greenwich Village. At her annual lesbian Christmas party in 1969, Louise asked me to dance, and I threw down my cane to partner her on my still gimpy knee. According to Louise, she and Bianca Lanza, one of her exes, saw me across the dance floor and argued over who would approach me. Louise won out, insisting that she had seen me first.

On our first date Louise took me to a downtown showing of the original *King Kong* movie. She wore a short skirt and tight top, and I loved her look—feminine Harpo Marx—and the sexy, confident way she moved. Louise had a head of ashy blond curls, blue eyes that slanted down into her cheekbones, and an infectious laugh. Although she was fair, the structure of her face and gently convex nose were clearly Jewish. "I do like a fair Jew or two," I wrote once, as if my Jewish father and WASP mother were beckoning to me from one person. She said "house" without the "w" sound because she was from Philadelphia, and boy, could she dance!

After the *King Kong* date, which showed me what knowing taste she had—the audience was all downtown hipsters—she asked me to go with her over New Year's to Philadelphia to meet her family and see the Mummers Parade, a drag event staged by working-class men in over-the-top feathers. We discovered how much we loved some of the same things (drag, spectacle, camp, and feminism). We also had sex, which went well.

Louise was just breaking up with the architect Phyllis Birkby. We were each emerging from our closed lesbian circles. Just as I had been making the rounds of the Patsy–Nancy–Elizabeth gang, Louise, Phyllis, and Bianca had all been with one another. The lesbian world was poised to crack open into something much more exciting. You could feel it on the streets, at GLF, and in the bars.

My love for Louise was part of that ferment. We read the new lesbian feminist writing to each other in bed, *Patience and Sarah* and *SCUM Manifesto*. We went to consciousness-raising groups, together and separately, sharing our excitement at each new revelation and our anger at the patriarchy and its male privileges. We both demonstrated on the steps of the Metropolitan Museum of Art for the inclusion of more women artists, and we went to It's All Right to Be Woman theater with hundreds of other young women, laughing and clapping at each reenactment of women's humiliations and triumphs. We were at the Second Congress to Unite Women on May 1, 1970, when a small group of lesbians calling themselves the Lavender Menace interrupted the program to demand the inclusion of lesbians, waving their mimeographed copies of "The Woman-Identified Woman." New York was one of the epicenters of the new movement, and were friends with or had friends who knew these authors and activists.[7]

Louise brought me new friends from her circle, Bianca Lanza, Carol Calhoun and Phyllis Birkby, who died relatively young, as did the novelist Bertha Harris. She opened the world of downtown art to me. We saw the avant-garde dancers Trisha Brown and Steve Paxton perform with their troupes and had tea with the painter Elizabeth Murray; I met the visual artists Harmony Hammond, Jenny Snider, and Joan Snyder (who was then married to my Stockbridge classmate Larry Fink, the photographer). We saw Andy Warhol films and talked endlessly about the meaning of feminist writing and art. Should it be realist, abstract impressionist, protest, or could it be anything by a woman? She turned me on to music that she thought I'd like and has continued to do so over the years. I discovered Willie Nelson through her and Schubert piano music played by Alicia de la Rocha.

Foreshadowing the marriage equality movement, we thought of ourselves as married, knowing that the rest of the world did not. When Louise drew up a "certificate of Holy Matrimony" for us, the only witnesses were our cats and dog. We never thought of the economic penalties we suffered because we couldn't legally marry. What would have

With Louise Fishman. New York City, 1971.

been the point? Legal marriage was as remote as the rings of Saturn. We lived our love in our apartment and among our gay women friends.

Around 1971, fired up by gay liberation, I wrote to my mother that Louise was my "lover" (that was the closest we could come to explaining ourselves). My mother wrote back implying she had known this, and that while she regretted not having grandchildren, I had to live my own life. When I told my father, I think he was embarrassed: too much information. He regretted that I was shutting out half the world, he said, and we never mentioned it again. It never occurred to me to retort that were I heterosexual, the female half of humanity would never grace my bed.

I bought three acres on a wooded hillside in the Berkshires, close to

Cummington, where I had gone to Belgian Village Camp. We had fun putting up tents, hauling in ice chests, and entertaining our circle of scruffy lesbian feminist friends over hotdogs and s'mores. Afterward, Louise and I would sleep in each other's arms, halfway out of our sleeping bags. She was affectionate and loving, kissing me and pinching my cheeks, calling me *bubela* and *Esther mein schwester*, reminding me of my sweet Jewish relatives. But she was also tough, so committed to painting and her career that I figured she would sacrifice anything, even me, if she were forced to choose.

When we met, Louise lived and painted in a small rented loft on Spring Street and West Broadway. Gradually, however, we spent more time in my apartment on 99th Street, between West End Avenue and Riverside Drive, because it had two bedrooms, and eventually Louise moved into it, reluctantly giving up her loft to save money. In the 1970s, the Upper West Side of Manhattan was more like the Upper Wild West. We lived right across the street from two single room occupancy hotels (SROs), one of which was called the Harvard Studios. These housed, at taxpayers' expense, junkies, petty thieves, and schizophrenics who, since the SROs were converted into condos in the 1980s, are now homeless.

Residents of SROs robbed the elderly; panhandled aggressively for "change"; and maintained an active social life of gambling, domestic violence, and drunken brawls. Our block was especially scary, but the entire neighborhood was crawling with an assortment of crazies who had been emptied out of newly closed mental hospitals and left to fend for themselves. Louise and I knew, of course, that these were human beings like ourselves, and in retrospect SROs were far more humane living arrangements than shelters or cardboard boxes on the sidewalk. Still, during this period Shirley was robbed twice in her elevator, and Louise and I, despite recognizing "in our hearts" that the women among them were "sisters," were always hoping we wouldn't get "cut or mugged." The day that somebody threw a bottle from the roof of one of the SROs that landed near my shoe was the day we went looking for another apartment east of Broadway, near Central Park. Reflecting on the SROs we had fled, I wrote in my journal, "Those people were too miserable and dangerous. If you ever forget your guilt about them, or your rage at the ruling class that people were ever made so sick, poor and ugly by a system, you certainly never, not for a moment, forget your fear of them. And since there was absolutely nothing we could do to talk with, control or help them, what option do you have in the end but to move away, if you can?" By May 1972, we were settled on 94th Street, between Central Park West and Columbus Avenue, in a floor-through apartment, smaller than 99th Street but with a leafy balcony overlooking pleasant backyards that are found in the interior of many residential Manhattan blocks. "This neighborhood reminds me of scenes, feelings from my childhood, when the city was a simpler but fascinating place full of promising futures and the unknown," I wrote.

This was the first time I had ever lived with a lover. My one model of lesbian domestic life came from reading about Gertrude Stein and Alice Toklas. In spite of (or was it in contradiction to?) my feminist convictions, Gertrude was still my gender ideal, a woman who created her own masculine persona. Together, Gertrude and Alice constituted a butch/femme couple I idealized. According to emerging lesbian-feminist majority opinion, butch/femme couples were an oppressive copy of heterosexuality. Since I was becoming a true believer I thought I should agree and yet I knew from experience it wasn't true. Anyhow, Louise was more feminine than I was, it seemed, and like Alice she was a good cook, but there the resemblance ended.

In the summer of 1970, we went to France and Holland, took in museums, bought bikes and a tent, and went camping in Collioure, in the South of France, where we were taken up by a French family and enjoyed ourselves a lot, despite getting rained on and bitten by mosquitoes. It was my second trip to France, and I loved the food, the carefully tended countryside, and the comforting waters of the Mediterranean. France was luminous for me, and this was where Gertrude and Alice had made their lives, on the Rue de Fleurus in Paris.

Back in New York I was bitter about being fired, and under the influence of Louise's artistic sensibilities and interests, and in the heady freedom of the feminist ferment, I accepted Shirley's proposal that we write a book together—she, too, had joined a consciousness-raising group—which quickly took the form of a double journal. We would write to each other but also write about our separate lives. "I'm tired of precision and professionalism," I wrote. "I'm tired of being an uptight, objective, write-up-your-grant-proposal-with-one-quarter-inch-margins type person (woman?), so I'm going to goof off (but I know there's something serious here)."

I had already been fired from Queens College; my book on drag queens, *Mother Camp*, had come out to no notice; and I had less to lose than before. In 1970, there were no memoirs by academics, no category of creative nonfiction. The book we ultimately wrote together and self-published, *Womenfriends*, has never counted toward academic promotion—quite the contrary. But as my academic career faltered, I was attracted to writing that was free of academic form and vocabulary. In *Womenfriends* I chronicled important events of my young life: coming out to my parents, loving Louise, and Shirley's and my struggle to maintain our friendship against the strains of her married life and my now fervent lesbian feminism.[8]

By May 1971, our writing had momentum, but there was friction between us. I was between jobs and writing almost every day. At an all-lesbian dinner party, I wrote, one woman had said, "Straight women cannot understand us, and we shouldn't let ourselves be watered down by them." Shirley was understandably threatened. Then, on June 5, Shirley found out she was pregnant, and she thought (correctly as it turned out) that it was a boy. This development threatened both our friendship and our overheated feminist world.

It was bad enough that Shirley was married to a man (even though I liked him) but becoming a mother to a son—that was too conventional, and it threatened the pact we had made that our relationship would be as important as her marriage. Shirley was going to become the mother I perhaps would never be. As we tried to thrash this out, I became ever more firmly attached to my lesbian identity and aware of how angry I was at the straight world in general, and at Shirley in particular. "Gay is angry! Gay is squished; gay is invisible," I wrote. "I must stop thinking and acting like a second class human being. . . . Anyone called my friend must put herself on the line; where does she stand?. . . My 'marriage' makes me an outcast, yours sets you up as a card-carrying member of the human race."[9] Then, to bolster my case against Shirley, I quoted "The Woman-Identified Woman," the political screed that was the foundation of lesbian feminist ideology: "Our energies must flow toward our sisters, not backwards toward our oppressors. . . . It is the primacy of women relating to women, of women creating a new consciousness of and with each other which is at the heart of women's liberation."

Within lesbian feminism there was, then, a blanket condemnation of "giving energy to men." Becoming pregnant by a man and then giving birth to a son seemed to reduce the woman to a vessel. (The Michigan Women's Music Festival, an important holdover from that time, made boy children older than six stay outside the main festival with minders.) "What," I asked myself and my friend, "would be a woman-defined pregnancy? . . . Pregnancy has been a symbol to me, just like fucking men was, of womanliness. I envied it, and yet, always rejected it. Pregnancy disgusts, repulses and fascinates me. It represents the cop-out, the easy answer, which I long for but cannot accept." I recognized that our abjection as lesbians was changing, and that although Shirley and I were not equal in the eyes of society, Louise and I were relatively privileged and could more or less live as we pleased. And so, I concluded, the struggle was against self-hatred, self-imposed limitations, not dreaming big enough.

Although I feared that Shirley might dump me for my diatribe, she provided affirmation, writing, "I love you; I think we will survive this," while admitting, "I never want to speak to you again." To Shirley I was the special one, the one with more status because of my professorship, and she accused me of not standing by her when some professional women had dumped on housewives, which, despite her part-time work in journalism, she mostly was. (In the last part of her life, she became mostly a grandmother.) In the end, attempting to compromise, we agreed that I would be intimately involved in the rearing of Shirley's child; brave new world, we would create revolutionary parenting arrangements.

The second annual Gay Pride Week was held in June 1971, culminating in a Pride March. I thought the danger of being photographed was too great, and I planned to attend the "Gay-in" at the end of the March in Central Park. But I had just had breakfast with "a bunch of dykes" who were all going, including Louise, and at the last minute I had to go or couldn't live with myself. I saw lots of gay people on the sidelines, too scared to join us, and I knew just how they felt. But I was embracing a radical vision of gay liberation. "The revolution is less authentic by every oppressed person it excludes," I wrote breathlessly in my journal, struggling with my repulsion toward a man swaddled in sheets who carried a sign announcing his membership in "the Pennsylvania Enema Society."

A second attempt at a "gay women's group" was shaping up, and I volunteered to organize the first get-together, inviting (among others) sister activist Martha Shelley and two women I had just met, Barbara Towar and Mary-Ann Dann, both of whom lived on City Island off the Bronx. Nothing like this had ever happened in our lifetimes, or ever in history: lesbians meeting to share experience and anger, blown forward by the hurricane of feminist ideology, seeing ourselves at the core of momentous change. I wrote in my journal that summer:

> Our energy pressured the walls outward until it seemed they must bend and buckle. In the second half of the meeting we went around, each woman telling where she was born, and giving a brief biography. There was complete silence as each woman in turn talked, broken only by a few questions. I hung on each word. I know this time in New York will be written about, studied by our descendants. Already, women in Paris translate *Sisterhood Is Powerful* and back issues of *The Rat* [the alternative newspaper that chronicled the counterculture]. Everything we do resounds. . . . I want to celebrate the group, write about it, to make portraits that will live on.

Barbara and Mary-Ann, the City Island dykes, were the women in the group I loved the most because, like me, they were "old gay," a concept that was just beginning to come into use to distinguish lesbians like us, who were gay before feminism and Stonewall, from the young women, some of whom were coming out through consciousness-raising groups and some of whom were declaring themselves "political lesbians," even though they were sexually attracted to men. Realizing that the world I'd come out in was dying made me want to memorialize, or even "romanticize," what would soon be forgotten otherwise.

When Barbara and Mary-Ann, both of whom were butch, had been lovers, they had built a houseboat out on the bay where Barbara kept a shotgun. One day, some drunken guys tried to tie up on the houseboat, and Barbara, terrified, brought out the gun and threatened to shoot. All bluff—the gun was unloaded—but the drunks motored off. I could have listened to Barbara tell this story a hundred times. Later, Mary-Ann and Barbara split up, and Barbara bought a "doll house" with a fecund garden on City Island. Mary-Ann still lived on the houseboat, guarding her solitude and independence.

On February 1, 1972, Shirley's baby, Ben, was born. At the foot of Shirley's hospital bed was a sign: "Mrs. Fischler." That day something in feminism died for me. No matter how much Shirley and I loved each other, we weren't going to march into the feminist future together. She was a conformist, I wrote angrily in my journal, who "wanted the conventional things, the marriage license, the financial support, the orange plush couch," a shorthand we had for financial and material comfort, "the circle of straight friends, the baby in a good hospital, the husband's name." By contrast, I wrote, "My mother and father are both rebels and adventurers, and I am like them. I haven't found the strength yet to accept what I already am, what I already have chosen. It's still a struggle to feel OK." I was in no mood to acknowledge that inside my best friend's conventional appearance was a stifled mutineer: honest, loyal, and brave.

When I complained to Louise that Shirley wasn't calling me after Ben's birth, despite the plans we had made to involve me in parenting, Louise said, "It's obvious; she's totally absorbed in something that has nothing to do with you." Shirley had called her mother in to help, and they formed a little bio-cocoon around her son. At the time it seemed like years, but her mother actually stayed for only a couple of weeks, during which hiatus in our friendship it became clear to me that Shirley wanted to be a MOTHER, which meant that I and even her husband, Stan, were to be kept in our more distant places. I had no interest in occasional babysitting. When, at the end of the month, Shirley asked if I wanted to take Ben once a week, I didn't. What I had wanted, in theory, was a reconfiguration of the nuclear family that would include me. But when that was off the table and it came down to the mundane work of child-rearing, I preferred teaching and writing. "Neither of us is a 'new woman' or a 'liberated woman,'" I declared in my journal. "We are just pushing the ball along with our noses."

/ / /

I still hadn't come out at Purchase or in any professional setting. For instance, at the beginning of March, Shirley and I gave a talk about our joint journal to a feminist group, disingenuous since we did not disclose the central conflict in our book, the struggle of straight and gay to remain close. Yet the lesbian feminist community was blasting off, and Louise and I were sky high. The gay women's group that we had started caught on, with others clamoring to join. As the groups had to stay small to be intimate, successive groups formed until there were at least ten.

On March 4, 1972, we had dinner with Barbara Love and Sidney Abbott, who had just finished writing *Sappho Was a Right-On Woman*,[10] one of the first lesbian feminist books to be published by a mainstream press. Despite their privileged background—they lived on lower Fifth Avenue; both were WASP and upper middle class—Barbara had lost her job when she had come out at work and been featured as an "admitted" lesbian on TV and in *Life Magazine*. Barbara's family virtually disowned her. While we were there, a former lover called, furious that Barbara might have blown her cover by coming out. Sidney didn't have a job, either, and they were getting desperate. That kind of story convinced me to stay silent. I was coming up for tenure again the next year.

The brightest star in the lesbian feminist firmament was the former downtown dancer and *Village Voice* columnist Jill Johnston. Louise and I had devoured *Marmalade Me*, and Jill was just coming out with a new book, *Lesbian Nation*.[11] Despite her bohemian charisma (she often wore a black bowler hat and leather pants with metal studs), Jill had been a married mother fifteen years before. "I sympathize-hate you," Shirley observed of Jill. A year previously, Shirley had read a review of *Marmalade Me* that presented Jill as "living theatre, living poetry, living joy." Shirley was resentful because, as she put it, Jill was "acting out life in toto, presenting a living drama of change and feeling. She is what I dreamed of becoming." I had met Jill at a party, so when I heard her speak about this new lesbian nation at the School of Visual Arts, she recognized me in the audience, much to my pleasure. I wrote in my journal, "She is tall, awkward although a dancer, charming, gentle yet oddly cruel, as I imagine extremists are. Hers is not a cruelty of intent, but a cruelty of detachment, of single-mindedness, of the artist mystic. Unlike Anaïs Nin, she will not fail as an artist through being too human."

To a woman in the audience who babbled on nervously about human liberation and men's problems, Jill replied, "It's OK if you want to stop partway, but as for me, I'm going all the way with this thing." Women's total political and sexual liberation, cultural upheaval, and the end of the patriarchy—this is what we imagined. Very soon after the School of Visual Arts event, Louise and I were invited to Jill's country house to talk about editing a collection of lesbian feminist writing that became *Amazon Expedition*, an important early collection of lesbian feminist writing.[12] The guests included Jill's young lover, Jane O'Wyatt; Phyllis Birkby, the architect, who was an ex of Louise's and part of her crowd; and Phyllis's new lover, Bertha Harris, a novelist, whom I hoped would recognize me as the writer I was aspiring to be. There was another couple, one of whom was acting as a sort of secretary.

The weekend was not a success for me. The others didn't seem impressed with my writing credentials, and there was too much similarity between Jill with her groupies (of which I was one) and my father's cult. When Barbara Love (who was not present to defend herself) was criticized for curling her hair in hopes of getting another media job, I remarked that Barbara was worried about paying the rent, and much could and should be excused on those grounds. "I like blimpies," I blurted out after Jane, who then suffered from youthful extremism even more pronounced than my own, announced self-righteously that she was a vegetarian. I left disappointed that what I had fantasized as a crucible event in my ongoing chronicle of the New York lesbian-feminist community was actually a somewhat uncomfortable gathering of people who didn't know each other, sort of like an academic convention.

Nevertheless, the book project limped along, and there was talk of Jill buying land on which we would establish a lesbian feminist school.[13] Once again, Louise and I trekked up to Jill's rented farmhouse. In an entry in my journal titled "Heavy Combat in the Egological Zone," I complained that our feminist commitment to amorphous decision making did not allow us to recognize that Jill was obviously the central person in these plans. When somebody proposed that the school might work better in an urban setting, Jill snapped, "You do your project; we'll do ours. This is a country thing. You're bringing negative energy in here." I objected: "Is it negative energy to bring up a question, or propose a different point of view?" There was no chance that Jill could have submitted herself to consensus decision making. She was egocentric, brilliant, and imperious, an intense and creative woman always on the brink of a flip-out. I left disillusioned and confused. Little by little, doubts were sneaking into my feminist certainties.

Two weeks later, I got a lesson in star fucking. After a meeting in the city to work on *Amazon Expedition*, Jill and the group of us went to a lesbian party. As we walked in, every single eye turned to Jill. I felt protective toward her; the young dykes at the party were devouring her with unconscious cruelty, making giggling remarks behind their hands. But meanwhile, Shirley, buried under piles of diapers and constantly distracted by homemaking chores, saw me as a wannabe star who was taking ideas that were hers or ours and avidly courting public recognition. I gave a talk about our work to a gathering of sixty or so women, including members of groups I had been in whose admiration and support were tangible. By my estimation, the talk was a great success, but it left me wondering: were people talking about me? Would I ever, like Jill, have every eye turn toward me as I walked into a room, and would I like it?

Questions of leadership and "stardom" were painful in second wave feminism. We young women were mostly from comfortable families, yet brothers had been favored and boys had sucked the air out of every room. In opposition to patriarchy and in line with "all men are created equal," we were committed to the proposition that all "sisters" were equally important, that decisions must be made collectively, and that everyone must be included. Yet the media wanted spokeswomen, and Jill was colorful and articulate. This made some women envious and resentful, while others were mixed up and conflicted.

My friend Martha Shelley came over one day in tears because her prominence within lesbian feminism left her confused about who she was. She'd been elated beyond reason when *Ms. Magazine,* the more mainstream feminist publication, asked her to do an article, but then she felt bad because maybe she was lording it over other women. So she wrote a half-baked article that, in part, was critical of *Ms.* They got pissed off and stopped taking her phone calls. Her feelings were hurt, and she had to face how much she actually wanted to publish in *Ms.*

In the months after Ben's birth, I wrote almost daily in my journal, immersed in meeting other writers and in the work and life of the lesbian writer Radclyffe Hall, the author of *The Well of Loneliness*; at that time, there was no biography of her other than the self-serving memoir written by her life partner, Una Troubridge.[14] Most of that writing is not included in *Womenfriends* and has likely been lost. I also wrote at length about Shirley, Louise, and Jill and a great deal about my Freudian analysis; the latter was as compelling to me then as it is stale to me now.

I did participate in antiwar rallies and demonstrations and wrote sometimes about what was going on in the world beyond my lesbian circles. But my feminist ideology was now the lens through which I viewed national and world events. The Vietnam War was dragging on and on, and Richard Nixon was president. My ex-communist parents had especially hated Nixon ever since he had red-baited Helen Gahagan Douglas to win the California Senate race in 1950, and the very sight of him aroused my ire at men, capitalism, corporations, and the hopeless state of the male-dominated world. In May 1972, Nixon announced that he was going to mine Hanoi and Haiphong harbors and bomb rail routes from China. Watching this unfold on television filled me with helpless rage.

Despite my socialist feminist analysis, which told me that capitalism is incompatible with social justice and that white men controlled the state, I confessed to loving American culture and American people. I was as American as the tough sidewalks of New York and the live oak-covered brown hills of California, even as American as the American Army, in which my grandfather had been a general.

Revolutionary attitudes do not sit easy on me, even though I am an outsider to the bottom of my angry gay heart. When Martha Shelley told me she could identify with criminals, I said the state may be evil, but so are the criminals. I had spent my young adulthood studying human beings as creators of various social orders, and the kind of peaceable, non-hierarchical, vegetarian, and female-dominated societies that more and more lesbian feminists idealized struck me as impractical and unrealistic. "Order is human," I wrote in my journal, "and America is an order—an unjust, two-faced order—but what is there to replace it? We need time to build a feminist community." Faced with Martha's Jean Genet–like attitudes, I cited Gertrude Stein as my precedent. Of course, Gertrude had loved America from the safety of Paris, and I was living in "the belly of the beast," as the most radical among us said. In the 1970s, that beast had intense indigestion, and my friendship with Shirley, my commitment to Louise, feminism, our dead-broke city of New York, and the whole planet seemed to be coming apart.

During our honeymoon period, Shirley and I had done a research paper on consciousness-raising groups, concluding that becoming a feminist was comparable to a religious conversion and just as powerful.[15] But, of course, I had been the one who delivered the paper at the Annual Meetings of the American Anthropological Association and thus got most of the public credit. Now, as I contemplated another project, Shirley said no; she wanted to write a sports book with some other woman. Male sports! I was horrified. So I wrote my next paper, on so-called primitive matriarchies—whose pre-patriarchy existence was an article of faith for many feminists—with my friend Paula Webster, who, like me, had anthropological training. (Paula and I argued that primitive matriarchies were a romantic feminist myth and had never existed.[16])

I finally came out to colleagues at a Ruth Benedict Collective meeting, the first time ever in any professional setting. (At that time I did not know that Ruth Benedict, a famous anthropologist, had been a lesbian.) This was a group of women, mostly anthropologists, who wanted to formulate a feminist perspective within anthropology, but for a time it also included Shirley, my Purchase friend Mary Edwards, and some others.

As the women were hesitantly responding to my brave declaration, most implying they'd known or suspected all along, Shirley snatched up her baby and stamped to the door, turning to accuse the group. She felt rejected, she said, and she was especially angry at me for being so "special" while she was just a mother and housewife. I couldn't believe she had chosen that moment, when I was at my most vulnerable, to publicly attack me. This scene was, as we both understood at the time, the "culmination of a long struggle" between us. "It's as if we each had two sets of hands," I wrote. "The upper hands are holding each other in love and support, while with the bottom hands we're punching each other in the kidneys."

This could have been a metaphor for second wave feminism as a whole, which had begun with a dream of universal sisterhood and, during the succeeding years, would split and split again over issues of race, sexual orientation, and ideology. We would have to recognize that women were and are in very different locations and situations, often in ways that pit them against one another. Still, second wave feminism changed me and the world for the better. Many of the indignities of my girlhood are gone, and barriers have been breached, if not removed. Shirley and I were both proud to have helped bring those changes about.

—— CHAPTER 8 ——

THE ISLAND OF WOMEN

I thought I might get tenure at Purchase College—after all, my dissertation was published, and my teaching evaluations were great—but I was still not palatable to the academic digestive tract. Queens College had quietly chucked me out, and at Purchase I caused a major case of heartburn.

Back in 1973, most assistant professors, at Purchase and elsewhere, were promoted if they fulfilled the basic requirements—then as now, a published academic book and several articles, competent teaching, and "community service," which means serving on committees. At Purchase, an experimental new public college, most faculty were young, all were eligible for tenure, and almost all, as I recall, got tenure, after which they could not be fired except "for cause," such as failing to meet classes.

Tenure review in higher education can leave the candidate with a bad case of PTSD. You are judged by faculty peers, those already tenured, and then by deans and administrators according to supposedly objective criteria that are all too easily bent to produce the outcome that one or more opponents (or supporters) want. The process is supposed to be secret so that you won't know who your enemies are or what they are saying about you. Although you are given a chance to respond to the academic review committee's written judgment, you are not supposed to know what the committee discussed in coming to that decision, and if it is negative, you are fired—not fired by a boss, not laid off, but judged inferior and unworthy, after years of low-paid and stressful preparation, by other scholars like yourself.

In the years since my firing at Queens, feminism had caught fire in academia, so I was no longer isolated. The savviest and most determined feminist organizer on campus was Mary Edwards, the feminist political scientist who was my close friend and ally. Purchase was so small, with fewer than one hundred faculty then, and Mary was so well connected to feminist faculty and staff that I knew who was on my review committee and what was being discussed at every step. The two male senior faculty wanted me gone, while the three junior faculty supported me. The factions could not agree, and they wrote separate letters, the positive one recommending immediate promotion and tenure and the negative one recommending that I be promoted to associate professor without tenure and be considered again for tenure the next year. Not only would this have been inhumane, considering the stress produced by the tenure process, but my supporters and I perceived it as a stalling tactic. One of the senior men accused me, in writing, of "teaching against marriage" and of being unfair to my male students. Mary organized some of my former male students to write a letter refuting the latter claim.

I still have the letter written by John Howard, then the dean of social science, supporting the promotion-without-tenure position. "There is a difference between being a feminist and being anti-male," he declared. The question raised by the committee was "whether that difference is blurred in Professor Newton's case," although the majority letter written by the three junior faculty brought this point up only to refute it. Then, despite positive evaluations of *Mother Camp* by outside authorities, Dean Howard argued that in the five years since the doctorate I had published only this one book and two articles, so my scholarly potential was iffy.

But my major alleged shortcoming was in community service. We were hiring, and Howard wrote: "She met with 4 out of the 5 anthropologists brought in but missed an interview with one candidate for a senior position, for reasons that were not sufficient." Organizing a group of female faculty (which led to our women's studies program), for instance, counted against me: "She seems to have largely been active in activities benefiting women."

In those fervent days before women's studies departments, feminism transcended the chain of command; from students to secretaries and faculty, there were women who saw the attack on me as an affront to the exploding feminist movement. Reading and rereading Dean Howard's letter, which I had not looked at since 1973, once again set my pulse racing. How have I lived with this anger? "She is a feminist"—meaning "suspect" and "not one of us" and possibly a lesbian (though I had not yet said so)—and thus "anti-male." Therefore, she is difficult and irresponsible and won't be a good colleague. My detractors had correctly sensed, however, that I was alienated from traditional academia, and, of course, my disaffection deepened with each rebuff and insult.

But feminism is not a bias. It is, in the academic context, a scholarly perspective motivated by values, as is all scholarship. Yes, I was angry at men's power over women, but I have never been unfair to male students. In fact, I took quite a few of them, gay and straight, under my wing. This was my form of parenting, of social responsibility. I had something to give these eager young beings: my commitment to scholarship and ideas. But what made me a special asset to Purchase undergraduates, many of whom were their family's first college student, was my belief in them. They were in college to attain some of the prestige and skills that I had inherited, and I did my damndest to make it accessible to them.

/ / /

Adding to the turbulence of that spring, my Freudian psychoanalyst suddenly terminated our sessions. I had been seeing Dr. Elise Snyder three times a week for three years. I called her Dr. Magnet because of the many ways in which she attracted me (otherwise called "transference"). I never told my father about my Freudian analysis, not wanting to hear his negative *pronunciamentos* about a rival type of therapy, and for the first time I was able to pay for it myself (though my health insurance paid for a lot of it—those were the days!). Psychoanalysis, for me, was a chosen odyssey, and I don't regret it. No longer was I trying to "go straight." I was following Socrates's dictum to "know thyself."

My students have found the Oedipus complex outlandish; Freudianism is an intellectual "fashion don't" on campuses. Insurance companies are partly responsible, because psychoanalysis is labor-intensive and can't be outsourced. Insurers prefer three-hour cognitive readjustments and, above all, drugs. But psychoanalysis is, or can be, a Western art of healing. Although I sometimes accused Dr. Magnet of trying to turn me straight, she helped a lot more than she hurt. I did not have the miserable experience of so many other gay people. I finished as gay as I started, but with more insight and inner strength.

/ / /

Meanwhile, Louise's and my "Holy Matrimony" was falling apart. The stress of the long tenure fight and the tortured end of my analysis did not help. But the biggest problem was that I had lost interest in Louise sexually. This was the first time I had been with someone long enough to no longer desire her. (It wouldn't be the last.) All the fights, all the rub and scrub of two people trying to live together, needing to compromise—something that I, the only child, was never good at—smothered desire. And yet, this explanation is too pat, for I still loved Louise and have never stopped loving her. At bottom, desire remains a mystery. Why am I erotically attracted to women? Why mostly feminine women? Why does desire die? When all is said and done, when all the hunches and theories have been laid out, I am not sure. But the result was clear: Louise took it personally and was hurt, very hurt.

We were spending a lot of time at Jill Johnston's country place in Huntington, Massachusetts (paying her some rent), plotting to start a feminist school or artists' colony and finishing our work on *Amazon Expedition*. On New Year's Eve of 1972, I had turned my face away when Louise asked for a kiss, a rejection she remembers still. Louise started saying that commuting to her studio was too much of a hassle. She wanted to move downtown to a loft, where she could paint and once again immerse herself in the art world. I hated the idea of a big open space, without definition, sort of like bathrooms with no doors. I needed my own, separate room. And, as Purchase was north of the city in Westchester County, moving south would add at least a half-hour each way to my already long commute. Every molecule in my body was screaming "no way," but to save our relationship, and out of guilt about my sexual failure, I agreed to move to a loft on Mulberry Street, in Little Italy, and Louise agreed we would build a room in the loft for me.

We had gone to a couples' counselor, who had instructed us to have regular cuddling sessions to restore intimacy, which appealed to neither of us. (By now I have accepted that, for me, without passion and romance sex is mostly too problematic, while Louise enjoys sex, period.) So we talked about an arrangement that was in the air then: having an open relationship. The third party was supposed to be just a sexual partner, not interfering with our primary coupling. We saw monogamy as an edict of the patriarchy that oppressed women, so open relationships were the theoretical ideal of lesbian feminism.

A colleague I'll call Rachel was a scientist who had been one of the junior members of my tenure committee. She was about my age, thin, and intense, with deep-set brown eyes under thick graceful eyebrows; she had a quick, precise way of talking and a big, toothy smile. Over the course of the tenure fight we were thrown together as conspirators, and I wondered whether she was flirting with me but discounted it, as she was married with two young children.

My wingman in this (and another affair to come) was a younger anthropologist, Judy Friedlander. She and I had become acquainted at the University of Chicago, and we were both members of the Ruth Benedict Collective. Judy told me that she had heard from Rachel that she was splitting with her husband and was "turned on by lesbianism." I wrote in my journal that if Louise and I went through with the non-monogamy plan, I might have an affair with Rachel.

Our affair was as sneaky as it was passionate, since we were both hiding from our partners. In the excitement of the moment we imagined ourselves like Plato's two halves of a being that longed to reunite. Gay and straight, science and humanities, perhaps. I wrote, "Phone call [with Rachel] improves spirits. Thought of long summer depresses. Thought of sneaky meetings in motels causes loss of appetite. But fantasy of open access to R. does not seem like solution either. Can't imagine life with R. Know and like life with Louise: shared interests, mutual respect, common friends. But beginning to see that passion possibly has unintended consequences."

In modern idiom: well, duh. Almost immediately Rachel told me that although she and her husband were barely speaking, she could not ask him to move out of their Manhattan high-rise, since it came through his academic job. It's not easy or simple to give up heterosexual privilege.

My two confidants were Shirley, as always, and a new friend, the fiction writer Bertha Harris. Both of them had been married and had a child each, and Bertha had been through an ugly divorce. She was a southerner, with a clever, cutting humor and high-culture sensibility (Mozart operas, experimental fiction) that seemed to contradict her round face and innocent blue eyes. (Bertha once famously said that the archetypal lesbian movie was *Jaws*.) She was in a relationship with the architect Phyllis Birkby, who had been with Louise just before me, and we were all involved in Jill Johnston's ill-defined lesbian feminist project.

Both Shirley and Bertha warned me against what Rachel's husband might do to hurt Rachel or me, or both. He had abused her in the past, and if he found out about our affair, he might try to take Rachel's children away from her. At that time, lesbians were usually considered legally unfit to be mothers. I consulted with a lesbian lawyer, who said not to worry about the "unfit mother" gambit, as it had never won in New York State, but Bertha said Rachel was crazy if she thought she could get out of the marriage without a confrontation. Her husband was going to California for the summer, and Rachel said she hoped he would find someone else more pliable and ask to get out of the marriage himself. Meanwhile, she was going to Woods Hole for the summer on some scientific project. Against every dictate of common sense, I was still hoping that Louise and I were on solid ground and all this wouldn't interfere.

/ / /

On June 6, 1973, Abbot Kaplan, the president of Purchase College, granted me tenure with the words, "You can stay here for the next forty years." In contravening my enemies and Dean John Howard, he was ending the campus uproar over my case and had been persuaded through the intervention, it was rumored, of his genteel feminist wife, who had liked me at a gathering of campus women that Mary Edwards had organized on my behalf. As a sop to my detractors, my promotion and tenure were granted but delayed one year, ensuring my salary would fall even further behind those of my male peers.

I wish I could have enjoyed my personal success and the win for feminist organizing, but I was too ambivalent about the prospect of spending "the next forty years" in academia and too exhausted to feel much of anything. Instead, I allowed myself to get caught up in the open-relationship mess.

Lesbians do not usually have the resources for an "open" relationship that both gay and straight men have, such as prostitution, escort services, erotic baths, and cruising grounds. So most of us never practice sexual or emotional "polyamory," as it is now called, or we wind up making god-awful messes, as Louise and I did. The lies and subterfuge brought out the worst in me and were a betrayal of my genuine love for her.

Shortly after this, Louise and I had it out. I confessed to her about my affair with Rachel, and she countered, to my shock, that she was having an affair with Bertha Harris, to whom I had innocently confided about *my* affair. In the fighting that followed, I fixated on the fact that when we had agreed to the open relationship, we had set the rule that we could not have affairs with friends. Louise had broken this rule more flagrantly than I had, as Bertha was part of our intimate circle, leaving me on higher moral ground, I thought, though Louise was not impressed. It was obvious that neither of our "other women" was just a sex partner.

It is ironic that just as I got job security at Purchase, the rest of my life fell apart. Louise and I were in crisis. Rachel had left for a summer research job with nothing resolved. We were supposed to meet one more time, but she telephoned to say she had to end our relationship because of her children; after that, I heard nothing from her. I was furious but also hoped she would change her mind.

I had no plans for the summer, so not knowing what to do with myself I took a quick tour of my New England friends. First stop was Walpole, New Hampshire, where my old flame Patsy and her partner, Elizabeth, were living in a 1790 house; as usual, I left feeling that my car was the wrong color and maybe I looked too dykey. From there I went on to

Northampton, Massachusetts, where Nancy Smith was spending the summer. I poured out the whole Rachel story, to which Nancy opined, ever world-weary, that I could get over Rachel in two weeks. "Read this," she said drily, handing me a murder mystery.

By the end of June, I was home again with Louise on Mulberry Street. Against all odds, we still enjoyed each other's company. To get away from the firecrackers over the July 4 weekend, she and I met up at Bianca Lanza and Carol Calhoun's place in East Quogue, on Long Island's south shore. When I told Carol about Rachel, she commented, "I'm surprised at you, Esther. I thought you'd have better sense." Never get involved with a straight woman is an adage (though frequently broken) in lesbian life.

On July 8, I went up to Boiceville, near Kingston, New York, to visit Shirley and her family. Back in June, she and I had met at an Italian festival near Mulberry Street to eat cannoli and enjoy the spectacle of people stuffing dollar bills into the clothing of the holy statues being carried through the streets on truck beds. Later that day, Shirley was crossing Amsterdam Avenue near her apartment when an errant gypsy cab hit her, shattering her ankle. She was in the hospital for some days, but I—preoccupied by my tenure fight and disordered personal life—visited only once, an omission that went into the ledger of friendship failures that Shirley and I marked against each other and still dredged up when the other upset us.

Sometime in the following week, the phone rang in our loft on Mulberry Street. Louise seemed to be always out with Bertha, but how could I object just because Rachel had dumped me and left town? To control this rat's nest of angry emotions, we were both pretending to a fake sophistication, and I was utterly miserable. I picked up the phone, not knowing that the call would lead to my falling in love with a Frenchwoman and spending six years in Paris.

It was my colleague Judy Friedlander. She and our friend Paula Webster, with whom I had written the paper on matriarchy, were in Mexico. We had all gotten closer in the Ruth Benedict Collective. They had rented a villa in Tepoztlán, near where Judy had done her anthropological fieldwork, and they were sharing the place with Judy's French friend Catherine Lawton. If I had nothing better to do, why not fly down and meet them?

My memories of going to Mexico with Shirley back in 1965 were mainly of the poverty and of the aggressive men. In the end, though, the hope of escaping from the Louise and Bertha situation and from my obsession with Rachel were so tempting that I flew to Merida, where Paula met me. The others were already on Islas Mujeres (Island of Women), off the coast of Yucatán.

/ / /

Paula was fleshy and Jewish, New York working class and witty. I envied her comfort in her own skin, swinging along in her long, brown spotted dress, sexy, confident, unconcerned, while I slouched defensively in my pants, shoulders hunched, like an apprehensive prey animal, afraid of unfamiliar surroundings. It was so humid in Merida that we could hardly breathe. Paula spoke some Spanish, and I straggled behind her through the *mercado*, buying a Mexican hammock and a Panama hat against the sun. Paula told me she didn't like Catherine Lawton much, that she was pretentious. But Catherine's friend was nicer: Dominique.[1]

On the overnight bus and boat to Islas Mujeres, exhaustion finally overtook me. I had lost a lot of weight and wasn't feeling well. When we got to Islas Mujeres, we tied up our hammocks in a bare white hotel room with a Casablanca ceiling fan. The room looked out on the sea and on Islas Mujeres's one dusty road, and there I slept through a day and night, oblivious to the honking motor scooters that the bored island youth were racing back and forth.

When Paula and I emerged from the hotel room, we walked down to the little beach. The sun was frying in the sky. Lying on a deck chair was this slender body in a yellow bikini. The woman was wearing a kerchief from which some blond curls escaped. She inclined her head to regard us from behind big, dark sunglasses; she didn't say anything, but she also didn't turn away. I wondered whether she spoke English. Her blank stare was unnerving. Who was this woman? As we walked away, Paula explained that this was the Frenchwoman she liked, Dominique.

The next morning, Dominique was again lying on the deck chair, reading. This time we approached, and Paula introduced me. When she took off her dark glasses I saw she was fair, with freckles and hooded blue eyes and that pinched look around the mouth that French people get from speaking their language. With no prologue she said, in excellent but accented British English, "I had a dream last night that I was marrying a woman." Her lack of a filter left me speechless, but Paula quipped, "Oh, what were you wearing?"

Paula, Judy, Dominique, and I spent that day on a hired boat with some Mexican tourists. Judy got into a flirtation with the sixteen-year-old deckhand, who told her, as Judy translated for us, "Older women are better; they are past danger." We laughed, and Paula said she'd be curious what it would be like to sleep with a sixteen-year-old boy. As we chugged by the ruins of the Mayan temple on the tip of the island, Paula remarked drily, "That's the ruins of the matriarchy, if I ever saw one," and flopped back on her elbow.

While the passengers and crew were eating lunch, there was a brief look—a *frisson*, as the French say, a little spark or shiver—that passed between Dominique and me. She asked me to light her cigarette, just the way Betty Silver had in the Michigan Union. I bent over her hands and our eyes, shaded by sunglasses, still met and held some seconds too long. My heart was already beating faster. My friends told me Dominique was ten years older than we were, in her early forties, and just recovering from a devastating affair with an Englishman; she was straight but had had one or two quickie affairs with women. A professor in Paris, she was the author of several books. It became clear that Judy and Paula had talked me up as the LESBIAN. Both Dominique and her friend Catherine were fascinated by the American women's movement—the second wave was barely getting started in France.

Dominique said later that she often acted out of unconscious motives—knowing I was a lesbian must have been why she was so impatient to meet me. "I thought you would never get out of that hammock," she exclaimed. (Several years later I met one of her former lesbian adventures and was nonplussed by how alike we looked.)

In my journal I described "the flirtation with Dominique," wondering whether it would be possible to have a "friendly intimacy" with no lasting consequences, though doubting I would be capable of it. I imagined Dominique as "a woman who is presented to me in the same manner as the tornado dropped Dorothy's house down in the Land of Oz." When Judy had called me, her friend Catherine alone had been mentioned, not any companion, and Catherine could have had an entirely different companion, or no companion, so that our meeting was not destiny but entirely random.

And yet for me, our affair felt ordained. Instantly her Frenchness intrigued me; her blonde Jewishness was aesthetically pleasing; her intelligence was sexy; and I couldn't wait to get her into bed. But that makes my impulse toward her sound so rational, and while those qualities were all real, overwhelming sexual attraction is never rational, and that is frightening—and thrilling. These great loves lead back to my mother, to the intensity of our original love, the oedipal triangle when she married Saul, and then her despair, from which I would always be doomed to rescue her and vainly try to win her love back.

/ / /

Two days later, Paula and I journeyed to Tepoztlán, where it was cold and soggy and there was nothing to do but sleep and write. Dominique, Judy, and Catherine had gone off to see ruins so Paula and I rattled around the enclosed villa. We went to Cuernavaca, where we mailed letters—no mail service in Tepoztlán—and Paula helped me buy a black-and-white-checked vintage jacket, white linen pants, and Mexican sandals made of Firestone tires, with deep tread. Dominique was coming back, and I was tan and fit from swimming, restored and confident. I was looking for a woman to admire me and to lie with during the afternoon rains. Two days later, Louise called me late at night, and we argued. She wanted me to come home, and I said, "What about Bertha?" I had no intention of leaving Tepoztlán before the end of the month that remained.

Still, I hoped that whatever happened between Dominique and me would be "just for now" and "light"—how could it be otherwise when we lived so far apart? There were the complications and commitments at home: my job, Louise, Rachel (though she had not returned my letters). The following night, when Dominique and I first made love, she said the same: "I hope it will be pleasant and not too deep between us." But she added, "I've been thinking about you more than I want to."

We made the awkward transition from the couch to the bed and gently explored each other's upper bodies and faces, and no more. I didn't want to rush it. I worried about her being "straight," though I reassured myself ("After all, women are women"), and I worried, that being older and French, she would be more sophisticated sexually than me, even though I knew that was just a stereotype (one that turned out to be true).

"Sensitive, very sensitive," Dominique murmured next to me before we fell asleep (*sen-si-tif* is how it sounded). "So far so good," I replied, and she laughed. "What does it mean, 'So far so good'?"

"Up to this point, everything's cool." This made her laugh more, and she asked whether "cool" meant "good." The last thing she said before she slept was, "So far, so very good."

So many things about Dominique gave me pleasure: her not-quite-native British English, the way the muscles around her mouth had been pinched by the pace and sounds of French. When she and Catherine spoke French, they sang like woodwinds. I liked her trim figure and the way her casual but well-fitting French clothes showed it off. I saw the dark blue of Nancy's French workman's shirt, the one she had painted in, in Dominique's blue-and-white-striped mariner sweater—with buttons along the top of her shoulder. Her hooded blue eyes and curly blonde hair. Her lively wit. A lot like Louise.

Although Dominique already spoke French, English, and German, she'd been attending the Spanish language school at the Centro Intercultural de Documentación (Intercultural Documentation Center; CIDOC), in Cuernavaca. When she returned to the villa carrying her books and passed in front of my room, she whistled to me—the confident older woman and her youthful lover. As with Nancy, I found the age difference compelling. Some years earlier I had been entranced by Tony Perkins and Melina Mercouri in the French film *Phaedra*. Perkins plays Mercouri's husband's son by a first marriage, and they fall into forbidden love. As I recall, my avatar Perkins wound up driving a fancy sports car over a cliff to swelling classical music while my heart pounded with tragic erotic excitement.

/ / /

During these early days, Dominique told me stories. The first was how she had fallen desperately in love with a well-known English sociologist, Michael, fifteen years her senior and married with children. He had

With Dominique. Tepoztlán, Mexico, August 1973.

strung her along, told her he loved her, said he would leave his wife. He attended a conference in Mauritius and took her along, stashing her in a posh seaside resort where she, having nothing else to do, waited trembling for him to return to her each evening. She was forty and wanted a child with him, but as time went on she realized he would never leave his wife. This was the failed affair that had plunged her into depression, medication, and even a clinic before she went to Mexico on impulse.

Even though I put this down to the predictable gullibility of straight women, her suffering moved me, and I lowered the obvious red flags. I was jealous when some nights she woke crying over him, but I was also drawn in by the prospect of supplanting him and rescuing her from her heterosexual misery, which to me at that time was a feminist as well as a personal project. (Is homosexual misery any better? Maybe not, but it's *my* misery.)

Dominique's other story, of her early life, was exotic and even more compelling. She came from a distinguished family of French Jews. Her grandfather had been a Hungarian immigrant who became a leading left-wing professor and public intellectual, first a leading Dreyfusard, one of those who supported the Jewish army officer Captain Alfred Dreyfus against the anti-Semites who accused him of treason, and then a founder of the Popular Front, an alliance of socialists and liberals during the 1930s. When the Nazis invaded France, Dominique's father, who was a doctor in the French army, turned his revolver on himself, leaving his wife, Sophie, and two young children, Dominique and her younger brother, Gilles, to fend for themselves.

The trio escaped to the south, which was not under direct German control. Dominique, then twelve or so, was given an assumed name and shipped off to a Protestant family for safety while Sophie kept Gilles with her. Dominique believed that her mother always favored Gilles. Both children wanted to be medical doctors like their parents, but only Gilles was encouraged. Dominique was always told she was too emotionally fragile. Resenting her brother was the bedrock of her feminism. Fervently attached to her mother, Dominique never forgave her, either.

Sophie Lévy, who had been a prominent doctor in Paris, found work in the south, but as the war ground on she felt less and less safe. In 1944, the French Gestapo, the Milice Française, arrested Dominique's grandfather, who was then living in Lyon. His wife elected to go with him. They were taken out to a rural road, and both octogenarians were shot point-blank. Dominique heard the news on the radio.

Meanwhile, Sophie Lévy had been tipped off that the Milice were coming for her. As Dominique heard the story, her mother, a woman of uncommon resolve and nerve, escaped out the back door of her clinic as the fascists were coming in the front. (When I exclaimed at her mother's bravery, Dominique cautioned, "It is not always easy to have an admirable mother.") Somehow Sophie collected her two children to escape over the border to Switzerland. Dominique was shocked; she could barely recognize her mother—a dark brunette with a no-nonsense expression and almost hawk-like face—who had assumed a blonde wig and pancake makeup to elude the Gestapo. When they got to the border, a guard asked, "Are you in danger of death?" Sophie answered, "Yes." A woman behind them answered "No" and was turned back.

My father had risked his life to fight the Nazis in Spain and elsewhere in Europe, and the Holocaust had been a theme of my childhood. I knew that my Aryan mother could not have saved me; the Nazis would have seen me as a Jewish target for extermination. Those facts were part of me but distant from my own experience. Dominique and her family had lived these traumas, and they had (most of them) survived. Her persecution and suffering bound me fast to her, wanting to protect her. The family's escape from the Nazis made her seem more special, intriguing. Hers was a history that was larger than life, epic and entrancing.

/ / /

Paula and Judy helped organize a women's meeting in Tepoztlán from among the American expatriate community. They included Margaret Fiedler, the estranged wife of the critic Leslie Fiedler, and an extraordinary woman named Anne de Neven.

Anne had walked out on two husbands (totaling twenty years of marriage), sent her two children away, and decided that her greatest need was solitude. Paula and I liked her and thought she was painfully up-front and courageous. But our French friends were filled with disdain. "If she hates men so much, why did she stay married for twenty years and make such a miserable failure of it?" said Dominique, while Catherine remarked acidly, "I can't believe any woman could have such conventional ideas on marriage." (Anne had thought marriage was to serve the husband.) Then, Anne belonged to the "mystical" side of the movement. Paula and I had grown accustomed to talk of "the goddess," astrological signs, and the tarot, while our French friends had no tolerance for what we now call New Age concepts.

The topic of one meeting was competition. Quite a few of the local expats were writers. I envied their having dropped out and contrasted it unfavorably to our group, who were employed by academia. I told the story of how I had given up writing after getting my college roommate Hilary to write a required sonnet for me, and that even before that, "I was totally intimidated by 'ART' and was clueless about how to express my own experience." I concluded, "Maybe I have wasted ten years of my life in higher education." The women made sympathetic noises. As we all saw it, I had been directed by "the patriarchy" to become a dry scholar instead of the true artistic (more womanish?) me.

But from the perspective of forty-five years, I have different regrets. I was a gifted scholar who was sidetracked by discrimination, by the struggle with my sexual and gender confusions in a hostile society, by the initial failure of my first book and so on. Not that I renounce my love of beautiful writing in any genre. The years I spent in college and in Paris, reading George Eliot and Henry Miller and writing amateur novels myself, made me a better writer and intellectual. (By now, the distinction between "objective" academic writing and "subjective" artistic writing has blurred, and on the whole that is a good thing.)

But the decade of the 1970s, when creative writing captivated me, was a period in which I could have been doing more scholarship and advancing my academic career. Back then I disdained the idea of becoming a famous scholar with an endowed chair, although in the long game I became well known and respected in LGBT studies. But like most accomplished queer people, especially women, I never broke out of the "You have a special (minor) interest" box we are put in. Now I am pissed that, largely because I am a lesbian and my subjects were queer, I was never considered for honors *as* an anthropologist or historian that I believe my work was distinguished enough to deserve. Every recognition, tribute, and opportunity has come to me from other queers. Without them and their support, I would indeed have been a bitter flop.[2]

/ / /

One of Louise and my failures had been in the minefield of lesbian feminist-approved sex. We hardly distinguished between men's social power and their sexual power. These ideas came to their logical culmination in the writing of Andrea Dworkin, who argued that heterosexual intercourse was an intrinsic act of domination. The end goal was to eliminate all hierarchies, and since sexual relations between ourselves was one of the few areas we could control, the lesbian feminist community exerted intense pressure—not to eschew sex, as is often asserted, but to have sex as far from the heterosexual script as possible. In the lesbian feminist context, this meant no dildos, no sadomasochistic role-playing, and no butch/femme. All sexual acts had to be reciprocal—or, at least, reciprocated. So if I was on top, then you were on top; if I went down on you, you had to go down on me; if I came, you had to come, and so on.

After Nancy Smith, I fell back to more of the butch-like, I'm-on-top mode that Betty Silver and the underwater dancer Nannette had taught me. It wasn't polite to admit that in middle-class circles, but anyhow sexual details were not talked about. When I first met Louise, I took her for a femme, which didn't mean I could tell her what to do. It just meant that femme was her gender identity and that I would assume a persona that took more initiative in bed. Louise came out of the bar life, too, and she was familiar with butch/femme; her first female lover, Mike, had been more butch than I was. Sexuality in our early years more or less followed that line, but as we both "converted" to lesbian feminism, we changed in unexpected ways. Louise was becoming less femme and more androgynous. She wanted to make love to me more, and I didn't like it. But then Rachel, whose demeanor was more feminine than mine, liked to pleasure me, and because I now knew what orgasm was, and this was a new relationship and had no set parameters, it turned me on.

By the time I met Dominique, despite her being feminine, I was convinced of the rightness of reciprocal sexuality and did not want to give up on orgasms. But it was turning out that Dominique was not comfortable with female body parts below the waist. One night I insisted that she touch me, and she had complied, only to withdraw in fright. I woke in the morning in a pool of my menstrual blood. We had been pushed into the same room by the arrival of Judy's sister's in-laws from Mexico City, and between the blood and the sound of their car arriving, Dominique jumped straight up and out. She was terrified they would realize we were sharing a bed.

After breakfast I saw her anxiously counting her Mexican money, and I joked that she was seeing whether she had enough to escape. She had to laugh, and we discussed how it was just as well that we were not so compatible sexually—after all, she was straight and lived in France, and our relationship was just part of the spice of life, pleasant and tasty. I felt relieved and wrote that if she couldn't make me come, I would never fall hard. But it was nice to have a French friend, and maybe I would visit sometime. That night I wrote, "Ever since I read of Susan Sontag's French friends I've wanted some too."

/ / /

I met Dominique in Cuernavaca, and she wanted to go to an elegant restaurant called Los Mananitas for a drink. We sat on a veranda while down below was a garden, which was more like a park, with parrots, peacocks, and monkeys. The waiters made a great show of serving us. I was drinking a daiquiri topped with orange and a cherry. The women looked like jewels, pale; one wearing a white hat resembled a doll. Precious little boys in shorts played quietly in the park while wealthy, paunchy old men talked at their young wives. A lesbian rendezvous was perfect for this park, I thought. It set the tone.

It made me think of Nancy Smith, who told me a joke that opened a world to me. Two elegant American women met for a drink in a Paris bar. One had a gorgeous hat. They began to fight, and finally one ripped the hat off the other, threw it to the ground, stamped on it, and flew out of the bar shouting, "So much for your fucking hat, Mrs. Cunt." Elegant bar-hopping American lesbians in Paris? I wanted so badly for that to be me.

Dominique laughed when I told her, but the peacocks and monkeys and lesbian rendezvous were making her more and more anxious. We took a second-class bus back to Tepoztlán, because the first-class bus, as frequently happened, was *discompuesto*, out of commission. As we sat down in the bus, surrounded by barefoot Indian women and young men in straw hats with farm tools, Dominique took my arm and whispered in my ear, "Only a drunken lesbian bitch would put her straight lover on a second-class bus. We should have taken a taxi. It's going to take a whole bloody hour to get back."

I was charmed that she referred to herself as my lover and called me a "drunken lesbian bitch." I wished I could have kissed her.

/ / /

Our stay was coming to an end, yet I felt more and more happy and relaxed. I was writing in my journal almost every day and enjoying our feminist life inside the villa. "I can't remember when I've felt so at home in my body," I wrote. My appetite had come back since the spring turmoil, and I was no longer semi-emaciated. Dominique set a good example. Her muscles lay smooth under her skin, and in France she skied, rode a bike, hiked, played tennis, and practiced yoga.

I resolved to brush up on my French and swim every day that fall. New York felt cramped; by 1973, some of the ideas of lesbian feminism were starting to seem like conventions, or even dictums. Clearly, Dominique figured, though confusedly, in my hopes. I could see even then that, emotionally, she had her ups and downs. Later I would learn that her trouble was worse than that.

One afternoon, Dominique met Paula and me at Ann de Neven's house and plunged into a black mood, apparently because we didn't leave right away, as she wanted. Not only did she stamp off in a snit, but later, as we lay in bed, she started to cry very suddenly, saying she was too weak and that she'd done the same thing with me as she had with Michael—gotten attached to someone who couldn't live with her and who was going away—and that she couldn't stand feeling jealous and possessive of me. "When I get back, it'll all crumble," she cried. "I won't be able to do anything that I want to—no commune, no baby, no work, no man, nothing." She was not comforted by my touch, and the next morning she woke up tight as a cramped muscle.

Mostly, though, she dazzled me with her elegance, warmth, affection, and charm. She would tease me, calling me "an American asshole" (it is easier to say naughty words in a language that is not your own). I knew she meant, "You're my American lover; you're my drunken lesbian bitch." And after weeks of saying she had to return to Paris early, Dominique changed her airplane ticket to stay into September, and we planned to go to Acapulco with Paula as a grand finale. Sunday, August 19, 1973, I wrote, was "the best day of my life." We planned to take the 2:10 bus into Cuernavaca to see a movie and buy some Mexican shirts. After lunch, though, we lay in bed sleeping and touching. How good it was, how healing. Her hand was warm, and I thought about how the Nazis could have killed her; other children were sent to camps and never came back.

/ / /

Ivan Illich had founded CIDOC in Cuernavaca in 1961. He had been a priest, and was a prominent intellectual in the progressive Catholic tradition. Revered by left-wing French intellectuals, he had just published *Deschooling Society*, an argument for dismantling the educational system in favor of peer- and self-directed learning as a means to bring about an anarchist society.

At the time, left-wing men typically saw the women's movement as a distraction from "the real issues," class and maybe racism. In fact, the radical branch of second wave feminism had emerged from the antiwar and civil rights movements over anger with the chauvinist behavior of leftist men. As well as studying Spanish, Dominique had joined a seminar run by Illich, and had been invited, along with two other seminar attendees, to give papers on "women."

The night before, I had proofread her paper, missing the women's meeting—on creativity—so I was furious when, on the bus to Cuernavaca, Dominique turned to me and said, "Michael will be wild with joy when he hears I've given a paper." Gritting my teeth, I suppressed my reaction, since I knew how nervous she was and didn't want to upset her further.

Dominique at her most attractive and sophisticated, in a long and well-cut cotton skirt, white linen blouse, and blue and red beads, read her paper on Victorian womanhood on a breezy open patio at CIDOC. Her delivery in English was clear and precise. Paula and I, who saw her as our feminist project, were as proud as mother hens perched in the back row of seats.

Illich was a tall, slender man with a severe face, tanned, a potent, powerful charmer. He decreed no interruption between the three papers, but after the next woman's presentation, which was obscurely related to his ideas about consumerism and the so-called convivial society, whatever that was, he enthusiastically held forth about how she had gone beyond Juliet Mitchell, without referring back to Dominique's paper, which was far more competent and worked out.

Then Jackie, a lovely young woman we knew from the Tepoztlán women's group, stood up to give her paper on the family. After five minutes, Illich flew into a rage and gave her three more minutes while shouting that her paper was banal, nothing more than could be read in cheap magazines. We knew Jackie had been Illich's special pretty pet; how could he be so abusive toward her?

Paula and I were furious, but although we thought that the others in the seminar were too tame to object, they did. Illich found himself with a minor insurrection on his hands, and he backed down slightly. Somehow Jackie did not crumble, but she also did not finish, omitting what would have been the most apropos points under the circumstances, about the role of the authoritarian father. After the seminar Illich came and sat with us, and we let him have it. He said it was his seminar, he was a teacher, and he could decide what was good and bad, what was relevant and what was not. It emerged obliquely that he was hurt that Jackie had not been working with him that summer. However, anytime the going got tough, he diverted with another charming story. Paula and I were terrified that he would kill us for our rebellion, and it was worth the whole thing to find out that he did or could not.

We were all in our several ways terribly upset by his behavior and our stand against him. Dominique, who had been as brave as anyone at the time, began to apologize for him. A poet we knew went home and read his book. Jackie left the table and cried, then found she could not work, rejoined us in the market in Tepoztlán, and spent the rest of the evening zoned-out. I got furious with Dominique for defending Illich and shouted that he was just like my charming dictatorial father and I'd had enough of that while secretly fighting off a fear that we brazen women had mortally wounded him. Paula delivered a speech about not letting "special people" get away with shit, to which Dominique responded that she'd always let her men get away with shit because they were "special"— but should she do it anymore? Later, Paula told me, Dominique went on to Judy for twenty minutes about killing Illich.

/ / /

We traveled to Acapulco by bus. I was reading Virginia Woolf's *The Voyage Out*, but her gorgeous prose intimidated me, and I recognized that whatever skill I had did not lie in her path, however scenic. My quest to find a new, creative voice for my writing always returned to Gertrude Stein, her life with Alice, and her associative, free-range, very American prose style. Psychoanalysis and the women's movement had made me more supple. What I wrote in Acapulco captures the style of what I was doing: "Acapulco is hot yes hot not a beautiful land even with palm trees and tropical fruits not a fair land but one all jumbled and everyone thinks always of money. To be poor is to think always and every minute of pesos when mixed with tourists."

We took a glass-bottom boat to Roquetta Island, which had a sweet little beach and more Americans than we'd seen before; not as many Mexicans trying to sell you things. And the great thing was we all went water-skiing. First Dominique skied around and around the bay, very competent. And then Paula, who was not athletic, let herself over the side, carefully. We had a young Mexican instructor named Angel who was feeling her up in the water, which she quite enjoyed. He did try to help her get up on the skis, too. I had never water-skied, but I was in my thirties and up to most physical challenges. I got up the very first time, and each time it got easier. How exhilarating it was to fly over the water as the ending of our magical Mexico!

/ / /

One night in 2010 I was walking my dogs through a sticky Florida night that reminded me of the Island of Women, where Dominique and I met, thinking about how Dr. Magnet had once said my problem was "object constancy." In experiments, when the mothers of certain children disappear momentarily behind a screen, these children panic because they can't believe their mother is still there. The physicality of my lover, her body against my body, her presence, her voice was always vital to me. Her leaving for the day felt like abandonment forever, and I would verbally kick and scream. When my analysis was ending, Dr. Magnet tried to comfort me by saying I would always have her with me, inside of me, which I dismissed as a bromide. But writing about Mexico has made me see that Dominique, who is behind the screen now because we live in different countries and have seen each other infrequently over the past thirty years, is still with me, inside me in these memories. Her warm hands, light-blue eyes, musical French voice live in my brain and blood, and she will be with me to my end.

When I did fieldwork in Cherry Grove during the 1980s, my dear friend Kay was an eighty-three-year-old whose faculties were diminished and who was barely able to walk. The Grove is on a barrier island, surrounded by the saltwater that Kay had always loved. I offered to wheel her to the ocean so she could see it. "No, dear," she said, tapping her temple. "I can see it better in my mind."

CHAPTER 9

IN-BETWEEN DYKE

For people with modest salaries living in buildings without protective doormen, life in New York City during the mid-1970s was scary. All kinds of public services declined, and the city, supposedly going broke, was reviled all around the country as a dirty, crime-ridden hellhole. When the city asked President Ford for a bailout in 1975, the *New York Daily News* ran the headline: "Ford to City: Drop Dead." Graffiti was everywhere—in subways and public parks; on busses, cars, and sides of buildings. Not only the ambitious murals on whole subway cars that are featured in glossy art books, but also scribbled "tags" that announced gang territory or just tough guy presence. Though it is no more invasive in principle than advertising, I hated it.

What was happening to the vigorous yet fairly orderly city of my childhood? Ruined and pathetic men wiped my windshield for quarters whenever my car was stopped, and street crime seemed to be around every corner, though Louise and I joked that because we lived in Little Italy, there would be no muggings on Mulberry Street. The sense of chaos and decline deepened during the oil shock of October 1973, with its around-the-block gas pump lines and desperate drivers siphoning gas from one another's cars. Our dispirited troops were shooting their lieutenants while giant planes sprayed the Vietnamese people with burning napalm and their forests with Agent Orange.

My commute by car from the downtown loft to the Purchase campus in the suburbs took well over an hour each way, and although I liked our quirky and motivated undergraduate students, teaching mostly felt like just a job. The ending of my affair with Rachel splintered the feminist circle that had rallied around my tenure case. Although Rachel had never answered my letters from Mexico, she had decided by the start of the fall semester that she wanted me back, and my "no" was interpreted by her as my "dumping" her, so much so that some former feminist allies refused to speak to me.

The feminist and lesbian feminist movements, whose consciousness-raising groups and political actions had enthralled Louise and me, also waned. The consciousness-raising groups were morphing into therapy sessions or were split by toxic personal conflicts. I daydreamed about Dominique, Mexico, and Gertrude Stein's Paris. The Tepoztlán gang— Judy, Paula, and me—saw one another fairly often, but they lived a long subway ride away on the Upper West Side of Manhattan. Still, Judy and I signed up for an advanced French course at the New School, and we hung out, reminiscing about Mexico and planning our travels to Europe.

We talked about living in a commune, but none of us did it. We talked about couples and wanting to escape them, about passion and its illusions and about special people not getting away with shit. But I stopped going to feminist meetings and stopped writing my journal, instead writing long letters to Dominique. Not passionate letters, because she wrote that she didn't ever want to be in love again. Her answers sounded more and more disjointed and strange. She called me long-distance from Paris in the middle of the night and another time from a London phone booth after having burst into her ex-lover Michael's house unannounced and telling him off in front of his wife. We assumed she was becoming the feminist she had seen in us, and we all wrote her confident letters, since what seemed to be happening to her was what we believed in. She wrote that she wanted me to come over during Thanksgiving.

She was waiting for me as I passed through customs at Orly Airport. Gone was the elegant Parisienne. Her clothes hung on her skinny frame, and her hair was a mop of barely combed blonde curls escaping from a cloth workingman's cap. Playing "Here Comes the Bride" on a harmonica she hopped from one foot to the other like a drunken sailor, keeping time to the tune. I didn't know whether to laugh or flee.

An elegant caped figure emerged from behind her shoulder and pointed me out to Dominique. The caped woman had to be Nicole Rougier, a gay friend and colleague she'd written me about. Dominique, playing another spirited round of "Here Comes the Bride," fended off my greeting hug with an offer of a rose.

"So you're here," she said.

"You must be Nicole?" I offered my hand to the woman in the cape. "How did you know it was me?"

"How do you do," said Nicole formally, with a proper British accent. "My dear," she said, taking me in, "it could have been no one but you."

"I want a coffee," Dominique said, running off to the airport bar on her toes without looking back at us.

"She's mad," said Nicole disapprovingly. "I don't know what's come over her. She's always been such a polite person, well-bred. I can tell you, this change is making me quite nervous."

"What makes you think she's mad?"

"See for yourself," said Nicole disgustedly, gesturing toward the airport bar, where Dominique was signaling the waiter with a great show of arm waving. Other customers were looking at her curiously. "Phoning people at all hours of the night," Nicole went on, "stirring up trouble. It can't go on like this."

"She'll be all right," I said with fake confidence for Nicole's benefit. "She's finally asserting herself, just blowing off steam."

"Perhaps," said Nicole doubtfully. "But I am glad to meet you at last," she said recovering her polite airs, and critically eyeing my crumpled airplane clothing. "Dominique has talked endlessly about Mexico. Everything with her these days is Mexico this and Mexico that. Has she told you about this man, this African she's taken into her flat?" Nicole asked as we dragged my bags over to the bar.

"What man?" Dominique's letters hadn't mentioned that.

"She means my black man, Jean, the one I ran into on the street," said Dominique gaily. "Nicole thinks I'm crazy to have taken him in, don't you, Nicole? Do you think I'm crazy, too?" She turned toward me accusingly.

"Maybe," I said, annoyed about the man. "What do you mean, you took him in?"

Dominique pulled off her checked hat and held it out to me. "How do you like it? Not bad, eh?"

"Terrible," Nicole interrupted. "You look like a ragamuffin."

Dominique downed her coffee in one gulp and wiped her mouth with the back of her hand, grinning at Nicole's censorious look like a demonic imp. "Nicole's mad because I'm so free," she said.

"Free, my foot," said Nicole. "You're overexcited."

"They all like me better when I'm depressed," Dominique accused.

"What black man?" I insisted.

"Ba ba ba baaamh," Dominique blasted out the opening chords of Beethoven's Fifth on the harmonica. Travelers up and down the coffee bar were staring. "I always wanted to be a conductor," Dominique said, oblivious, "but they don't let girls do that. I'm learning the saxophone, though."

Nicole fastened up her cape with long, elegant fingers. "Very nice to have met you at last," she said. "I must be off. I hope your stay here," she glanced pointedly at Dominique, "will not be too trying. Goodbye, my dear." She dismissed Dominique with a little peck on each cheek. "Be good to your guest."

"What do you think?" Dominique asked, nodding after her retreating friend.

"Impressive," I said. "A very handsome dyke."

"Dyke, dyke," she mimicked, "that's all you lesbians think about."

"I'm not sharing you with some man," I said. "You should have told me."

"Oh, for goodness sake. I'm not sleeping with him, if that's what you're worried about. Let's go to the car. I want to show you my apartment."

She walked off, leaving me with my luggage. As I struggled along behind, she told me over her shoulder that she'd met Jean in the street, where he'd been collecting money for some Third World cause. They'd begun talking about racism, and eventually it came out that he'd been sleeping in the Métro, so, of course, she invited him to stay with her for a while. "Spread the wealth," she said. He had brought his white girlfriend, who was also more or less living there. "It's a nice little commune," she said, "just like Mexico."

On the way back to her place on the Left Bank, she was not concentrating on driving, and we had several near-misses. She talked non-stop. Her English trip had been a huge success. She'd dropped in on Michael and his wife and told them both just what she thought of the way she'd been treated. And that prick Michael had acted so hurt. Yes, it was upsetting but worth it—worth every minute to see the looks on their faces.

And then there'd been her impromptu speech at a big women's meeting at a London university. Why were they wasting time with all those boring scholarly papers? They should be talking to each other, really talking, the way we did in Mexico. And at her university job she'd told them off, too, the stuffy bores. Yes, she was telling them all off. I hadn't heard the half of it. She'd never felt so free, so uninhibited. And she backed the car into a parking place with a gashing sound as she scraped the huge Citroën parked behind.

"Watch it," I cried.

"I'm born again, and all you can think about is a little scratch."

"If you feel so great, how come you look so bad?"

"I suppose you mean tired? I can't sleep. The nights are bad," she admitted. "I've been writing my memoirs."

"Now you'll sleep, with me here," I bragged. She needed steadying, and the wilder she sounded, the more I tried to make myself solid and confident. She was someone whose wild freedom I had dreamed of in feminism and I was someone she thought would see her through it all.

"Are you really here?" she turned to me, suddenly defenseless and vulnerable on the sidewalk. But before I could frame my reassurance, her expression changed again. "I want you to see my apartment. I've lived here for ten years, but I've decided to move, so it's the last time. The view of Paris is wonderful. I need light. Can you live without light? But the Left Bank is getting too crowded, not as nice as it used to be. Here, I'll take one of those bags, my poor American. It's six flights up."

What was going on? The emotional volatility that I'd seen in Mexico had morphed into this frantic nuttiness. She did sleep a little better with me there for the week, but not much. At night, the energy fueling her acts of defiance turned inward. She looked like someone in a centrifuge who was going to go splat. During the day the demons drove her: early-morning phone calls to friends and old enemies, shoplifting, playing her saxophone on the street. She told her publisher she would do translations only of women's work from now on. These symbolic blows against the real and imagined oppressors gave her childish and enormous satisfaction. But at night she just burned and burned:

> Tiger, tiger
> Burning bright
> In the forests
> Of the night.

She was fond of reciting Blake. That day she had tried to invite a crazy man who called himself a prophet up for lunch, but I had stopped her.

"Why don't you turn on the light if you can't sleep?" I said. It was no use my trying to sleep. Her body against mine was hot and crackly.

"I hung up on my mother. I told her not to call me anymore."

"Why don't you turn on the light?"

"I will. I'm going to phone her."

"It's three in the morning. What do you want to say?" As she turned on the bedside lamp, I saw her face breaking apart. "To tell her that she ruined my life. She crushed me. I wanted to be a conductor. I should have been a lesbian."

"It's not too late."

"It *is* too late," she insisted, bursting into noisy tears. "I'm too old now. You don't know what a curse a family is. I hate them, anarchists, Jews, the family name. I wish the Gestapo had gotten us."

"What? Don't say that," I said. "Here, have a Kleenex." She stopped crying and blew her nose with a loud honk.

"What do you know?" she cried. "What do you know about anything? You've always done just what you wanted. I'm nothing. I've never done anything."

"That's not true," I said, incredulous that this accomplished woman could be so down on herself. "I haven't done just what I wanted at all. I wanted to write and I gave up. Remember all the stuff we talked about in Mexico? Communes, getting out of the system, doing just what we wanted, feminism. You're doing it all. We just went back to our regular lives." She had exposed my ambivalence toward order, toward the monthly paycheck, toward academia. Yet her suffering was plain to see.

"You should come and live with me for a while," she said. "Take that leave you were talking about."

"Maybe I will. But I thought you didn't want to be in a couple. Nothing deep, remember?"

"That's right," she said fiercely. "I want to live in a commune. Be with the people."

"What people?" I asked. "If you mean Third World people like Jean, I don't trust him. He's taking you for a ride." Jean had struck me as an amiable con man, and I had talked Dominique into ousting him and his girlfriend for the week.

"Paranoid," she accused.

"That's true."

"I had some sexual fantasies about you, just before you came. While I was reading 1001 *Virgins*. When the insomnia started."

"What's 1001 *Virgins*?"

"You know, pornographic stuff, masochistic. . . . It was so long since I'd felt anything sexual."

"Do you want me to make love to you?" She nodded tentatively and turned out the light again. I held and kissed her for a long time, laying my hands all over her, soothing the demons. Finally, she relaxed a little and I was able to make her come. But as I lay congratulating myself, she suddenly jerked upright and snapped on the light.

"It's no use, no use," she cried.

"What's no use?" I reached for her, but she was out of bed and pacing the floor. Unruly blonde curls dwarfed her haggard face. I thought of one of those little French kings whose beaky faces were surmounted by mountainous wigs. I sighed and turned over in bed. She'd been running me ragged, with the struggle to adapt to Paris and the strangeness of everything.

I heard her honking away on the saxophone in the next room. She'd been teaching herself to play the main themes from Beethoven's Ninth Symphony. I laughed aloud thinking of her threat to take the sax to her office. She was so comical, and I understood as only a solemn person can what a release that was. Now she started clacking away at the typewriter, working on her memoirs.

I struggled through what she had written so far with the aid of a dictionary. Her writing was poetic and also very funny. Everything I had wanted to write. It's not fair, I thought; she's not even conscious, not trying. It's just happening to her. It's a compulsion, she had told me. I have to do it. If only I had a compulsion. But no, I was left with the dull task of disciplining myself.

At a jarring crash from the other end of the apartment I jumped out of bed and ran down the hall. She was standing in the kitchen with tears streaming down her face, a big china plate held over her head. The fragments of another were on the floor. "What's going on?" I yelled.

"It's no good, no use!" Her arms came down over her head like a whip and I ducked behind the doorjamb just as the plate hit the floor. "It's no use," she was jumping up and down. "I'll never be anything but a princess. Useless. I can't have men anymore, and now I won't be able to have women, or anything, anything!" She turned toward me as if to explain, pointing at the broken china. "It belonged to the family," she said.

"Come back to bed," I said, without coming any closer.

"No. It's no use. I can't make love to you."

Although Dominique, who had no experience of gay life and did not identify as femme, that is how I saw her, and her independent femininity along with her attraction to me fit the profile. Though it did not change the kind of woman who appealed to me one bit, lesbian feminism presented a prescriptive sexual script of sexual "equality." In line with these ideals, I had told her in Mexico, it had to go both ways. I still had no nuanced understanding of how butch-femme intimacy could be re-worked.

"OK, OK. let's just be friends then. You can still count on me."

"No," she said. "I don't want to be your friend. I wouldn't want to see you anymore."

"Well come back to bed anyway."

"I can't sleep." But she seemed calmer.

"I'm exhausted," I said. "Will you be all right?" But she wasn't listening, and she walked past me, leaving the mess on the floor, and sat down to the typewriter in the living room. I went back to bed. Clickety-clack went the typewriter at full speed.

/ / /

"What are you doing?" Dominique asked me, superfluously.

I was packing my bags. "I have to go back to America tomorrow morning, remember?"

"You're leaving me," she said. "I've been difficult, I know."

"That's true. But I wouldn't have missed it."

"Really?" She sat down next to me on the bed. The summer freckles were gone from her face; her skin was gray and taut. She looked ten years older than before, but her light-blue eyes were so alive I looked away for a moment, disconcerted. She was all there, present, listening. "You've been very patient," she said, taking both my hands in hers. Her sweet smell enveloped me. "Don't leave me," she said. "Why don't you throw it all up, stay with me. I need you near me. We're like sisters."

"OK. Sisters then."

"That's not what I meant," she said.

"You know I have to go back to work."

"Shall I come for Christmas vacation, the way we planned?" she asked. "Will you still be living with Louise?"

"I don't know. Maybe not. We can't seem to get out of the mess. Hey, are you going to be OK? Maybe you should go and see your shrink."

"No, no shrink. He's just another repressor. He'd dope me up the way he did when I got so depressed before. I don't need him. I feel wonderful!"

"Not quite," I said. "You can't eat, can't sleep. You need to get your balance. You've turned your world upside down. Terrific, I'm behind you all the way. But enough is enough. You can't live this way."

"You don't like my shoplifting," she accused.

"That's true. I think it's childish. But that's not the point."

"Don't be so pompous. You always think you know what's best. I'm sick and tired of people knowing what's best for me." She was getting worked up again, and her crazy energy filled the room.

"OK, have it your way." I started packing again. She put on Beethoven's Ninth, loud, and played along with the harmonica. I was almost packed. She went over to the stereo and swatted the arm, which squeaked crazily over the record and came to the center, ticking. I winced.

"What about Christmas?" She turned on me, fiery.

"Yes, come. I want you to come. But what about you and me? Since we can't really sleep together . . . that is, I told you I couldn't go on this way forever, if you didn't make love to me. I can't live that way anymore. It was OK for Mexico, but now something's got to give. You mean a lot to me. Couldn't we go on as friends?"

"No! No, I told you no before, it just wouldn't work. I don't want it."

"Well, what do you want me to do then?" I said angrily. "I'm through with straight women. I told you that, and now I mean it!"

She stopped pacing and stood shaking her head. She seemed to push outward, filling the space. I sensed an enormous effort.

"I'm not straight, not any more. I'm . . . I'm bisexual." She made it sound dignified.

"Congratulations," I snorted. "Prove it then, if you're so bisexual as all that."

"I will." She jumped on me and her momentum pinned me down against the bed so suddenly that reflexively I struggled and tried to push her off. But I couldn't budge her.

"Don't fight me," she panted. "You belong to me. I'll show you." I let myself go limp and closed my eyes. It was true; somehow I did belong to her and was only waiting to be claimed. My shirt was opening, my pants coming off magically. I felt her face in my breasts; she was hot and fiery as a dragon. She took me in her hands and rolled me away, rolled me and rolled me until I was fluid and then, dissolved. At last I opened my eyes, feeling bewildered and subdued. We were separate again, and she was raining kisses on me. Then she got up triumphantly, seized the saxophone, and played a full chorus from the Ninth with terrific verve and many vigorous honks. I could make no effort and pulled the covers over me. The last sound I heard was the clack of the typewriter.

I hardly noticed the Atlantic the next day for the erotic clouds that enveloped me. Now I had the mutual sex my lesbian feminism told me I should have. I would make love to Dominique, and she would make love to me. My head was swimming with ideas for that novel I'd been thinking of writing. Of course, it was going to be about our affair, about Mexico and Paris. About an hour off the American shoreline, I began to draft a letter to my dean asking for a semester's leave.

/ / /

Back in New York I was hardly reading anthropology anymore, in thrall instead to feminist writers such as Kate Millett, Anaïs Nin, and Doris Lessing. Half-consciously I associated scholarship with the masculine part of myself that I later called "the Biographer," an entity who was nothing but the facts ma'am, with no room for play or creativity.

Louise had opened the art world to me. I knew it had not treated Nancy Smith well, but with feminism many things seemed newly possible. The creation of beautiful art offered a way into inner truths that had been revealed to me through my psychoanalysis, rather than objective "standards" about which I had serious doubts. ("Art," wrote Shirley, always available to puncture my pretensions, "he was an uncle who died in a car crash, and Aunt Sylvie never mentioned him again.") I was at a passionate, questing stage of my life. If success in the university no longer beckoned or seemed possible, I needed a new meaning and purpose, and my medium had always been writing; I thought of writing a novel.

But when the euphoria wore off back in the States I got nervous about Dominique's condition. She wrote me that she was feeling a bit better and had gone on a drug I had never heard of, Lithium. I consulted Dr. Magnet, who diagnosed a bad case of manic-depression (now called bipolar disorder). Dr. Magnet told me that "they" always think the manic phase is wonderful. "If it hadn't been for those awful depressions," Dominique wrote to me, "I'd have never gone on Lithium."

/ / /

I didn't know what to expect from Dominique's Lithium "cure." She had come to me at Christmas on the downslide, dragging around like a sick cat; all the steam had whooshed out of her. I had tried to play nurse to her melancholy while secretly wondering whether our plans to spend the next summer and fall together could possibly be real. How could I write a novel while supporting her mood? She kept telling me to come. She said that she believed in my novel as I had believed in her. Sometime in the spring, her letters from Paris got more cheerful. She was working on her new apartment, a new translation. Things were looking up.

Even during Dominique's Christmas visit, Louise and I were both still living at the Mulberry Street loft like angry and disappointed roommates. But in late winter, alone in the loft at night and lonely, I had gone to Bonnie and Clyde's, the restaurant and bar where all the lesbian feminists were going in 1974.[1] As I was talking with friends, I turned to see Louise walk into the bar with Bertha Harris. Louise was wearing a tie. Anger and hurt boiled over. Despite all my egalitarian principles, Louise loving Bertha and wearing a tie could not be my partner. (If anyone were to wear a tie—not that I like ties—it had to be me.)

My dear friend and colleague Mary Edwards, along with a group of other Purchase people, had rented a large house in the Westchester suburbs, near the campus, and the smallest room was empty, so I moved in. The Rye House was the real deal, the communal living that I'd always thought I should want and that we had lived an idyllic version of in Mexico. I liked being close to Mary but didn't know the other people that well and was lonely and cried a lot over the break up with Louise.

During that spring I filled the gap by hanging around with my lesbian students. I was particularly drawn to Sybil Meyer, a slender, dark-eyed, thoughtful child of Holocaust survivors. Her girlfriend, Debbie Roth, had pressured me to come out publicly at Purchase, saying how much it would help gay students. Though terrified I told myself I had tenure now. Would the sky really fall? Only once before had I admitted to being gay in a professional context, during those meetings of the Ruth Benedict Collective, but surely word had got around, especially in the aftermath of the Rachel disaster. So still dry-mouthed with fear I started by telling my students, then some colleagues.

The May before my departure for Paris, I made a bad move: I had an affair with a Purchase undergraduate. Of course, there were extenuating circumstances; aren't there always? I hadn't seen Dominique since Christmas. I was in my early thirties, coming out of a bad breakup, ripped from my New York City social world, and painfully lonely.

Yet there's no escaping the fact that what I did next was not only foolhardy but cruel. Beth, as I'll call her, was in her mid-twenties. She was part of the lesbian student group and had come to Purchase through a Westchester program for underprivileged youth. Having just graduated, technically, she was no longer my student. Blatantly Irish in appearance, with fair skin, a round face, and huge blue eyes, she had been adopted at birth by a poor Italian couple who had raised her Catholic. She smoked, drank, and swore a lot; she was known for her competence and had been the head resident adviser and right-hand woman of the female dean of housing, on whom she had a crush.

I don't recall how we wound up fucking each other in my single bed in the Rye House, but it was energetic and hot. Like my old flame Patsy, Beth turned out to be more butch than not, and she was a confident lover. Now that I was past the "don't touch me" era, I enjoyed butches without, Patsy aside, having the profound emotional attachment that femme women aroused in me. But Beth dialed my number. She was one of the many alcoholics that I'd wanted to save, and she was insecure underneath a tough working-class persona that pleased me as much as her vulnerability. Beth, Mary, and Paula were calling out "special people," privileged people like Dominique and, I had to admit, like me. My mother had been a fallen princess, and I was her flawed prince who had been raised to root for the workingman's Brooklyn Dodgers and scorn the capitalist Yankees. These conflicts had always gripped me. And though back in college I had turned my back on gay life for my scholarly ambitions, the working-class lesbians who had ushered me into gay life never let go.

I had told Beth from the beginning that I was going to France for the summer, and maybe for the fall semester; that I had a lover there and planned to write a novel. On my last day in New York I stood in a bookstore in front of a row of paperbacks, my fingers on *The House at Pooh Corner*. "Beth," I called to her over the row of books. She wasn't really looking at books but was pacing up and down the rows. Beth was nothing if not energy, somehow stored up and generated by the disasters in her short life. Some people are broken by misfortune; Beth had been created by it. Some mysterious law of personal chemistry was at work in her, converting misery to determination. Her hands were thrust into her jacket pockets, and the usual cigarette dangled from her mouth.

"Yeah baby," she answered, in her husky voice, turning the row and coming toward me. The sight of her squat, square body sent a thrill down my spine. Searching her big blue eyes, I saw she was just as much in love with me as she had been five minutes earlier.

"You ever read *Winnie the Pooh* when you were a kid?" I asked, knowing what her answer must be.

"No," she admitted. "What is it?"

"It's a great kids' book." I reached down and took hold of her shoulder. "Listen to this": "Pooh began to feel a little more comfortable, because when you are a bear of Very Little Brain, and you Think of Things, you find sometimes that a Thing which seemed very Thingish inside you is quite different when it gets out into the open and has other people looking at it." Beth cocked her head to one side, blew out a stream of gray smoke, and gulped in another drag. "It sounds like that Gertrude Stein stuff you were reading to me last week."

"Jesus, punk, you're smarter than hell," I said, leaning over toward her to feel the electricity between our bodies. "I wouldn't have thought of that."

We left the bookstore and walked slowly down Broadway. Though she was six inches shorter than me, and ten years younger, she steered me down the sidewalk with her hand on my elbow, all authority. We didn't talk for a few blocks, both thinking of my flight to Paris the next day.

"Esther," she said slowly, "do you really respect me?"

"What do you think?" I said, trying to be tender despite my annoyance at her question. But I saw from her clenched jaw that she wanted to hear me say it. "I respect you as much as anyone I've ever known. Don't you believe it?"

"Then why did you call me 'punk' back there in the bookstore?"

"Oh, Christ, I offended your working-class pride," I said laughing, trying to take the sting out of it. "I called you a punk 'cause you are one, you, my short, fat, working-class butch husband, and don't you forget it," and I pulled her to me. I knew there were people on the street, but the urgency of that flight tomorrow and her need meant more. We stood together touching on Broadway, two vulnerable figures protected by our indifference to the passing cars and pedestrians.

"Listen to me, bitch," she almost growled into my ear, but even her breath was tender. "Gertrude Stein and all her pals are dead, dead and buried. I know you got to go. I respect your going to France, for your work, but damn it, you come back to me. Come back as soon as you finish what you need to do." She pushed me back to arm's length and fixed me with those big blue eyes set in her plain, round Irish face. During the month of June I'd made no promises about when I'd come back. I could see each of the heavy black lashes over her eyes, the sweat dampening the short brown hair, her square body planted like a fireplug on the sidewalk. A taxi horn sounded on the curb and I jumped. Beth's shoulders sagged suddenly; she didn't release my elbow, but two tears slid down her cheeks.

I succumbed: "Yes, I promise, I will, darling. I'll come back as soon as I can."

Beth walked on again, brushing the tears off her face and lighting a cigarette. "Oh, Beth, you fool," she chuckled to herself, "how you do go on." I walked on next to her, matching my longer strides to her short, quick ones, cursing myself. I'd wanted to leave the country free and clear. Why did I promise her? I had engaged with these two utterly different lovers and made them stand for butch versus femme, America against France, populism against elitism. No matter how it turned out, one or all of us would get hurt.

Armed with a large supply of good typing paper and my Olympia portable typewriter, I boarded a plane for France in June 1974, full of apprehension. But I had promised Dominique, and she was expecting me.

CHAPTER 10

PARIS FRANCE

Tanned again, well-groomed, and lightly freckled, more attractive than ever, Dominique met me at Charles de Gaulle Airport on a warm June day. She was back up to a good weight, her clothes fitting perfectly. It seemed we were starting all over again. Who was she, now?

Dominique had bought a fourth-floor walkup in an ancient building in the Le Marais neighborhood on the Right Bank. Once the Jewish quarter, it was close to her university and just beginning to gentrify. She'd had the flat renovated and filled with modern, elegant furniture. Her lesbian friend Nicole Rougier, who had come by to greet me, approved. It's got *le standing*, as the French say, meaning "class."

Nicole was charming and friendly, having forgiven Dominique's crazy episode of last fall, since Dominique paid for it afterward with a two-month depression. Nicole preferred to think of it all as hereditary imbalance. Wasn't Dominique descended from high-strung anarchists and revolutionaries? Hadn't her father killed himself? And now a wonder drug had cured the problem, and Dominique was acting quite normal. Except that now she was calling herself a lesbian, in private, and Nicole approved, though she only halfway believed it. Midlife conversions were outside Nicole's lesbian experience.

It was nice to see a familiar face, and Nicole was just the same as when I had met her six months ago. "Place des Vosges, I like it," said Nicole, suggesting a nearby café for drinks before dinner. Horsily handsome, slim, Oxford English with a stylish French accent, Nicole was wearing a white blouse with a wide collar, knitted vest sweater, gray twill pants. Expensive, and everything matched. Dominique, also elegantly dressed, always seemed to have a Q-tip–size chocolate stain on her blouse, a little rip in her sleeve, or subtly mismatched socks, endearing imperfections. Impulsive, chronically ambivalent and a worrier, yet capable of great tenderness, she was a charming, highly intelligent princess with "issues," who tended to stamp her foot or sulk when frustrated; usually in a hurry, she leaned forward when walking and sometimes even walked on her toes. She had a mercurial temperament, with manic highs and devastating lows that were ameliorated but not erased by the wonder drug.

/ / /

The French, as personified by my French girlfriend, had a genetic need for exotic vacations, so the next day, June 30, 1974, we headed for the resort town of Les Arcs in the French Alps. Already I was obsessed by thoughts of the novel I had come here to write.

We passed thousands of funny little cars, each crammed with vacation gear and a standard-issue French heterosexual family. "I hate the restaurants on the auto route," said Dominique, dug in behind the wheel of her little gray Peugeot sedan. "Horrid." I knew what she was thinking, just what my mother always said . . . thousands of fat, white, hairy people in ill-fitting shorts, sticky-faced kids buying balloons, candy, atmosphere of crowding, orange drink and hotdogs. Dominique thought for a moment. "Aristocratic response," she admitted. "The lower middle class on holiday."

We arrived at the chalet where a friend of Dominique's was staying. Dominique remarked that the sheets look grimy. "Fastidious," I teased her.

"Don't tell me you don't mind," Dominique smiled back. "I know you do."

"Oh, no, I've overcome my class background," I said drily. She laughed in my face.

My head was working overtime on my novel. I was going to write about Dominique, I decided; she would be at the core. But what was the relationship of so-called fact to fiction? Afraid of violating reality . . . or was it fear of getting in over my head? Kate Millett wrote in *Flying*, her memoir of becoming a famous feminist after writing *Sexual Politics*, that the third person felt false to her as she documented her life.[1] Jill Johnston had said to me, justifying her first-person writing, "What else is interesting besides myself? Novels are boring."

/ / /

At a local restaurant Dominique looked at me over the fondue, smiling tentatively.

"I think you are more attached to America than I am to France."

I gazed fixedly into the fondue pot; a touchy subject was coming up. "Yes, maybe it's because of the movement."

"No, it's not just the movement. For example, I don't think you're really interested in learning a foreign language. You haven't traveled that much or known many foreigners."

"Maybe I'm less ambivalent about American culture than you are about French culture. Of course, there's lots of horrible things there, crazy things."

She persisted. "I don't see how you can say you like American culture if you dislike the politics so much as you say."

Nixon, the Vietnam War, so terrible. "It's the political set-up there I don't like, not so much the culture."

Silence over the fondue. Neither of us was satisfied. I had told Dominique the day I arrived about my affair, expecting she might tell me to go back to America, but she hadn't. Yet I knew this awkward conversation was about whether I was going to stay in France or go back to America to Beth.

"I love France," I said, "no question. But I'm ambivalent, too. Want me to say more?"

She made that funny little French sound, a sudden expulsion of air, like blowing across a Coke bottle or like an infant blowing its lips.

"Sure" (the French could never quite get that "r" sound right), she said. "Go ahead."

"Well, France has always meant the past to me. You know, Gertrude Stein, the American dykes in Paris, and I guess Hemingway, not that I'm a Hemingway fan, but American writers of the '20s and '30s. And . . . it's elitist . . . "

She made a gesture of brushing a blond lock out of her eyes. "And so the next step is to get involved with a working-class woman? You can't change your class. Something always gives you away."

She was so direct I wanted to slither away, and under the table I started wringing my napkin. "Not to change it. That's impossible. But I've noticed that people of my class are not exactly helping to make changes I want to see. I guess, what I mean is, I want to transcend my class." The French saw no contradiction between being affluent and being left-wing; Dominique didn't seem to know what I was talking about. No wonder. I was pretty vague, ashamed to accept her accusation that I'd "transcended my class" by sleeping with Beth. It sounded like a typical liberal crock of shit.

"For instance, I thought it was a big forward step when I started to have Jewish lovers." Why did it always come back to the woman I was with? "Started with Louise, then Rachel, then you . . . but you're not so Jewish?" I said, eyeing her blond hair and blue eyes.

She was instantly indignant. "What? I *am* Jewish!" Yes, of course she was—more Jewish than I, what with the Nazis, gassed relations, the barbed wire at the Swiss border. Her slightly bent nose and her small teeth, somehow not French. "My middle European teeth, my dentist calls them," she had told me.

"But the class thing . . ." I persisted.

"I don't see what you mean."

"You wouldn't see my class attitudes, because you're my same class, so they aren't directed at you."

"Which attitudes?"

By class attitudes I meant condescension, privilege, taking advantage. Should I have replied that my attraction toward her fair skin, her mastery of languages, her trim and healthy body, tennis, skiing, tasteful clothes, exotic accent, academic position, these were also my class attitudes?

But love, after all, is not quite explained in political terms. We are all swathed in symbols, wearing our past like feathers stuck in an exotic headdress; a southern accent or a sweater that shouts out "working class" or "dyke" or "French," yet love in the end eludes even sophisticated explanations.

On our way out of the restaurant, a foursome of young French heterosexuals eyed us maliciously, and one of the men sang out, "*Au revoir, Monsieur-dame*," the standard French way of addressing a male/female couple, which was how they were publicly denouncing us as lesbians. After that I had a dream that I was going to meet Shirley and Hilary, my college roommates, only I had a husband, who was malformed, and I had to carry him over my shoulder. My freaky butch self.

/ / /

We continued on to Belley, a provincial town famous for fine cooking, so I could view Bilignin, Gertrude and Alice's summer place. I bought a red T-shirt that said "Belley, Sports en Pleine Aire" that I have carefully saved, though it is now much too small for me.

On my trip to Paris the previous Thanksgiving, Dominique and I had gone to Gertrude and Alice's grave in Père Lachaise Cemetery, and for many years I wore one of the black beads that were scattered about the burial plot around my neck. Someone took a photograph of the two of us at the grave, with Dominique looking wild and tormented and me in 1970s platform shoes.

At Bilignin we actually knocked at Stein and Toklas's former house, and the current owner, a French matron, came out and showed us the garden and the wall where so many pictures of Gertrude were taken. All the locals had loved Gertrude and Alice, she told us, and thinking how they had survived the Nazi occupation of France there I had to agree, though research has shown they were probably also protected by collaborators in the Vichy regime.

By the time we got back to the country house just outside Chartres that was owned by Dominique's mother, I had decided to try to write a novel that overlapped my experiences in Mexico and France with my

Dominique and I visiting the graves of Gertrude Stein and Alice B. Toklas, Père Lachaise Cemetery, Paris, November 1973.

childhood and youth, and how I wanted to live like Gertrude Stein. Even though I was faithfully keeping a journal, "real" artists, creative ones, write fiction, I assumed.

Dominique's doctor mother, Madame Lévy, had built the house after World War II. Even if I'd never met her, I would have known from her house that she was competent, sensible, and intelligent. Although it was set well back from the little paved road that ran by it, almost all of its large windows faced the other way, down a sloping lawn that ended on the bank of a small, placid river. This side of the river had been built up in the years since the war and was becoming a suburb of Chartres. But the far side was still farmland, and in August through the trees fringing

Dominique. Bermuda, 1970s.

the river you could see the haunches and heads of a small herd of perfectly white cows.

Our days were balanced and harmonious. Up by nine, breakfast in the kitchen, then the click-clack of our two typewriters until lunchtime at one o'clock. Lunch of French bread, pâté or ham, cheese, tomatoes, yoghurt on the lawn leading down to the river, if the weather was nice. Then a couple of hours of reading in the sun. In the late afternoon we played music together, flute and piano, or canoed on the river, and just before dinner there was tennis. After dinner, which we usually made together, although Dominique was the better cook, we read or wrote letters or occasionally went next door to the neighbors' larger house to watch TV, especially if there was an American movie on.

The whole set-up was so ideal that we both began to feel nervous, for after all we were supposed to be radical. One afternoon we took the chance of lying on the back lawn after lunch in a compromising pose. Dominique had taken her shirt off to get the sun, and I was lying in her arms. "Some nice lesbian photographer should come along and take our picture," I joked, and just then the next-door neighbor emerged from the trees. I jerked up just the second before. Had she seen us or not? This French housewife sat down beside us perfectly at ease, even though Dominique had not had time to put on her shirt. "Don't be embarrassed," she smiled. "If I had breasts like yours, I'd show the whole world."

/ / /

Dr. Lévy had arrived from Paris a few days before, but her bedroom was on the ground floor, and until we were sure that she never came upstairs, we slept in separate bedrooms. In the middle of the night I woke up, tormented by insomnia. The sky through the window was beginning to lighten, and a strong wind jostled the house. Hopeless to sleep, so I turned on the light and read science fiction for three hours. At seven I began to feel drowsy when I heard a slam. *Dominique is leaving me, leaving the house*, I thought, and sat up more wakeful than before. Finally, I tiptoed into the next room. Dominique sat up in bed, white, drawn and untidy. She tossed back the covers and came to me. "Oh, tootsie, what's wrong?" She pronounced it "*toot*-sie."

"I couldn't sleep," I said into her shoulder. "I thought you were leaving."

"Come back to bed," she said, and got in next to me. I lay clinging to her, one leg thrown over hers, my head on her chest.

/ / /

Dominique and her mother had reconciled since Dominique's breakdown last November. But it was apparent that Dominique had a conflicted, resentful and anxious love for her of a kind that I was all too familiar with. *Madame le docteur* at seventy was the opposite of clingy, full of her own projects, sewing up bedspreads, gardening, arranging the fall hours of her Paris household staff: the maid and secretary.

Though she fussed over Dominique, clearly thinking her daughter lacked common sense, this matriarch who had escaped the Nazis was not the motherly type. Her short, well-cut gray hair, hawk-like features, solid arms and legs, and precise French belonged to a commander, not a Madonna. Yet she was polite to me, even kind and generous. Though she must have suspected I was sleeping with her daughter, she made me welcome on condition this was not said. She was content, perhaps, to see Dominique happier, after so steep a nosedive, and if so she was as admirable as Dominique had always said.

As a youngster, Dominique had endured many gatherings of her mother's friends, no-nonsense professional women in smart tailored suits and stout shoes, and vowed not to become like them. She would be feminine and have men in her life. Forty years later, she wondered whether her mother's friends might have had a point.

"You ought to meet Hélène she said one day. "She's one of those ancient lesbians, nearly eighty."

"Did your mother ever say she was a lesbian?"

"Of course not. My mother told me you could live as you liked in private, as long as you didn't talk about it. That was their attitude, those women."

"How do you know, then?"

"Hélène got rid of her husband after she'd had two children, and lived for twenty years with a 'friend,' who died years ago. Hélène's never gotten over it."

"A woman friend, I take it?"

"Yes, a ski instructor. Besides," she finished impatiently, "if you meet Hélène, you'll see for yourself."

Madame Lévy's face dissolved into a doting smile at the mention of her old friend. Hélène was this, Hélène was that, had been one of the biggest, most important doctors in Paris, had taught her everything she knew about medicine, had been a ranking tennis player, semiprofessional sports car driver, had known everyone who was anyone in literary and artistic circles. Madame Lévy picked up the phone on the wave of her enthusiasm.

"She hardly ever goes out anymore, since she retired and her friend died. Even to see me, though she lives quite near here," said Madame Lévy while dialing. "But I keep trying. She shouldn't allow herself to become a recluse."

Miraculously, it seemed, Hélène agreed to come over, and Dominique and I were directed what to buy at the market (the best beefsteak, good cheese, more fruit), how to arrange lunch (in the dining room with the good silver, not in the kitchen). Madame Lévy whizzed away to fetch Hélène, who was now too old to drive.

When we got back from shopping, seventy-year-old Madame Lévy and eighty-year-old Hélène were discussing a murder case that had been in the papers for days. Of course, they were speaking French, and I noticed I was following along better.

"Here are the children," Madame Lévy interrupted, ignoring Dominique's wince at having nearly forty years subtracted from her adulthood. These women still had power over her. Hélène rose stiffly from a deep chair, and Dominique advanced to accept the required greeting, a peck on both cheeks.

"The girl looks more lovely than ever," Hélène commented to Madame Lévy. "You must be proud. And this must be the American friend?" Suddenly she smiled and held out a pack of cigarettes. Gauloises unfiltered. They killed my throat, but I took one anyway. She produced a heavy monogrammed gold lighter. I cupped the Gauloises and bent to her hands. They were trembling and brown-spotted but large and well defined. As I straightened up, our eyes met.

It was true, then; I had not entirely invented myself. Here was one who had come before me. Hélène's white hair was thinning at the forehead and cut short. Baggy workmen's trousers obscured the shape of her body. A white sport shirt opened at the collar to reveal the net undershirt that, Dominique had told me, Hélène had always preferred to a bra. Though the room was warm, she did not remove her worn, beautifully made cardigan sweater.

Madame Lévy's tailored dignity looked matronly next to her friend. And now she was bustling around like an excited girl on a first date. "This is the most comfortable chair," she told Hélène, who ignored this advice as Madame Lévy signaled us into the kitchen. But as we began cooking lunch, she rushed in to supervise and instruct us: "Hélène always drinks whiskey before lunch."

While they drank, Dominique and I sat like obedient children. Madame Lévy launched into her bête noire of the moment, a plan by the City Council to build a public walk on this side of the river. It was impossible! Outrageous! Nothing but the spite and greed of a bunch of grasping peasants.

Though she had told this story several times before, none of Madame Lévy's indignation was lost in the retelling. "Awful," Hélène nodded supportively, "such a successful house you have here, and if this goes through, it'll be necessary to move. Imagine, all the common types going by with transistor radios!" Hélène took out another Gauloises, offered me one, too, and lit it, and advised a lawsuit against the City Council.

We left them over a patronizing discussion of the merits and faults of various younger doctors. Though the meal was simple, Dominique was nervous about the cooking; Hélène liked her food just so. In fact, she complained that one could no longer get good-quality beef. Yet she seemed amazed at the tastiness of the frozen spinach, as if freezing were a new-fangled invention. The subject of food led her to restaurants, and then to La Pyramide, the three-star restaurant near Lyons. With lofty relish she described the choices offered in each course and the quality of their wines.

"But I always feel stuffed after these fancy meals," Dominique protested.

"My dear, it is not necessary to do more than taste each course," rumbled Hélène. "You young people know nothing," she continued, indifferent to Dominique's sullen expression, "and of course you refuse cheese, you refuse the salad, and perhaps even the dessert. The menu is 125 francs and it's very reasonable, considering what you get, considering you can go into any dirty bistro with pretensions and pay eighty francs, while dining disgustingly, whereas at La Pyramide you get . . ." and she rolled off the courses again, "and as soon as you have finished your hors d'oeuvre it is taken away, very discreetly of course, the service is like nothing you can find in France anymore," and she went into a crotchety discussion of labor costs and bad food, ending with detailed instructions on how to drive to La Pyramide. "Yes," she finished, rising with difficulty from the table but declining the helping arm Madame Lévy extended. "I am aristocrat by inclination, though not by birth."

Once again, we trailed them into the living room. Had she known Gertrude Stein? That was all I could think of.

"What is this typing, typing we hear all day long?" Madame Lévy asked me.

"I'm writing a novel," I offered.

"On what subject?" Hélène demanded.

"It's about Gertrude Stein," I said evasively.

"Oh? You are too young to have known her."

"It's a case of worship from afar," I said. Hélène smiled. Her face changed. I understood that until now she'd been on automatic.

"Of course, the first novels of great writers are always autobiographical," she said. "Ah, yes. That woman Gertrude Stein. I met her at . . . Adrienne Monnier's bookshop, perhaps at one of the evening readings."

"Were you ever at her home, Rue de Fleurus?" I asked.

"No, I don't think so. No, I believe I only met her once or twice, at Adrienne's." She rambled on about the bookstore, Sylvia Beach, and her medical student days. Finally, I brought her back to Gertrude Stein. "An awful woman, like a block of stone," she said irritably, making a large square in the air with her solid hands. "Expressionless. I assure you, that portrait by Picasso, though it was very like her, erred on the side of flattery."

We'd all humored the old tyrant for hours, but this was too much. "Let me show you my photograph." I returned with my most treasured portrait of Gertrude and Alice. They are standing side by side, a finger's distance from touching. Gertrude looks vulnerable, almost shy, in a baggy jacket and shapeless skirt and, improbably, a stovepipe hat. Alice beside her is haunting in a full-length suit with appliquéd flowers.

"Yes," Hélène said, peering over the image, "this is certainly marvelous, marvelous." She leaned toward me, almost excluding Dominique and Madame Lévy from the conversation. "I would say this was taken about 1925, by their clothing."

"Hmm, no. I think a bit earlier, but after the war."

"Well then, 1923, do you say?"

"OK," I agreed. "Is it true she had a wonderful voice?" Hélène stiffened and, pretending not to hear me, told a little anecdote about James Joyce, to whom she had given medical advice. Madame Lévy was not to be put off. As Hélène paused to light another cigarette, Madame Lévy repeated in French, "Is it true that Gertrude Stein had a wonderful voice?"

Hélène's wrinkles set stubbornly. The Gauloises dangled from her lower lip. She wasn't going to give Gertrude an extra centimeter, but she couldn't lie. "Ehh, well . . . yes, but she talked to very few people. Picasso, Hemingway. . . . She didn't talk much. She had hardly any womanly charm."

I was surprised that a masculine woman like Hélène would judge Gertrude Stein on "womanly charm." Hélène was holding my photograph in one gently trembling hand. "Yes, remarkable, this." She blew out a stream of smoke on a sigh and coughed. "They were a remarkable couple," she said finally. Was she forgiving Gertrude her lack of femininity? And herself for being so different?

Hours after Hélène had gone, Dominique was still fuming. "What a stubborn old witch!"

"Yes," I admitted.

"Such a snob. She still makes me feel insignificant."

"She must be lonely now."

"That's true," Dominique softened. "Did you get what you wanted?"

"Not really. It's crazy that I couldn't just ask her things."

"Like what?"

"Like how was it to be gay then, way back."

Dominique shook her head. "That would be indiscreet. That's how she'd see it."

"What's she got to lose now?"

"Pride," Dominique said. "Respectable people don't discuss sex."

"It's not about sex. It's about how to live," I protested. "We've lost our history; people like Hélène and me can't really talk. Most of the time we can't even find each other. What a bad butch she is!"

Dominique frowned. "Don't say that. You're as bad as she is."

"We're really the same person," I teased.

"Hélène's no feminist. You'd better not turn coats. There always was something suspicious about you." She was half-kidding. "Hélène's always so full of herself. *Je m'en fous des vedettes* [to hell with stars]."

"Really? Do you think you can?"

"Yes. To hell with all stars," she repeated belligerently.

"Even me?" I teased.

"You? You're no star, you idiot." She pulled my ears, a gesture I adored. "I only thought you were. You only look imposing. Now that I see how dependent you are . . ."

"It's all over?"

"Of course not. I was attracted to you for the wrong reasons, maybe. But now it all balances out. It's a wonderful change. . . . I don't feel oppressed by you."

"I like you, too. And you're so pretty."

She flushed. "You are as bad as Hélène."

"Did she tell you that, too? I'll break her fingers."

Dominique's mouth twitched, but she thought she shouldn't laugh too much at this kind of possibly sexist banter. She glanced at her watch.

"Forget your watch." I hooked my hand behind her neck, pulling her toward me with a sharp little jerk.

"Come, my little cabbage," she whispered. Only it sounded so much better from her mouth against my ear: "*Viens, mon chou.*"

/ / /

In August, Nixon resigned. We were still in the country, but my former student Debbie Roth was visiting, so I could commune with another American. Although Dominique understood what was going on in the States politically, she didn't respond to it in her gut. Debbie was only twenty, but she and I were in the same Nixon-hating groove. We tried to imagine how the folks at home were taking it, how were they celebrating, what was the feeling in the streets of the cities?

Meanwhile, the contrary force I thought of as "the Biographer" was impeding my novel. Not a friendly character, and definitely him, always with me, reading my letters, even writing them. In a way he was an ego booster: I would be famous one day, future generations would want to know everything about me, just as I had wanted to know everything about Gertrude Stein and her circle. The Biographer also collected data on my friends. I was generous enough to think they would be famous, too. He recorded all of our movements and changing relationships; monitored our intimate details. But as much as the Biographer made me feel important, he also insisted on historical accuracy, criticizing and putting down my attempts to fictionalize, which I thought of as creative. I was years away from resolving this internal conflict. Now I have made peace with the Biographer, and she is a butch intellectual who likes to write.

I decided to try writing without my shirt and bra. It was acutely uncomfortable, which at least gave me something to write about. When we were in Switzerland, Dominique had shocked me by casually typing topless. I had never seen or imagined any kind of intellectual work without clothes. She said then that I must feel a contradiction between writing and the female body, and she was right.

Not that there wasn't every reason to go shirtless: the weather was heavy, muggy, and even the white cows were sprawled in the field. How often had I sat in a too tight bra envying the men their bare chests?

Not only is a man acceptable at the beach with a bare chest; his chest is positively commanding at a typewriter.

All doors in the house were open because of the heat. Dominique had a colleague at the house, Odile, and they were working together on translating an essay by Juliet Mitchell. I could hear Odile working away downstairs on her typewriter. Dominique had gone off to town. My fear of invasion, ever present, tripled because I was half-naked. But the big problem was disgust. My five pounds overweight, the sweat, my breasts hanging in front of the hard, black little machine . . . useless appendages, with no muscles, no function (since I would not have children) but an erotic one. I put my shirt back on so my breasts wouldn't spoil my French vacation.

Dominique and Odile and I ate lunch on the lawn looking down toward the small, placid river. Odile was a big woman, busty, encased in a fawn-colored underwire bra. They discussed the many problems with the Juliet Mitchell translation. I had never realized what a skill that is. It's not just one-to-one word equivalence; it's transforming one thought system into another. They asked me for help on the very hardest parts: what did this mean? I could almost always puzzle out some words in English to explain. Then the two of them would chatter excitedly in French until they'd agreed on a translation. They were saints, for the Mitchell text was the worst kind of academic, overwritten English, mostly about Freud's theory of the castration complex.

Odile was what they called *feminisante*, very feminine, with a calm temperament and a lively sense of humor. She joked all the time about spilling the milk, tangling the typewriter ribbon, wearing platform shoes, all because of her castration complex. She explained what I already knew: that according to Freud, women could never be liberated, because we would always be blocked by envy. "Juliet Mitchell," I joked, "*son complex de castration, et, son orchestra*," mimicking the signs you would see all over France announcing concerts. My French was improving.

/ / /

Dominique and I talked about my writing and the problem of writing about lesbians in general. We needed a new vocabulary. Writing about lesbian sex was the most frustrating. All the words and even images were too clinical, such as "clitoris" and "vagina," or pornographic, crude, and male-created, such as "pussy" and "tits," or trite, like the idea of melting, or flowery and too sweet, like "her little pearl."

One night, we were lying in bed enjoying what was then our favorite book, *Le corps lesbien* by Monique Wittig.[2] Sometimes Dominique read it to me in French. But I always asked her to translate, because French poetry was too hard for me. She read me one poem in which the metaphor is of the lover burning her, and it was so rich, maybe ten or fifteen different words and ideas about burning. And it had broken free of that straight model; it really grasped the idea and the experience of lesbian sex. "Well, shit!" I said. "She succeeded. She found a new way to do it. There's nothing I admire more than an artist tackling a problem head-on, and if she happens to succeed, then I fall at her feet."

"Yes," said Dominique thoughtfully, her frown of concentration deepening the crease between her light eyebrows. "It's interesting work. Someone should translate it."

"I know some writers in the States who'd be thrilled by this," I said. "Wittig's stuff is hard to read, but she's worth it."

Dominique laughed and took off her owlish glasses; I could see the ring of light gold in the center of her deep-set blue eyes. "It turns me on," she said, shifting her body toward me. The table lamp backlit the line of her cheekbone, as graceful and intended as a painter's stroke.

Her face touched mine, and she kissed me—not the dry, tight-lipped pecks she always gave me before, but with her mouth open, loose, probing. How she had changed! When she was "straight," it was easier for her to let me touch her breasts or her cunt (see, that word again, but what to do?) than for her to kiss me. So I knew what it meant that she was kissing me now, and my nerves tingled. Then I rubbed my face over her torso, as brown and comforting as a horse's neck.

"You know who did pretty well on sex?" I said into her side. "Gertrude Stein. 'Toasted Susie is my ice cream,'" and without waiting for a reply I settled into the angle between her thighs, gliding over the exposed red flesh, swollen and glistening between cushions of gray and blond hairs.

/ / /

Paris in late September had a festival atmosphere that seemed to be celebrating my release from teaching for the next four months. People were jaunty in the streets, springing along in the cold, and the flat tourist boats on the Seine looked fuller than they had in June. Young people were on their way to new jobs or new terms. Older people were smartly dressed, workmen in blues digging up streets. Everyone was back from August, the *"mois de congée"* when all France takes a vacation.

My condition was laughable, I decided. Of all the banal, worn-out ideas, that of taking four months off from a teaching job to write a novel in Paris was right up there with the moon in June and *Singin' in the Rain*. I was not going to starve in a garret, either. Dominique had given me one room to myself, just to write, in her chic duplex in the ancient 5th arrondissement of Paris. Dominique still believed in the "nobility" of the artist, or artistic enterprise. In spite of my protests, she said, "I am your Alice." She was too independent to be an Alice, and I was not wealthy or gifted enough to be Gertrude, but she was right to the extent that writing a book was special in her eyes. Writing, for her, was more worthy than digging up the street; the French do respect writers and artists.

/ / /

In the chic women's bookstore on October 1, I saw a handwritten notice: "Those interested in an English-speaking women's group, call Susan." It turned out that Susan had been trying to get a job teaching conversation at Dominique's college for two years; I probably could have had that job for the asking. The man who headed the American studies department, whom Susan had tried to make a connection with in vain, was Dominique's officemate. Susan said all jobs were given out through personal connection, which we agreed was a bad thing, while I reflected silently that Dominique's love for me was the magic that made this period in France, and all the goodies going with it, possible. As always, this thought confused me. Did I love her for herself? And yet, even though it clashed with my Gertrude Stein fixation, there was something romantic about seeing myself as her kept lover.

Meanwhile, Susan the American was telling me on the telephone that the women's group didn't really want new members, as they were going through a stage of personal testimony. But she herself thought that even having visitors was a good thing. For instance, a recent visitor had said that, although she was married, she was passionately in love with a woman and thought she was a lesbian. "It was wonderful that this woman spoke, even though it caused an uproar in the group," Susan said.

"Well, I can see where I would be upsetting," I said, taking a deep breath, "because I am gay."

"Oh," said Susan on the other end. "Oh, are you? Well would you be willing to come to the group and talk about it? And how about having dinner with me and a few other women before the group—say, this Friday evening?"

Up to this point, she had offered nothing more than the telephone number of another lost American and had hedged about the group. I couldn't believe her reaction to my coming out. It was the first time in my life that someone had thrown out the red carpet because I was gay. In the past, they wanted to ride your queer ass out of town before sundown.

/ / /

After my idyllic stay in the French countryside I knew I was going to stay in France for the year but had not told Beth back in the States. Why was I refusing to let Beth go? The most selfish reason was sexual: I wanted to come. Often with Dominique I would initiate our lovemaking, or she would invite or entice me with tenderness, flirtation, or seduction. To say I liked this is an understatement. Dominique enjoyed surrendering to my advances, but after her manic outburst the previous year, she almost never took command and was not quite comfortable even reciprocating. How was I going to get off? Did I want her to "take" me, as I "took" her? How to imagine that without feeling feminine? She had become so much to me, why should I reproach her for something she wasn't? Yet this need—for what? genital pleasure? submission?— refused to go away. It nagged at me in the night.

Under a full moon we stood in a narrow street on the Isle St. Louis when Dominique said to me, "Play Mr. Hyde," so I brushed my short hair down over my forehead and stuck out my front teeth in fangs, pressing her back against the building. We both liked it, and she said, "Oh, don't. It's scary," and then, "Do it again."

Sex, even gay sex, was so confusing. These were the personas we enjoyed, that were natural to us. No matter how we tried to change it, and despite my dependence on her, in our erotic drama Mr. Hyde was always me, and she was always the blonde victim.

/ / /

As the autumn went on, my life in Paris began to seem bleak. There was never any sun. Time hung on me. One after the other, we got bad colds. I stopped going to my daily French class; writing was out; and I lay in bed reading Victorian novels, facing the usual discouragement. They, Emily Brontë and George Eliot, knew what they were up to. Although I had written a hundred pages or so, my autobiographical novel seemed absurdly feeble in comparison.

During the colds I began to feel my dependence on Dominique in a new way. As it was so obviously true that I could barely exist for an hour in Paris without her, she began to seem unbearably precious, magical, and dear. Her smile was the only possible substitute for the sun that never appeared, and at night I clung to her as if she, and not my own heart, were the source of body heat.

Then Beth called me from New York. The long-distance phone did nothing to fade Beth's signal, which as always was forceful and unswerving. She put it to me that she still loved me and was waiting for me. "Do you still love me?" As always she got right to the point.

"Yes," I said weakly, after a hesitation.

"You lie," she said angrily. "I want some direct answers. It'll do you good to be direct with me."

I still prevaricated, and after I put down the phone, there was an agitated twenty-four hours during which a painful knowledge coagulated. "I can't love Beth," I said to myself. "Dominique owns me." Of course, I could have gone back to the States at any time and I still had my job, so on the face of it, the thought that Dominique owned me was melodramatic and absurd. Yet it described my state of mind—or was it my heart? The mild resentment that had gone with this idea, "Dominique owns me," had evolved into acceptance by September. It seemed to be a fact about which it was pointless to have moral scruples and that I could no way change. Finally, I wrote to Beth that, as I put it, "I am no longer free."

I reached this conclusion around the same time that I went with Dominique to see a pornographic film that gave shape to my growing anxiety. Such books and movies had played almost no role in my life. The fact that the female masochism and male sadism often portrayed there turned me on was not an enticement. On the contrary. My fantasies, rather lacking in initiative, were always susceptible to stimulation. For instance, I could not watch horror movies, no matter how fake. My lesbian convictions about feminist sex had been seriously threatened by not being able to put down *The Story of o*. But when Dominique announced that she wanted to see *Emmanuelle*, which had made a splash in France, I found that I wanted to see it with her rather than have her go alone.

Slick, colorful, featuring attractive actors—in contrast to the two such movies I'd seen in the past—this movie told the "story" of a young wife who is initiated into "real womanhood" through a series of sexual adventures. The setting was a Far Eastern country, maybe Vietnam or Thailand, where decadent, idle, and extremely wealthy whites seem to have nothing better to do than drink, smoke dope, and fuck each other. The "Orientals" were a Greek chorus of brutalized strippers, rapists, and dope heads.

In the key sequence, after a couple of warm-up lesbian episodes, the heroine is initiated into total sexual submission by a mysterious older white man, who never fucks her himself but orders her to be raped by a series of Asian brutes. At the end, she willingly pulls up her dress and offers her behind to the winner of a boxing match, in front of a crowd of grinning natives. All the while, the old white guy is lecturing her on the art of eroticism, the true sensual nature of woman, and the evils of monogamy.

The sharp edge of my outrage against this sexist, racist film was blunted by the unwelcome (but not completely unexpected) discovery that it had only heightened my lustful passion for Dominique. I could not make sense of my contradictory reactions to the film, disgust slugging it out with desire. I cast myself and the privileged life I was living with Dominique (which I had just chosen over a future with working-class, up-by-her-bootstraps Beth) as equivalent to the idle, rich and perverse decadents in the film.

Dominique found these fears laughable. Her views on sexuality had always been more French, less judgmental toward varied forms of eroticism, than mine. There was all the difference, to her, between two women enlarging the sphere of their sexual activities in a context of mutual love and the brutalized, impersonal fucking in the film. And what kind of parallel was there between our comfortable but square Parisian existence and the colonialists in the movie? She rejected my bugaboo word "decadent" out of hand, pointing out that by straight standards, homosexuality was decadent.

/ / /

Early in December, I flew back to New York to sign paperwork for my leave from Purchase. Right from the beginning the trip went badly. Judy Friedlander had lent me her Upper West Side apartment. One night I woke up sweating, thinking I'd heard a scream. I'd been unnerved by the suicide of a member of Paula Webster's consciousness-raising group, who had just started her first college teaching job and was so devastated by criticism from her superiors that she stopped functioning: the middle-class nightmare. Soon she couldn't pay her rent, and there was no backup. She had jumped from her ninth-floor apartment to her death.

The night before her suicide, over the scratchy transatlantic phone, Dominique, her voice trilling with excitement, announced her plan to go skiing with some French dykes she had met; she would not be in Paris when I returned at the end of December. Telling her how upset this made me—after all, I was crossing the Atlantic to be with her—had no effect. She was going, and it would all be fine. These French movement feminists, lesbian mostly, were like our lesbian feminists at home: young, chaotic, and self-absorbed; busy adoring Monique Wittig, who was still living in Paris then, and one another. I admired their struggle. Paris had been a great place for a circle of wealthy, cultured women who happened to be lesbians, but rotten for starting a lesbian feminist movement. Unexamined and triumphant heterosexuality was all-pervasive. It was one thing to ignore it and go about your own business, as Stein and her friends were able to do, but much different to challenge it, to make a counter-appeal to women.

/ / /

Louise and I had settled into our new situations. She took me to a showing of the dancer Yvonne Rainer's experimental *Film about a Woman Who . . .* The irony of Louise and me watching this movie—about a breakup so brutal that Rainer tried to kill herself—was lost on neither of us. Louise admired Yvonne's rigor, her integrity, and said the movie was as good as *Scorpio Rising*, Kenneth Anger's experimental gay film that had been a cult classic and that Louise described as the first movie made by "people"—that is, artists, not Hollywood.

Louise had made her peace with monogamy: "I am monogamous— there are certain things we won't change in our lifetime—I don't feel bad about it." She talked about the energy she got from Transcendental Meditation: it was a choice, life-supporting, to meditate. The energy could go into her work. Painting.

As physically striking as ever, a slender, Jewish blonde, with paint-stained hands, Louise wore a red-and-green-striped sweater and her old khaki painter pants that I remembered from our earliest days together. Our breakup was a turning point in her life, she told me. She had chosen then to break not just with me but with all those "mommy-daddy" priorities of other people. "My work is really first now." I said I was stuck in between the mommy-daddy priority and the work priority. Oh, she said, from what I heard—secondhand, of course—it seemed you were choosing in terms of people, not work.

The next day there was a negative review of Rainer's film in the *Times* by Nora Sayre, who dismissed it as tedious, pessimistic, and narcissistic. This seemed to me an attack on women's art in general and on the novel I was writing in particular. Far from being narcissistic, Yvonne's movie was analytic—only the subject of analysis was "love" as it affects women. Sayre didn't even try to understand what the movie was about and dismissed it as having no interest for audiences, as if she didn't want people to go to see a film she secretly believed was subversive.

In *Film about a Woman Who . . .* Yvonne Rainer explains her suicide attempt as the outcome of total disillusion with love, crashing into her refusal to tolerate the loneliness of living outside personal relationships. No subject could be of more interest, I thought. The review struck me personally, since by Sayre's standards the joint journal that Shirley and I were revising, *Womenfriends*, would also be dismissed. Shirley said there was a growing trend away from criticism of "personal" relationships: "There'll be a revival of heterosexual romanticism."

"No," I said.

"Just you wait and see," she said with absolute conviction.

Dominique and I talked again on the phone, and her refusal to consider coming back to Paris for New Year's Eve left me crushed.

Shirley said, "What does her reaction have to do with your good feeling? You felt pure commitment. Be glad—it doesn't happen often. Now you're falling apart from fear of it, not fear of how she's treating you."

"Dominique owns me," I repeated, "and I feel like there's nothing I can do about it."

"That's a myth. She can't possibly own you. Maybe she's keeping you, but that's your choice. And she's not going off the deep end if you leave. Everyone knows that lithium stuff really works. So maybe the reality is that the myth covers up how deeply you feel committed to her."

"Uh, well . . ." My face went all funny in the way it does when I can't hide a strong emotion.

"Maybe you better keep up the myth." Nothing could get by Shirley.

/ / /

Louise and I went to Phyllis Birkby's annual mulled wine party, a gathering of movement lesbians. The wooden stairs in Phyllis's Chinatown building were dirty and partially blocked with derelict-looking wood scraps. Phyllis the architect was always redoing her apartment, but from year to year it was never finished.

We are getting older, I thought unhappily (though I was only just thirty-four). Old friends and enemies sat down together with groans and sighs. All had put on weight: Kate Millett, my friend the novelist Alma Routsong, and the others. Was it so long ago that our brave lesbian consciousness-raising group was new and revolutionary? Alma said it's not a political statement anymore just to be a lesbian.

Louise loved our lesbian friends at the party, but in general she didn't have time for feminists anymore. The movement helped her, but she was moving on, she said. She didn't like the lesbian feminist lifestyle, their petty politics. Those women never understood her work. Her painting had always been abstract, and lesbians were admiring work like Judy Chicago's *Dinner Party*, plates in the form of vaginas. Instead of seeing herself inside a feminist art community, she was painting for herself and a few close friends who understood what she was doing.

As usual, Phyllis showed our favorite home movies, and my friends settled in battered armchairs and on the floor to watch with pleasure-filled, uplifted faces. Phyllis shot *The Kite Film* on the beach on the South Shore of Long Island; it starred Louise, me, and some other women as we tried, and finally succeeded, to fly a kite in the ocean breezes. It's a beautiful tableau, the ocean, and the sand in the wind, the happy energetic women: a metaphor for the excitement of the young movement.[3]

/ / /

I had flown back to Paris with apprehension, dreading being alone over the holidays. Debbie Roth and Sybil Meyer, my former Purchase students, were traveling through Europe and planned to stay with me in Dominique's apartment for a week or so around New Year's. I expected that Dominique would at least call me, but the phone didn't ring. And didn't ring. I was furious and so hurt. One night, by chance, I picked up the phone, which was dead. I should have felt better, since our failure of communication was possibly technological, but the same phrase played over and over in my head: I fell in love with you, and you don't care.

When you plummet into a psychic abyss, the insights of psychoanalysis don't help. Your adult status doesn't mean anything. You can't stand back and say to yourself, "Oh, grow up!" The dependence that had made me so anxious in the fall, the depth of my commitment to Dominique, that primitive fear of abandonment, the lack of structure and support in Paris all culminated in a meltdown. Several nights in a row I got drunk on brandy to fall asleep and would wake several hours later, sitting up sober. Once I dreamed I went everywhere with a broken, rusty ax, which malicious men and boys were pressing to my face, making bloody gashes.

When Dominique returned, finally I hoped our Parisian life would return to normal. But it soon developed that the new women in her life were living the same frantic, passionate life that Louise and I had lived five years previously, filled with feminist meetings, melodramatic love affairs, and political certainties. Dominique was besotted, not with any one of them, but with all of them and the women's movement they were just inventing. I belonged to that lesbian world I had just found in New York, which was sadder and maybe wiser, where my friends were coming off their feminist high and were talking about living with one partner, working hard, and not going to many meetings. Dominique and I were badly out of sync.

/ / /

Dominique had been depressed by our fighting, and depression always lessened or even erased her interest in sex. I was pestering when she said, "You know what decadent people do? They put jam and things on each other and lick it off."

"OK," I said, "let's find out if the decadent people are right." I would have done almost anything to connect with her. She ran downstairs to get honey while I yelled down to bring up the tube of sugared milk, too, condensed and sugary milk they have in France. She came back up with both, and while we laughed a little nervously, she put honey on my breasts, and one after the other she sucked it off. The decadent people were quite right: the feeling was wonderful, a textured feeling to the contact between lips and nipple.

Then I put the honey on her, which we both liked, and then the thick, yellowish milk. It dribbled off and oozed off her nipples. I liked looking at it as much as sucking it. Now we were both excited, and I thought, If she comes first, then she'll fall asleep and I won't get to come. So I sat astride her, and she made me come, deep inside me for once and not too fast. But then she said that she was sleepy and didn't want me to touch her, a reversal of our usual script.

The next day, we took a boat ride on the Seine, and each time I touched her made me hot again. I couldn't get a response from her, and she said she just wasn't feeling sexual. "I'm three hundred kilometers from my cunt," she said. Searching for a way to turn her on, I thought about how often she'd talked of wanting to tie me to the bed and sometimes to have me tie her down.

When we got home later, I said, "OK, how about this fantasy that you've talked about so long but never done?" Just saying this made me hot. Dominique got out some twine she'd been saving for months for this but never used. I got my knife (I try to always be prepared) and, cutting four pieces the right length, I tied her to the bed. I tie knots pretty well. When I'd tied up each arm and leg, in turn, I'd say, "Now, move," but she really couldn't. It was scary to think that nothing stopped me except how much I held myself back.

It seemed as if I'd never seen her loveliness before; I'd never felt as free as then to look at her, strolling around and around the bed, smoking a cigarette, looking at her strong legs spread wide. My naked eye saw every freckle, every hair, every muscle, how they all connected around her bones. Finally, not because I was tired of looking but because she was waiting, I sat down on the bed next to her and ran my mouth all over her skin and muscles and touched and bit. She liked it and tried to rise up, but she really could not move, so nothing rose but her nipples and cunt under me. "Now you want me, don't you? Don't you," I said into her mouth. "Now you want me. Say it. Say it."

"Yes, I want you," she murmured from her throat. So I put my hand between her spread-out legs. I ran my hand over her, wet and big, then I grooved my fingers into her inside as far as I could, and I fucked her like she never let me, with my whole hand all over between her spread-out legs, and she came then, and I wanted to make her come again, which she never wanted and didn't this time. Something in me wanted to force her, but she said no, and I pushed down that impulse.

That night I dreamed I was a white person in India with a penis. I met a beautiful young Indian woman with black hair piled up on her head and sparkling eyes. She said that for a fee, which all white people could afford, she would teach me how to really use my penis. She seemed to take me for a man. I thought about correcting her but didn't because I liked how she looked up to me, not just for being white, but for being a man, although it was strange, knowing I was a woman.

There was another white man in her house—a decrepit gentleman waiting to sleep with my woman, his hat in his hand. She smilingly brushed him aside, saying that she was going to take care of me this afternoon and he'd have to wait for tonight for his turn. He didn't like it, but she preferred me, and there was nothing he could do.

The beautiful dark Indian woman took me into her small bedroom. She undressed, saying, "Now, where's your penis?" We both looked down, and there it was, on me, swelling up, standing up. I was a spectator of my own miracle. She said, "Now put it in me." I fell on her with my arm under her ass, pulling her toward me. I put my penis in her. All the time it was harder and bigger, all the way up and in her. It felt so good, so good. I jammed it in her, turning all ways in and out, pulling her up to me again and again—such a feeling, such a thrill. She was saying, "Here and here and there and turn and go," and I could do everything with this penis. *So this is what it's like being a man*, I thought, through all the pleasure and power of screwing her. After she came (but did she really come? There's a doubt. Maybe she made it up, would make it up again tonight for the old man with the hat), I fell asleep in her rumpled bed with both hands over my penis, thinking, *Now I've got it, I'll never let it go.*

In the morning I told Dominique my dream, which made her look uncomfortable. "Next you'll be wanting to wear a dildo and fuck me tied to the stairs," she laughed, to show this was ridiculous. But then her face darkened. "It's horrible. I don't want to think of you with a penis. I don't mind a penis on a man—it's natural—but not on you." She paused, then she said very definitely: "I don't want a penis."

/ / /

The women's movement in France was built around cliques that were glorified by the name "*tendance differente*" (different [political] positions); they proposed that the divisions grew out of abstract ideological differences. The writer Monique Wittig and the shrink Antoinette Fouque were the central figures of two such *tendance* groups that were hardly on speaking terms. Antoinette's group, Psych et Po, whose name stood for "psychology and politics," called Monique a sellout to the capitalists, partly because Monique gave *Les nouvelles lettres portugaise*, a feminist book "find," to her commercial press, Seuil, to publish, bypassing the Librairie des Femmes, a press of which Antoinette was the editor-in-chief. Where there's smoke, there's ire. Antoinette was an intellectual so pretentious that Dominique, with the highest doctorate France offers, felt intimidated.

One winter night, Dominique and I went to a meeting of the Feministe Revolutionaire (FR) at which Monique Wittig was the dominant figure.[4] In my journal observations of the FR women I cast a jaundiced eye on the French anarchist feminism that Dominique was so enamored with:

> The FR women were supposed to decide how they would relate to the *locale* or meeting place that they use. The center had been bought or rented by one woman who got an inheritance, and who had organized a group which was responsible for keeping up the meeting place and its cafeteria. Different groups used the meeting room, of which FR was the largest. The responsible group was already losing money and they wanted the center to be used by lots of different women, but then some straight women who came with their children were freaked out that some of the lesbians there were kissing.

> The meeting started about 8:30; dinner is late in France but the meeting had to end before the Métro closed at 12:30. About sixty youngish FR women were there smoking, looking defiant, holding hands with their lovers, sleeping and sitting all over the room like sheep in a pen, very friendly. The responsible women were sitting at one end of the room on a table looking defensive. They complained about losing money and about the FR women scaring away the straight women.

> Finally there was a group silence while women whispered to each other and something or nothing was happening. Here and there, women starting leaving. Then someone said, "Well, I guess there's nothing else to say or do about it now," and everyone seemed by a mysterious process to agree that the meeting was over, so they all started leaving and talking and hugging-kissing on each cheek and making plans for the weekend. It was all friendly and active, and the responsible group just sat there mad. Nothing had been decided.

Psych et Po, in contrast, was organized and authoritarian. Dominique and I attended one of their meetings at the Librairie des Femmes, the swanky feminist bookstore that was their home base. Nobody seemed to know who owned the bookstore or the associated press, *des Femmes*, but rumor had it that the backing came from one woman's huge inheritance. The bookstore occupied at least half of a nice old building in an expensive part of town. The meetings were not open, unlike the FR meetings, where anyone (female) could just walk in, and we were invited specifically to discuss the possibility of publishing a French edition of Shirley's and my book, *Womenfriends*.

Antoinette Fouque, whom everyone said was the big shot of Psych et Po, had told us that the meeting would start at nine. But when we arrived, all polished and shining, a woman said that the meeting wouldn't start for a while because Antoinette had gone out to eat. Although Antoinette was not the one with the big money, the more we heard, the more it seemed she really was the big shot. So we went to an imitation English pub on the corner to have a drink. It seems the subway's closing didn't bother these women, who had private cars or could afford cabs.

Around 10:30 we paid a lot for our drinks and went back to the bookstore. On the second floor we saw a nice kitchen. On the third was a large, airy room for meeting with a shiny wood floor. Forty or so young women were sitting neatly on cushions around the walls in a semicircle, so all could face Antoinette who sat on a chair by the door.

Antoinette seemed slightly older than her acolytes; more casually dressed, chubby, short with curly black hair. When tea had been passed around, Antoinette went, "Shhh," and the meeting started. Antoinette asked another woman with a notebook what was to be decided that night. The notebook woman read out a list of book titles and dates that I couldn't quite follow. Antoinette kept interrupting, and the notebook woman seemed a little scared. A woman across the room said something to which Antoinette replied ending in *"tu comprends?"* meaning, "get it?" which sounded like a put-down, and the whole group laughed.

"What is her power," I kept asking myself, but whatever it was, she was sure of it. Quite quickly the subject of our book came up. Antoinette decided that the press would do the book if Shirley and I accepted their terms, which were just as tough, I thought, as any commercial publisher might offer. Then there was a general quiet and whispering around the room, which clearly meant that this was decided and now Dominique and I should leave, because we weren't part of the group.[5]

The FR women hated the Psych et Po women and spread vicious rumors about them that may or may not have been true. Most of the rumors accused Antoinette as an editor of fucking over authors and as an analyst of fucking over her patients. Some FR complaints were class resentment: Antoinette and her group bought expensive, nonpolitical, luxurious things for themselves such as trips to exotic parts of the world and camelhair blankets.

Like most second wave feminist groups, FR purposely had no official rules or structure; these were seen as "patriarchal." Everyone being equal had the apparent advantage that no one was indispensable and everyone was autonomous. For instance, Monique Wittig, whom those in the know called Théo, could have been a leader in FR, but she refused and was instead a kind of magnet toward which everyone, unofficially, was drawn. When she left for the States, where—tired of penury—she accepted a professorship, her leaving did not disrupt FR unduly. She died in Arizona in 2003, having never returned full time to France.

But you couldn't imagine the bookstore *Psych et Po* women without Antoinette. Because of her, tea was served; there was an agenda; and decisions were made. But I hated the adoring looks on the followers' faces and the way they tee-heed when Antoinette made a joke. I bet her followers felt like kissing her feet and yet would have laughed to see her slip on a banana peel. When that "great leader," my father, who had scared everyone, got dementia, the followers all scampered off.

/ / /

At a third French feminist meeting, more academic than the other two, a professor named Hélène Cixous spoke to the audience from an auditorium stage. She wanted to plan a feminist studies conference for the next year in Paris. Cixous had very short but fashionably shaped hair and wore a see-through skirt. I thought you'd have to be darned sure of yourself to wear that skirt. She said she had been to an exhibition of women's painting and heard some female artists trying to speak about creativity, but instead they were stuttering, they could not be articulate, could not express themselves. This convinced her that women's greatest need was to "*prendre la parole.*" We don't exactly have the idea of *la parole* in English. It means "the word" and it means "language" and it means "the power of expression" and it means all of those things and even a little more. Hélène repeated that the top feminist priority was for women to "*prendre la parole*," to take and hold the center of the stage, just as she was doing right then. And all of the women in the audience seemed to agree.

After the meeting, I asked Dominique whether she agreed with Hélène that it was so important for women to "*prendre la parole*." She nodded. Well, then, I said, that's what Gertrude Stein spent her whole life doing: taking and holding the center of the stage, struggling to express herself and insisting that it was good. In a way, she helped us all to *prendre la parole*. And if this is the highest ideal, then Alice sacrificed herself, if it was a sacrifice, to this idea that women—or, at least, a woman—should take and hold the center of the stage.

/ / /

There was a saying that I learned in French class—"*C'est toi qui fait la pluie et le beau temps*"—which means, "It's you who make the rain and the good weather." It seemed to me to epitomize my dependence, but Dominique didn't think so. So to tease her and show off my French, I said, "Well, then, *c'est toi qui m'amene par le bout du nez*" (It's you who lead me by the end of the nose), which I had also had learned that day. "Oh no," said Dominique, "it's you who lead *me* by the end of the nose." I saw she believed it, too. Someone might think, since I always wore pants, and she was wearing a skirt, that it proved it was I who led *her* by the end of the nose. But it proved just the opposite. She knew I disliked her wearing skirts, which made me look more mannish in contrast. I did not want the masculinity that was my second nature to be quite so obvious.

/ / /

What did I really want from Dominique? Aside from my separation anxiety, apart from my loneliness and isolation in a foreign country, my primary goal was still the autobiographical novel I had come to Paris to write. Each time I planned to write, it seemed to take hours to start. No one believed in my novel, but they didn't disbelieve, either. It just was not real. This is what Alice did for Gertrude: she kept saying, "Yes, I believe in your book. I will make a home for you to write that book I believe in." Dominique had opened her apartment to me and supported my writing, but she had her own life, mostly apart from me, and she was always running here and there. To me our life did not have stability, and I had nothing like the attention from her that I had enjoyed back in the summer.

I wrote three pages and took them to her. I had told her that the novel was autobiographical, and when she read the pages, which was about one of our fights, she exclaimed, half-joking and half-annoyed, "I want my name on the cover of this book."

"Yes," I said, "just like Gertrude put Alice's name on the cover of her book when she called it *The Autobiography of Alice B. Toklas*."

/ / /

It was sometime in March that an American friend of Dominique's came to dinner. Harriet had her doctorate in psychology but had given up her profession to live in Paris, where, she complained, she had to teach English to live. She was short and triangular in a baggy dress, with long, shapeless hair and a small, intelligent face. She talked fast with a New York accent, and there was a scared kind of energy in her.

Harriet was trying to write a play, but she had gotten no further than doing a lot of research. A friend told her she had changed her play into a learning task. Already I liked her better than any of the other young Americans I'd met in Paris. She mentioned she had met a man who knew Gertrude Stein. "Oh, are you interested in Gertrude Stein?" I asked, very curious, as Harriet was not like any of the other lesbians I'd met. It wasn't even clear that Harriet was a lesbian, yet I'd never met a straight woman who cared about Gertrude Stein.

"Oh yes," she replied. "Gertrude Stein is the reason why I came to Paris. I've always wanted to live in Paris, and she is a big part of the reason why. But, you know, she said she was afraid people would remember her for her personality and not for her work. Well I'm one of those people. I read everything about her personality, but I don't read her work."

We checked out our fan credentials. Harriet had read the Sprigge book; she had read *What Is Remembered*; and, of course, she had read *The Autobiography*.[6] She asked excitedly, twisting her rings around her pudgy fingers, "Have you seen the movie?" a documentary about Stein and Toklas. "Have you been to Bilignin," her country place. We were sitting on the edges of our chairs, eyeing each other with respect.

"You see," said Harriet, "I don't know if she was a genius or not. What matters to me is that, without anyone believing it except maybe Alice, she just kept on working her whole life because that was how to live for her."

"But she *was* a genius," I said. "At first, I was only interested in her personality, too, but lately I've been interested in her work."

"I don't know about that," said Harriet. "I'd like it better maybe if she wasn't a genius. What I like is how she believed in herself, and I'd like it better if that was all her life proved. People's lives are always justified afterward by what they produced, but Gertrude's life can only be justified because she did what she wanted."

Dominique was shooting resentful looks my way because there were two other guests and Harriet and I were only talking to each other. Ignoring the looks, I took Harriet up to my room to show her my photographs of Gertrude and Alice. I had one poster showing Gertrude and Alice in front of the atelier Rue de Fleurus.

"I've never seen that one," said Harriet, "but I recognize Alice's dress."

"There's a real fan," I said, "someone who recognizes Alice's dress from other photographs."

Underneath this photograph I'd tacked up this fragment:

How many acts are there in it.
How many saints in all.
How many acts are there in it.
Ring around a rosy.[7]

"Oh, gosh," Harriet exclaimed, "you see, my play is going to be about St. Theresa. When I found out that Gertrude had written about her, I looked into her life and somewhere I read that St. Theresa was the only woman in history who achieved cosmic humanity. So I wanted to write a play about her. But," she said sadly, "I can never finish doing the research to start writing the play."

I told Harriet that Gertrude Stein was also a big reason why I came to Paris. And I suggested that we get together and help each other to work. Harriet was scared by the idea that I might help her to start writing her play, but she accepted, with the caveat that she didn't want to be pressured and didn't want any concrete suggestions. "Here, peel these potatoes," I said and she laughed, saying, "You must be the pressuring type."

/ / /

We went to a meeting of the Feministes Revolutionaires. In the end, the responsible women had fixed up the meeting place themselves, with a library, reading space, and toy shop. The framed paintings of a certain Susan Schwartz were shown on the walls. One could eat couscous for ten francs and drink wine or Coca-Cola. It was young and gay and the meeting started late.

Théo Wittig passed me a note that she liked Bertha Harris's novel *Confessions of Cherubino*.[8] She was going to get coffee; the meeting was a down. An angry woman demanded to know who had written a tract that was given out at the demonstration against the Year of the Woman. Why was it signed Feministes Revolutionaires when only one woman wrote it?

Théo preferred to have coffee and to talk about Bertha's novel. She said I should have come to the feminist gathering in Amsterdam. No, I said, I am writing a novel and didn't have time. But, said Théo, in Amsterdam there was energy; it wasn't a place that made you feel bad. The angry woman kept wanting to know who made the decisions. Someone replied that everyone followed their desires. One of Dominique's friends said she didn't like Amsterdam and there was no such thing as lesbian politics. The party was great, though. "What is lesbian politics?" she asked rhetorically and answered herself: "Lesbian politics is more and better parties."

/ / /

Céline Lavalle was the former lover of Dominique's handsome friend Nicole Rougier. A substantial forty, she was a professor of English literature and spoke English fluently, with precise diction. Her voice was mellifluous, viola-like and sometimes ascending to higher woodwind notes. She made extra money translating from English to French, including academic texts and some crappy American films that she dubbed into French.

Céline invited me to her apartment, letting it be known that she wanted to see my novel. I spent a frantic afternoon going over everything and removing all mention of sex (not easy since before computers, "cut and paste" meant using scissors and tape). Dominique didn't want Céline, who even though a lesbian was also a colleague, to see into our sex life. I was surprised at how much I had written about sex and surprised at how anxious Céline's interest made me. Céline admired my American paper and black three-hole binder: "Why, anything could look good on this paper!" I was ashamed to have ruined such fine paper with my nothing words and ideas. Céline had high standards. She had warned me in advance that she might find my work so alien that she could say nothing about it. Nothing *intelligent* about it, she amended. But if so, I wasn't to think that that meant it was shit. "Shit" was the exact word she used.

She took a sophisticated view of things and was condescending about Dominique. "She'll never be, she is not a lesbian," said Céline, who saw herself as the true magnetic north on the gay compass.

"Well, if she's not," I said, "my presence is surely embarrassing." Céline sat a bit drunkenly across from me in her living room, crossing and re-crossing her legs. She always wore skirts, but sensible long ones. She told me that since her son was born, she no longer kept up her appearance and that she didn't care about romance. Like so many French women, she dyed her hair to hide the gray but kept it off her eyes with utilitarian bobby pins.

"When Nicole and I met Dominique," Céline said, "she was blind to our relationship and so concerned with men. Obviously she was attractive to women, and I thought, *What a shame she throws herself away on elderly Englishmen*, but I don't at all see how someone can change at our age. I, for instance," she said, lighting up one of her English cigarettes, "since I no longer care for romance, could live with a man as easily as a woman, but that wouldn't make me like other women." She meant Dominique's living with me didn't make her gay. "And another thing," she went on. "If she really is a lesbian, she'll have a problem after you, if I may be permitted to say 'after you.'" Her voice rose to the higher note, as if this were a question, but disregarding my frown she continued blithely on. "She'll have a problem like I had at one time—that is, she's not feminine enough to attract one type of lesbian, yet she hasn't the authority to attract the other type." She took a drag on her cigarette and considered for a moment. "Of course, she could solve it by having a much younger woman who couldn't help looking up to her."

I said something about butch and femme, which she brushed aside. "You can call it what you like," she said "but it's a question of complementarity. Unless you find someone who is your double, there's bound to be complementarity, and people of different temperaments are attracted to each other." Céline would never say that opposites attract, as she never talked in clichés if she could help it. To avoid the banal in anything was her religion.

"If people aren't the same," I said, "doesn't the question of dominance come in? Take Gertrude and Alice. Wasn't Gertrude dominant?"

"Gertrude and Alice are a legend for me. They cannot be a model. My model would be rather Virginia Woolf and her circle."

"Well, if you're not interested in Gertrude and Alice, you won't be interested in my book," I said, wanting to add, *Don't bother to read it.*

Dominique arrived. While eating in the lengthy French way a dinner of roast beef and baked potatoes and salad and wine and bread and cheese, Céline told a joke in her melodic clarinet of a voice:

A new father is waiting anxiously in the hospital. The doctor comes out to him, and the father asks, "Is it a boy or a girl?" The doctor says, "Well, first I have to tell you something about the baby."

"What's the matter?" asks the father, anxiously.

The doctor says, "Well, you, see its hand is . . . well, it has no fingers."

"Oh," says the father. "That's not so serious."

"But, you see," says the doctor, "the hand is missing, too. And, actually, there's no arm."

"But," says the father, "you can do a lot in life with just one arm."

"But," says the doctor, "actually, the other arm . . . well, it has no arms."

"That's bad," says the father, "but at least it can run around here and there."

"No," says the doctor. "I hate to tell you this, but it has no feet. In fact, it has no knees. Well, let's face it: it hasn't got legs, either. And it's blind, and so on."

At last the attendants bring out one ear on a cushion for the father to see. The father leans over the ear saying, "Are you all right?"

"You'll have to shout," says the doctor. "It's deaf."

I couldn't stop laughing, especially loving the ear being brought out on a cushion, so French. Her timing was perfect, and the joke was so gross, it made me think of my old love, the painter Nancy Smith's joke about the two American lesbians fighting in a Paris bar, the one she told me so long ago that made me want to go there, the one that I had repeated to Dominique that day in the Cuernavaca bar. "So much for your fucking hat, Mrs. Cunt."

/ / /

One Saturday afternoon I visited my new friend Harriet's apartment on the Rue des Abbesses. It was my first visit to Montmartre, but coming up out of the Métro it still felt agreeably like a village. From Harriet's window there was a view of the Eiffel Tower and the new surrounding skyscrapers.

Naturally, we ate lunch. Harriet was Frenchified to the extent that nothing could be talked about without eating or drinking. I told her how much I had thought about her saying that St. Theresa had entered the cosmic, and how the book I was reading said that the lives of saints are masterpieces of experience.

"That's very interesting," said Harriet, "but it's not what I said. What I said was that Simone de Beauvoir said that St. Theresa was the only woman in history whose personal experience became a human struggle."

"Well, that's a different idea, but I like that, too, and is it really so different?" And I went on to explain that Gertrude Stein thought that people like that were geniuses.

"As I said before," Harriet replied, "I don't want Gertrude Stein to be a genius. If she's a genius, she doesn't encourage me. And that's one of the things I like best about Gertrude Stein—that she encouraged the creativity in other people. By the way," she went on, "do you understand what Gertrude saw in Alice that held her so long?"

"What?" I exclaimed. "That's an odd question. It's the other way around. The answer to that is so obvious."

"How is it obvious?" asked Harriet. "Gertrude gave Alice a life she could never have had on her own, which is why Alice stayed. But why did Gertrude stay? That's the question."

"Have you heard people say that Alice was oppressed like a wife and so why did she stay?" I asked. "Lots of women say it was just like a straight marriage."

"That's ridiculous. For one thing they lived without men, so how could it be like a straight marriage?"

The next day Harriet called to say she'd started working on her play. "Now I'm one step closer to failure," she sighed.

/ / /

I went to Céline's to hear her verdict on my novel. She welcomed me warmly. No wonder, now that she had the upper hand, knowing all about me and how I'd staked a whole year on a laughable fantasy. She didn't say I was a lousy writer. She didn't say I was good, either. If she thought I had talent, she'd tell me, I thought, but I waited three hours without hearing reassurance. Instead, she piled up the critique while I listened like an obedient student.

She said I didn't understand the French people. Why hanker after an old dream of Americans in Paris that is dying but not dead enough? The exciting thing in Paris now was not art but the intellect.

"But I am not an intellectual anymore. That's why I came here—to get away from that."

"Whatever you intended, you haven't succeeded yet," she said authoritatively. "You'll have to rewrite it. Or, if you want it to be commercial, you'll have to put in more sex" (the sex Dominique made me take out). "You know, it's not daring to write about lesbians today."

/ / /

I left Céline beyond humbled—more like crushed—deciding to throw out my novel. Céline had such a lofty perspective; she had transcended the mundane everyday of lesbian life, in which I was still enmeshed. Gradually I gave up the dream: reliving Gertrude Stein and her creative circle in Paris, not going to happen. Me, the author of a brilliant novel of lesbian life and love. Not really, not at all.

Dominique and I stayed together for four more years, mostly in Paris. Without any clear purpose, I still kept ample journals, as was my habit. Because vacations and travel are sacred to the French, we went to Sardinia, Holland, the South of France, California; we fought and made up, went to feminist conferences. We met some French lesbians who became beloved friends with whom we traveled and enjoyed lengthy dinners with artfully presented and great-tasting food. In order to know them, since they couldn't speak English, I finally became fluent in French, as Dominique had always wanted.

But in 1979 our shared life began to come apart in one of those lengthy and tortured breakups that could end in depression, or worse. We had both run out of sabbaticals and unpaid leaves. In that age before e-mail and FaceTime we were defeated by the expanse of the Atlantic Ocean. She had tenure in France; mine was in America. Would I really be content to teach English as a second language in Paris? In the end, though alienated from academia, I had to admit the depth of my attachment to job security and professional status, as well as to teaching, which I mostly loved. Scraping together the down payment on a studio apartment back in my home base, the Upper West Side of Manhattan, I resigned myself to what felt like defeat.

—— CHAPTER 11 ——

BUTCH REVISITED

In 1980 I turned forty years old, and my life to that point seemed a failure. Dominique and I were breaking up, and I was losing her and my treasured French connections. The novel I had gone to Paris to write was abandoned as a flop, and no one was interested in any of my three books or feminist-inspired articles. A homophobe attacked me in a skating rink and broke my wrist in three places. My only accomplishment was quitting smoking after several failed attempts. No matter how downhearted, I still wanted to live the second half of my life.

My youth had been privileged, unconventional, and tortured. Thanks to a native intelligence, strong constitution, and upper-middle-class parents, I had endured and acquired an elite education. But the burden of fear and shame I carried as a masculine woman who loved women in an age of state-sponsored terror, which was then our situation, shadowed and nearly eclipsed my successes. By my early thirties, still professionally closeted, I had been ignominiously fired and was lucky to get the only job offered to me, at an undergraduate state college with a low salary and high workload. At least I could live in New York City, where I had grown up, and among the gay people who had been so hard to find.

And yet, as it turned out, the most fulfilling part of my life was just beginning. The creative turmoil in lesbian and gay communities that was happening as I was turning forty reinvigorated my teaching and writing and showed me how to accept and even insist on the butch identity that framed the second half of my life. Looking back, 1981 was the turning point.

/ / /

In 1981, for the first time in some years, I attended the Annual Meetings of the American Anthropological Association, casting about for a point of reentry to my academic career. A gay male acquaintance, Larry Gross, flagged me down in the hotel hallway.[1] He said that some gay anthropologists had formed an interest group within the American Anthropological Association, which was then called the Anthropological Research Group on Homosexuality (ARGOH), the name chosen to imply that its aims were simply scholarly rather than motivated by gay identity. However, ARGOH was made up entirely of gay men, and Larry thought that they needed some female members. With charm and persuasion Larry overcame my reluctance to be a token woman. Evelyn Blackwood, then a graduate student, and I were the only lesbians, but we got busy recruiting others.[2]

In this way the gay men, some of whom were none too eager to have lesbians make annoying demands, were part of my entrée back into the professional world, just as they had been to finding the gay world in Chicago in the 1960s. Before long, I became president, and so did Evie. Over the years, ARGOH grew, and as we gained confidence, we changed the name to SOLGA, the Society of Lesbian and Gay Anthropologists, a scholarly and activist group that encouraged young scholars, gave prizes for outstanding work, and pressured for recognition within the American Anthropological Association.[3] In SOLGA I renewed my friendship with Ellen Lewin,[4] whom I had met through feminist networks many years before, and I made other wonderful friends, the first group of queer anthropologists I had ever known and no doubt the first such formal group that ever existed. Many of these colleagues had read my book, *Mother Camp*, and told me it had been important to them.[5]

Before this, one of the few people aside from David Schneider who

At the Moulin d'Andée Conference. From left to right:
Dominique, Clare Coss, me, Blanche Wiesen Cook,
Carroll Smith-Rosenberg. France, June 1979.

had praised my work was Gayle Rubin. In 1971, Gayle, then an undergraduate anthropology student at the University of Michigan, had come
to New York with the intention of meeting some lesbian and feminist
intellectuals. We also had a mutual interest in the Paris expatriate lesbians (she wrote an essay on Renée Vivien, the symbolist poet and lover
of Natalie Barney), and we hit it off.[6] Subsequently, still an undergraduate, she published her famously erudite essay, "The Traffic in Women,"
which attempted to integrate feminist, Marxist, and French psychoanalytic theory.[7]

In June 1979, Gayle had attended a scholarly feminist conference organized by Dominique together with the feminist American historian Carroll Smith-Rosenberg.[8] Gayle wanted to get together privately, so Parisian cafés were where I began to resolve the conflict between the lesbian feminist sexual script and my felt sexuality that had so confused my relationships with Louise and Dominique.

During the ten years since she'd come out as a lesbian, Gayle said, she'd had two kinds of dissatisfaction. One was cultural and political. The trend in the movement was away from gay consciousness and toward merging feminist and lesbian consciousness. That had always made her uncomfortable, along with matriarchy, goddess worship, and the whole notion of "women's culture." We were in agreement about that.

We also agreed that there was something, in sexual terms, that the lesbian feminist movement had swept under the rug about butch and femme. There was some truth in that older butch/femme system, we still thought. Yet the roles before Stonewall had been too rigid. Gayle said that although she looked and felt butch, she didn't fit into the butch role sexually. What did she mean by "not butch sexually"? I asked. At this point I learned why Gayle had wanted to meet in private. Her sexuality didn't exactly fit into a butch model, she said, because she had discovered she was a sadomasochist submissive and had become part of that sexual subculture.

I was shaken by her admission that she was part of the leather world of sadomasochistic (S/M) sex. She seemed so incompatible with my stereotype of sadomasochists. I noted, "She's got one of the sweetest, most innocent faces you'd ever want to see."[9] Before she came out to me, which must have taken great courage, I had vaguely suspected that Gayle was interested in S/M but found the thought so "abhorrent" that I brushed it off. I had met some leather men in the course of my fieldwork with drag queens, so I knew they could be cultivated, well-mannered, and fun. But their sexual practices—cock rings with sharp metal studs, whip collections, what little I had seen—were upsetting to me despite Dominique's and my mild private foray, and I associated the leather subculture with gay men, not lesbians.

Yet I couldn't help being somewhat supportive. Here was a friend owning up to a sexuality even more deviant and taboo than my own. Was I going to indulge the same sense of superiority that straight people held toward me? I expressed my belief that S/M fantasies were widespread in our culture and that the taboo measured their power, and owned up to sometimes having such fantasies myself and to having acted on them in a mild way. To prove it, I showed her the scene in my novel based on the episode when I had tied Dominique to the bed and later dreamed I had a penis. Aside from saying she found it very erotic (which, coming from her, I took as a compliment), she said women should not deny themselves symbols that give them access to the experience of men. This was why transvestitism was good: it was one sex appropriating the experience of the other. She deplored the trend away from butchness and dykiness.

Discovering S/M had brought all this into focus for her. She thought the big mistake was saying that lesbianism and feminism were the same thing. This did a disservice to both. People were trying to justify what they were doing (being queer) with a political ideology (feminism), which, though correct in its own domain—the oppression of women—really couldn't explain sexuality.

This mirrored both my sexual confusion and my problems with so-called politically correct feminist evaluations of drag queens, the subjects of my first book and the objects, often, of my admiration. You were supposed to think that drag queens were sexist and degrading imitations of women, which I always knew wasn't true. Not that drag queens couldn't be sexist, but so could politicians and taxi drivers. Female impersonation had to be seen in the context of the queer community, where it had its roots and fabulous foliage. The whole idea of the correct political line was dangerous, Gayle said. Feminism was largely correct because we were alert, because we said truths, not because truths had been handed down on tablets. And we had to continue to change, to search; otherwise, there'd be hardening of the movement and tyranny.

/ / /

In September 1981, I received a letter from Carole Vance, a feminist anthropologist at Columbia University. She was organizing a conference on women's sexuality at Barnard: would I like to participate? Her letter sat on my desk for a few weeks while I wavered, still feeling so alienated from academia, but I respected Carole and finally thought, why not?

With Gayle Rubin, two nerd butches. Ann Arbor, Michigan, 2017.
Photograph by Holly Hughes.

Upon returning to America in 1979, I had been struck by the rapid growth of a kind of militant feminism whose sole focus was to condemn pornography as a, or even *the*, principal tool of "the patriarchy." I knew very little about pornography (my ARGOH friend Larry Gross would later screen some of the gay male kind for me), but this obsessive focus on pornography struck me as wrongheaded, and I was further alarmed when the anti-porn feminists started making common cause with right-wing Christian groups.

Carole's invitation made clear that the conference would be the beginning of a contrary way of looking at pornography in particular, and at sexuality in general. In this planning group I experienced a more sophisticated and nuanced kind of feminism and made new contacts and friends, especially, as it turned out, the feminist literary critic Julie Abraham, who was then a graduate student at Columbia.[10] One day, the anthropologist Rayna Rapp, a close friend of Gayle's from their Michigan connections, came into the seminar room waving a sheaf of papers. "This is going to change everything," she exclaimed, out of breath and excited. It was a draft version of "Thinking Sex," Gayle's famous elaboration of the ideas she had shared with me in Paris. This one essay not only inspired the Barnard Conference planners; it also became the primary template for sexuality studies, which has since been incorporated into most women's studies departments. The Barnard group championed women's sexual freedom, as opposed to the anti-porners, whose feminism descended from nineteenth-century sexual double standards (women are or should be sexually pure, and men should be, too). It was the Barnard group that alerted me to the extraordinary essay by the working-class intellectuals Amber Hollibaugh and Cherríe Moraga titled, "What We're Rollin' around in Bed With."[11]

While reading this essay I got hot flashes and cold chills—not metaphorically but in my actual body. With nuance and a spirit of fearless exploration, Amber and Cherríe addressed the same questions about lesbian roles and sexual relations that I had been trying to figure out since Betty Silver had picked me up at the Michigan Student Union and Gertrude and Alice had become my idols. The essay is not outdated, and its lessons are not limited to homosexuals. Undergraduate students, especially the women, are still confused about what it's OK to want or not want from their partners and what to want for themselves.

After first dismissing the idea of "politically correct," power-free sexuality, Amber and Cherríe go back and forth about what they really want in bed, describing how they each experience desire. Amber identifies as femme; Cherríe identifies as butch, and they affirm the importance of roles in their sex lives. Amber writes:

> I begin to imagine myself being the woman that a woman always wanted. That's when I begin to eroticize. That's what I begin to feel from my lover's hands. I begin to fantasize myself becoming more and more female in order to comprehend and meet what I feel happening in her body. I don't want her not to be female to me. Her need is female, but it's *butch* because I am asking her to expose her desire through the movement of her hands on my body, and I'll respond. I want to give up power in response to her need. This can feel profoundly powerful and very unpassive.

Cherríe answers, "But don't you ever fantasize being on the opposite end of that experience?" Amber answers,

Well, not exactly in the same way because with butches you can't insist on them giving up their sexual identity. You have to go through that identity to that other place. That's why roles are so significant and you can't throw them out. You have to find a way to use them so you can eventually release your sexuality into other domains that you may feel the role traps you in. . . . Quite often what will happen is I'll simply seduce her. Now, that's very active. The seduction can be very profound, but it's a seduction as a femme.[12]

Amber lived in San Francisco then, but she was a long-distance member of the Barnard planning conference, and on her next visit to New York, we met, and she seduced me exactly in the way she had described. We stayed together for almost ten years.

My Paris talks with Gayle, ARGOH/SOLGA, the Barnard Conference on Sexuality, and "What We're Rollin' around in Bed With" all came together to resolve my confusion (if not all my issues) about sexuality, gender identity, and feminism of the previous years. It was OK to be butch; for the first time in my life, I embraced it without ambivalence. Gertrude Stein expressed the enduring paradox of butch identity when she said, "Thank god I was not born a woman."

Sexuality is a central part of it, but identifying as butch does not determine who is on top or any of the mechanics. Being butch in bed is about attitude, intention, fantasy, like my dream of having a penis and fucking the beautiful Indian woman: exciting, and all in my head. You needed a woman who understood and responded to your female masculinity; I knew then that I would never be with another partner who was attracted to me but ashamed of who I was, who did not consciously identify as femme.

As to restarting my academic and writing career, I had a lot of help. Already by 1979 I had begun to teach undergraduates about the history of sexuality and eventually to offer an introduction to lesbian and gay studies, for which I was repaid handsomely by the gratitude of students who were desperate for knowledge and affirmation. Then I found the new scholarly feminist and queer networks through ARGOH and the Barnard Conference. But the specific person who pushed me back into the pool was my friend from the Paris Conference in 1979, Carroll Smith-Rosenberg, the feminist historian at the University of Pennsylvania.[13]

With Amber Hollibaugh, probably at the Dyke march, New York City, about 1982.

There was an attraction between Carroll and me, but instead of jumping into each other's arms on the rebound (Dominique and Claudia Koonz, Carroll's partner at the time, had recently stunned us with the news of their clandestine relationship), Carroll encouraged me to get back to scholarship. We shared a common interest in the Paris expatriate lesbian community, and the result was a co-authored paper, never published in English, about the impact of the sexologists, especially Havelock Ellis, on the so-called New Woman, a generation that came of age at the beginning of the twentieth century. I was especially focused on the mannish/"invert" author of *The Well of Loneliness*, Radclyffe Hall, the first lesbian I had ever heard of and "known."[14]

But as Carroll and I worked on the essay, we started pulling in different directions, and the end result was two papers—one by her on the sexologists, whom she saw as a mainly negative influence on the New Woman, and one by me, which saw the sexologists' insights as more central to the formation of lesbian identity. My paper became "The Mythic Mannish Lesbian: Radclyffe Hall and the New Woman."[15]

With my spouse, Holly Hughes, in the 1990s.

Now I had connections: I was known to a growing group of feminist and gay scholars, and the essay was published in *Signs*, the premier academic feminist journal, the first peer-reviewed journal in which my work ever appeared. The essay examined the historical evolution of the mannish lesbian role, beginning in the late nineteenth century and culminating through Radclyffe Hall and her novel, which, partly because of a sensational trial when it was banned in England and partly because it was accessibly written, was a worldwide best seller and, for better or worse, disseminated the image of the mannish woman as the iconic lesbian figure.

In writing "The Mythic Mannish Lesbian," I had found a way to integrate my love of women, my female masculinity, and academic writing into one functioning, coherent person. In 1985, I was invited by Martin Duberman to co-chair the informal group that would ultimately lead to the Committee on Lesbian and Gay Studies, part of the City University of New York (CUNY) system. Marty wanted to attract women to the group (which met for years in his living room in Chelsea), and with the help of my friend from the Barnard Conference, Julie Abraham, and Melinda Cuthbert, then a graduate student at Yale, we did just that.

There I met queer scholars from a range of disciplines who gave me respect and urged me on.[16] Being turned down for a full professorship at Purchase was, after so many rejections, a horrible experience, but I have to admit that it pushed me to undertake a big new project of documenting the sixty-year history of Cherry Grove, an LGBT island vacation enclave near New York City, which became, among other things, my ticket to full professorship. During the 1980s, commercial presses started to be interested in publishing queer scholarly work, and since that time I have received some of the honors and respect that had been missing from my early academic career.

Dominique's friend Céline had wanted my novel to be about intellectuals in Paris because, according to her, it wasn't daring or significant to write about lesbians. But after all, I was not avant-garde. I just wanted to be the subject and hero of my own story. I belong to a people that have been rendered either invisible or stereotyped as comical or sinister. Although Céline was right about my novel's failure, and I eventually realized that memoir would be a far more congenial form, the essence of the novel and this memoir is the story of the first half of my life as I want to tell it.

Narratives embedded in minority experience are often justified as being actually about something "more important"—say, "human suffering." But abstract suffering is just an abstraction; it is always you or me who suffers. If I aspire to "make our experience a human struggle," as my Paris friend Harriet had said, it is not through denying or "rising above" myself.

At the climax of her melodramatic yet hugely influential novel, Radclyffe Hall broadened her lens to focus on the abjection of all queer people. Her writer-heroine Stephen Gordon imagines that the world's suffering inverts are trampling her in "their madness to become articulate through her," a prediction that came true more than she ever could have imagined.

During my lifetime, the novels, memoirs, and biographies of Stein, Hall, and others, such as Oscar Wilde, Paul Monette, Ann Bannon, and Audre Lorde, influenced me greatly and gave me courage, solace, and exemplars. These queer authors were concerned about how their writing would be judged from an aesthetic perspective that marginalized them, but they also wanted to be a portal through which readers could see others like themselves and take hope. This is the tradition I aspire to, and this memoir is an homage to those who came before, with the hope that it will help others to find and express their voices as they carry on.

NOTES

INTRODUCTION

Epigraphs: Munt, *Heroic Desire*; Shteyngart, *Little Failure*; Munt, *Heroic Desire*.

1. Sigmund Freud, "The Psychogenesis of a Case of Homosexuality in a Woman," in *The Psychoanalytic Review* 24 (1920).

2. For a pioneering and sympathetic description of this time period in working-class lesbian life, including both butch and femme roles, see Elizabeth Lapovsky Kennedy and Madeline D. Davis, *Boots of Leather, Slippers of Gold: The History of a Lesbian Community* (New York: Routledge, [1993] 2014).

3. Everyone involved in my intellectual training believed fervently in the supremacy of nurture (culture), as opposed to nature (genetics), in shaping human life. This was a reaction against the nineteenth-century social Darwinism that formed the basics of eugenics and, eventually, Hitler's Final Solution. The discovery of epigenetics (gene expression) leads the way toward a more unified and nuanced understanding of causality in human life.

4. The character of Ziva David, played by Cote de Pablo in the hit television show NCIS, is a more modern representation. Gorgeously feminine, hard-headed, and stubborn, she is totally believable as an agent who shoots straight and kills bad guys when she has to, can physically level any antagonist, and parries word for word with the man she secretly loves but keeps at a distance. As in *Dirty Dancing*, the powerful erotics of their relationship lie in the tension between them, not in conventional heterosexual love scenes.

CHAPTER 1. A HARD LEFT FIST

1. In his later years, Saul and his fifth wife, Joan Harvey, founded a theater group called the Fourth Wall that produced plays that promoted their political/psychological viewpoints, especially aimed toward children.

2. Jane Pearce and Saul Newton, *The Conditions of Human Growth* (New York: Citadel, 1964).

CHAPTER 2. A WRITER'S INHERITANCE

1. Lucia Gilbert, "Letters from Next Door," *New York Tribune*, November 13, 1869, Lucia Runkle scrapbook, vol. 1, 9, 13, Esther Newton, personal papers. I don't know how she felt about the Pullman strike of 1894, with its violence against the Pullman workers, but sympathizing with strikers might have been a bridge too far. A recent search of the Library of Congress's Chronicling America site, where historical newspapers are digitized, revealed that my great-grandmother was even more successful and prolific than I had realized: it showed ninety-three examples of her work into the twentieth century in multiple newspapers, not just the *Tribune*: http://chroniclingamerica.loc.gov/lccn /sn84024441/1896–01–13/ed-1/seq-5.

2. Lucia Runkle scrapbook, vol. 2, 71, Esther Newton, personal papers.

3. American Biographical Library, "Women of the Century: Runkle, Bertha," in *The Biographical Cyclopaedia of America, Volume 2: Daughters of America* (New York: J. T. White, 1892), 116.

4. American Biographical Library, "Women of the Century," 116.

5. Bertha Runkle, *The Helmet of Navarre* (New York: Century, 1906); Bertha Runkle, *The Truth about Tolna* (New York: Century, 1914); Bertha Runkle, *The Scarlet Rider* (London: Andrew Melrose, 1915); Bertha Runkle, *Straight Down the Crooked Lane* (New York: Century, 1915); Bertha Runkle, *The Island* (New York: Century, 1921). If, as my mother thought, Bash persuaded my grandmother to stop writing, it took him a while. They had married in 1906. I found no evidence in her papers that she wrote anything after 1921.

6. Saul's brothers' descendants are all named Cohen; his sister, Dobie, told me that she changed her name to something less Jewish-sounding because of discrimination she suffered in the working world. Saul changed his name to Newton in the 1930s, claiming that his non-Jewish wife at the time got him to do it, a story my mother disbelieved.

CHAPTER 3. MANHATTAN TOMBOY

Epigraph: Koestenbaum, *The Queen's Throat*.

1. On October 5, 1945 Eleanor Roosevelt attended a dinner to raise funds for the school: see https://www2.gwu.edu/~erpapers/myday/displaydoc.cfm ?_y=1945&_f=md000148. According to Paul Mishler, Mead cut off involvement in the school and took her own daughter, Catherine Bateson, out of it when the director, Norman Studer, came under suspicion of being a communist in the early 1950s. Paul C. Mishler, *Raising Reds: The Young Pioneers, Radical Summer Camps, and Communist Political Culture in the United States* (New York: Columbia University Press, 1999), 101. Although neither parent was active in the Party during the 1940s, the book's subtitle describes the cultural and political atmosphere in which I was raised until 1951.

CHAPTER 5. BABY BUTCH

1. "The Hanna farm property was purchased in 1948 by Hans K. Maeder who founded the Stockbridge School on the site. The school, a private school for adolescents, operated from 1949 to 1976 and was notable for being completely racially integrated from its inception." https://en.wikipedia.org/wiki/Stockbridge_School.

2. Bacon's legacy was discussed in the college newspaper the *Michigan Daily*, and I find it worth quoting almost in full because it was from this article that I learned that my college tormenter had succeeded in a man's world through dogged talent and was probably a lesbian. Probably, she saw herself the way I did before feminism—as an exceptional woman very different from her co-ed charges who needed protection:

> Deborah Bacon served as the University's dean of women in the 1950s, at the end of an era when University officials acted as parents to female students—enforcing dress codes and curfews and discouraging interracial dating.
>
> When students revolted against that system as the '50s gave way to the more tumultuous '60s, Bacon became the lightning rod in a controversy that would end in an upheaval of the University's relationship with students and the elimination of her office. "She was a person of very conservative views at a time when that was the norm, but the norm was changing," University historian Margaret Steneck said of Bacon, who died in her apartment at 98 Friday.
>
> Bacon's life was marked by conviction and energy. Born in 1906, she worked at a women's prison and served as a nurse at a missionary hospital in Alaska. During World War II, she enlisted as an Army nurse, landing at Omaha Beach six weeks after D-Day and tending to Gen. George Patton's army in frontline hospitals across Europe. After the war, she earned her doctorate in English at Columbia University and at age 44 was appointed dean of women at the University of Michigan. . . .
>
> When Bacon took over the Office of the Dean of Women in 1950, the University tasked her with carrying out its traditional philosophy: to act in loco parentis—in the place of a parent. That meant doing as most traditional 1950s parents would do with young daughters: controlling where they lived, how they dressed and whom they dated. Bacon took to the job with characteristic vigor. "She believed in the social structure as it was at that time, and she believed in enforcing it," Steneck said.
>
> Enforcing that social structure meant keeping a close watch on female students to protect them from moral harm. With few exceptions, unmarried women were required to live in University-approved all-female housing, where they were subject to strict curfews and dress codes, and where University officials could scrutinize their dates and visitors. These methods, Steneck

noted, were then common on campuses across the nation and widely popular with parents.

But as the decade went on and the '60s approached, students grew increasingly discontented with what they saw as the University's intrusive approach to their personal lives. And Bacon, in particular, became a target of their protest. Chief among the students' complaints was Bacon's alleged practice of discouraging white women from dating men of other races. "None of this was new," Steneck said. "Dean Bacon was enforcing it at a time when the cultural mores were changing, the Baby Boomers were arriving on campus, and the students just weren't going to have this. It just no longer was rational or reasonable."

Eventually, a group of *Michigan Daily* editors and other students, led by then-*Daily* editor Tom Hayden, gathered accusations and evidence from female alumni—including complaints that Bacon had severely punished women for visiting with black men after hours and had written to a white freshman's mother to inform her that her daughter had been dating black men—and in 1961 presented them to the administration.

In the summer of 1960, my former roommate and lifelong friend Shirley Walton was pulled out of college by her parents, and she spent the summer with them in Washington State, where, like me, she had a botched and life-threatening abortion. In retrospect (although my memory of this is hazy), I think that Dean Bacon must have called her parents because she was dating an African American. Her life course was drastically altered, and she moved to New York City, where she eventually finished her bachelor of arts at the Columbia University School of General Studies.

The *Daily* article continues,

Within months, the University established a committee, led by Law School Prof. John Reed, to examine its relationship with students. The committee's report recommended a sea change in the University's philosophy toward student life—beginning with the elimination of Bacon's position. In September 1961, after months of controversy and uproar from alumni, Bacon resigned from her post and took up teaching in the English department.

"The *Reed Report* was the foundation of the place of students at the University today," Steneck said. "They felt wholesale change was necessary in the relationship between the University and students, including dismantling the offices of the dean of women and dean of men. Dean Bacon's resignation, which was a forced resignation, was one of the first steps in that change."

The Reed Report's recommendations spelled out the end of the administration's paternalism toward female students. Throughout the rest of the decade, the University would make most of its residence halls co-ed, abolish curfews and allow women to live off campus. And with the deans of men and women eliminated, the administration's power to punish students for private infractions—a power Steneck said those offices had wielded absolutely and with little oversight—was severely reduced.

Steneck noted that the upheaval in the University's relationship with students in the '60s was one of the most powerful examples in the University's history of student-driven change. "I think there's a feeling on the part of students today that you couldn't make a difference," she said. "These students felt that they could, and they went out and did it. The University changed, and absolutely for the better." . . .

Bacon never married, and she is survived by a niece, two nephews and longtime friend Elsie Fuller [with whom she had lived for years], among others (Donn M. Fresard, "Former 'U' Dean of Women Dies at 98," *Michigan Daily*, November 23, 2005, http://www.michigandaily.com/content/former -u-dean-women-dies-98).

3. John Malcolm Brinnin, *The Third Rose: Gertrude Stein and Her World with Photographs* (Boston: Little, Brown, 1959).

CHAPTER 6. ANTHROPOLOGY OF THE CLOSET

1. James West, *Plainville, U.S.A.* (New York: Columbia University Press, 1945).

2. I am not sure of the spelling of Ady's nickname and don't know her given name, because David's Google entries do not even mention that he was married, which is a grave injustice. It was common then for women to get a bachelor's or master's degree in anthropology and then give in to prevailing low expectations by marrying another anthropologist. The woman would then keep the man's household, raise his children, interview the women at his field site without getting credit for it, and type his notes. David knew that this was wrong, but he still urged Sherry Ortner, after she married Bobby Paul, to give up her own career, advice that she resented and, fortunately, did not heed.

3. The students were Vern Carroll, Cal Cottrell, Charley Keil, Liz Kennedy, Martin Silverman, and Linda Wolf. Later he also mentored my friends Harriet Whitehead, Bobby Paul, and Ben Apfelbaum. Linda Wolf eventually left anthropology; Ben Apfelbaum fled to Canada to avoid being drafted into the Vietnam War; and Cal Cottrell died tragically and young. The rest of us became professional anthropologists.

4. U.S. Department of Labor, Office of Policy Planning and Research, *The Negro Family: The Case for National Action* (Washington, DC: U.S. Department of Labor, 1965).

5. Esther Newton, *Mother Camp: Female Impersonators in America* (Chicago: University of Chicago Press, 1979), 76.

6. Charles Keil, *Urban Blues* (Chicago: University of Chicago Press, 1966).

7. Many years later I reflected on these issues in Esther Newton, "My Best In-

formant's Dress: The Erotic Equation in Fieldwork," *Cultural Anthropology* 8, no. 1 (1993): 3–23, reprinted in *Margaret Mead Made Me Gay: Personal Essays, Public Ideas* (Durham, NC: Duke University Press, 2000), 243–58.

8. There were no University Institutional Review Boards then or when I began my second fieldwork, in Cherry Grove. These internal boards, designed to protect the welfare of study subjects, have also been a serious pain in the butt for social scientists—most especially for those who have wanted to study (especially young) gay people, who have been seen as vulnerable subjects.

9. I did not know then that lesbians were routinely doing drag at the Community Theater in Cherry Grove and perhaps in other places that were not commercial and not accessible to the public: see Esther Newton, *Cherry Grove, Fire Island: Sixty Years in America's First Gay and Lesbian Town* (Durham, NC: Duke University Press, [1993] 2014). Theatrical performances by wow are documented in Holly Hughes, Carmelita Tropicana, and Jill Dolan, eds., *Memories of the Revolution: The First Ten Years of the WOW Café Theater* (Ann Arbor: University of Michigan Press, 2015). One of the Brothers was Lisa Kron, who became the first openly lesbian writer to win a Tony Award for writing the book and lyrics to the Broadway hit *Fun Home.*

CHAPTER 7. LESBIAN FEMINIST NEW YORK

Epigraph: The paragraph is from my failed novel, *Alice Hunting*, which found its way into the Kessler talk "My Butch Career" in 1996, along with several photographs of Gertrude and Alice

1. Esther Newton and Shirley Walton, *Womenfriends: A Soap Opera* (New York: Friends Press, 1976). *Womenfriends* was inspired by, and part of, the thriving world of books self-published by lesbian feminists or published by small presses and bookstores. During the 1970s, Shirley co-owned (with Sue Perlgut and, later, with Karen London) the feminist bookstore Djuna Books in Greenwich Village.

2. *Mother Camp: Female Impersonators in America* was first published by Prentice Hall in 1971. It went out of print after a few years but, through David's influence, was picked up by the University of Chicago Press and published with a new introduction in 1979.

3. In the long run, and the big scheme of things, although my book was ignored by academia generally, and by anthropology specifically, for many years, it actually was noticed by younger queer scholars, including Judith Butler in *Gender Trouble: Feminism and the Subversion of Identity* (New York: Routledge, 1990), and Gayle Rubin. I quote from an (unsolicited) e-mail from Gayle Rubin not only because it flatters my work but also because it so movingly illustrates how damaging the nonexistence imposed on us by the state and the dominant culture was and how powerful visibility is for the transmission of knowledge and pride from generation to generation:

I don't know if I have ever told you just how much of an impact you had on my own scholarly trajectory; if I did, belay this message (I do repeat myself these days). But here's the short version[.]

Back around 1973, I had finished up my basic course work in anthropology and was starting to think about how to do a gay dissertation. Actually, the initial plan was to do a dissertation on lesbians. In any event, I went to the library to see what I could find and didn't find much: Fortunately, *Mother Camp* had just barely been published, and I found that. And I found Simon and Gagnon's *Sexual Deviance*. Those two books made me realize that I didn't have to go to New Guinea or the Amazon, but that it was actually feasible to study . . . queer populations here in the US. And through you and the Simon/Gagnon collection I also ran into much of the conceptual apparatus that sociology had produced that gave this kind of work many of its theoretical tools (you know, the usual: Becker, Goffman, Simon, Gagnon, et al.—basically the stuff David Schneider told you to go read).

That was just the beginning. Since there was no one in my department who did anything remotely like this, I pretty much had to figure out how to go about it. And you were my role model for this academic career, in so many ways: an out lesbian, a brilliant scholar and theorist, who did this amazing ethnographic study on a gay population. So you were kind of my "doctor father" in absentia, a lodestar who could always help me get my bearings. I really don't know what I would have done if I hadn't run into *Mother Camp*, there in the stacks of Hatcher.

And it's funny, because I also knew you in other registers—mainly through women's liberation and later, lesbian politics. And you were a huge influence on me in those areas as well; but the anthropology trajectory was its own thing, separate somehow from the movement contexts.

So, it bears repeating: thanks for blazing those trails and making my career as an anthropologist both thinkable and possible. (Gayle Rubin, e-mail to the author, October 22, 2017)

An afternote: as an undergraduate at the University of Michigan I knew a circle of gay men that included the writer Edmund White and a librarian named Ed Weber, who quietly accumulated books about gay life, including *Mother Camp*, so that Gayle was able to find it in the Hatcher Graduate Library in 1973.

4. Jo Freeman website, The Women's International Terrorist Conspiracy from Hell, http://www.jofreeman.com/photos/witch.html.

5. Based on Jo Freeman's description of the skit satirizing women's condition that was performed on the boardwalk in 1969. Her website also features photographs of the protest: see http://www.jofreeman.com/photos/MissAm1969.html.

6. I have notes provided by my friend Kathryn McHargue Morgan from meetings that took place at my apartment on West 99th Street on September 21 and September 28, 1969.

7. Originally self-published by Isabel Miller (Alma Routsong) in 1969 as *A Place for Us*, the book was reissued under the title *Patience and Sarah* by Ballantine Books in 1971 and, more recently, as Isabel Miller, *Patience and Sarah* (Vancouver: Arsenal Pulp, 2008). Louise and I read SCUM Manifesto as a mimeograph that Valerie Solanas was handing out at feminist events in New York. *Valerie Solanas, SCUM Manifesto* (London: Verso [1971] 2004). "The Woman-Identified Woman" was a ten-paragraph manifesto written by the Radicalesbians in 1970. It was first distributed during the "Lavender Menace" protest at the Second Congress to Unite Women, May 1, 1970, New York City. It is now considered a turning point in the history of radical feminism and one of the founding documents of lesbian feminism": see https://en.wikipedia.org/wiki/The_Woman-Identified_Woman; Radicalesbians, "The Woman Identified Woman," in American Queer, ed. David Schneer (Boulder CO: Paradigm, 2006, 232–35).

8. Our book is now an intensely personal and detailed historical document of the most fervent period of New York feminism from 1970 to 1972.

9. Newton and Walton, *Womenfriends*, 12–13.

10. Sidney Abbott and Barbara Love, *Sappho Was a Right-On Woman: A Liberated View of Lesbianism* (New York: Stein and Day, 1972).

11. Jill Johnston, *Lesbian Nation: The Feminist Solution* (New York: Simon and Schuster, 1974); Jill Johnston, *Marmalade Me* (New York: E. P. Dutton, 1973).

12. Jill Johnston, Bertha Harris, Esther Newton, and Jane O'Wyatt, eds., *Amazon Expedition* (New York: Times Change, 1973).

13. This idea ultimately found fruition in Sagaris, a lesbian feminist summer institute that flourished for a few years. The sagaris was an ancient double-headed ax related to the labyris, which had become a lesbian feminist symbol.

14. Lady Una Vincenzo Troubridge, *The Life and Death of Radclyffe Hall* (London: Hammond, Hammond, 1961).

15. Esther Newton with Shirley Walton, "The Personal Is Political: Consciousness-Raising in the Women's Liberation Movement," paper presented at the Annual Meetings of the American Anthropological Association, November 1971, and published in Esther Newton, *Margaret Mead Made Me Gay* (Durham, NC: Duke University Press, 2000), 113–41.

16. Esther Newton with Paula Webster, "Matriarchy and Power," *Quest* (Winter 1975). A further revision of this paper was undertaken by Webster and reprinted as Paula Webster, "Matriarchy: As Women See It," in *Toward an Anthropology of Women*, ed. Rayna R. Reiter (New York: Monthly Review, 1975).

CHAPTER 8. THE ISLAND OF WOMEN

1. "Dominique" is a pseudonym. At her request and urging, I have changed the names of all of the still living Frenchwomen.

2. For a more in-depth treatment of the effects of academic homophobia on my career, see Esther Newton, "Too Queer for College: Notes on Homophobia,"

in *Margaret Mead Made Me Gay: Personal Essays, Public Ideas* (Durham, NC: Duke University Press, 2000), 219–24.

CHAPTER 9. IN-BETWEEN DYKE

1. Bonnie and Clyde's was the most important lesbian feminist bar in Manhattan throughout the 1970s. The upstairs was a restaurant, as I recall, and the bar was downstairs. In the early 1970s, the space was the favorite hangout of politically active young white lesbians. Later it was "taken over" by young black lesbians. The last time I ever went there, I was pushed around on the dance floor by black women who, I assumed, saw it as "their" space, possibly the first such lesbian space that was not in Harlem. The pernicious effects of our racist history combine(d) with an overall shortage of lesbian space: see http://lost womynsspace.blogspot.com/2012/01/bonnie-clydes-bar.html.

CHAPTER 10. PARIS FRANCE

1. Kate Millett, *Flying* (New York: Alfred A. Knopf, 1974); Kate Millett, *Sexual Politics* (Garden City, NY: Doubleday, 1970).

2. Monique Wittig, *Le corps lesbien* (Paris: Éditions de Minuit, 1973). The book was published in English as Monique Wittig, *The Lesbian Body* (New York: William Morrow, 1975).

3. These, along with Phyllis's other films and papers, are in the Sophia Smith Collection at Smith College.

4. At the time, I knew nothing of its history, but the group had apparently split off from the main left-wing feminist group Mouvement de Liberation des Femmes (MLF), which had formed out of the student and worker rebellion of 1968. Wittig and Fouque had both belonged to the original group but split over ideological differences.

5. *Womenfriends* was never translated into French. As I recall, Librairie des Femmes withdrew the offer due to the cost of translation, which they wanted us to pay for.

6. Elizabeth Sprigge, *Gertrude Stein: Her Life and Work* (New York: Harper and Brothers, 1957); Gertrude Stein, *The Autobiography of Alice B. Toklas* (New York: Literary Guild, 1933); Alice B. Toklas, *What Is Remembered* (New York: Holt, Rinehart and Winston, 1963).

7. Gertrude Stein, *Four Saints in Three Acts: An Opera to Be Sung* (New York: Random House, 1934).

8. Bertha Harris, *Confessions of Cherubino* (Ithaca, NY: Daughters, 1972).

CHAPTER 11. BUTCH REVISITED

1. Larry Gross was then a professor at the University of Pennsylvania and is now the director of the School of Communication at the University of Southern California. By indicating the current status of my colleagues, I point to the gradual (and still partial) institutionalization of LGBT studies that began in

academic publishing and then emerged, mainly in the women's studies departments that themselves had gained footholds beginning in the 1970s. In both cases, the impetus came from intellectually and politically powerful protest movements.

2. Evie is now an emerita (retired) professor at Purdue.

3. The group is now called the Association of Queer Anthropologists (AQA), a change that was designed to include transgender colleagues without just adding another initial to "lesbian and gay."

4. For many years, Ellen was unable to get a full-time, tenure-track job. But finally, after prolific publishing, academic service, and feminist connections, she became a full professor at the University of Iowa.

5. Although Prentice-Hall, the original publisher, had dropped *Mother Camp* in the mid-1970s, at the urging of David Schneider, the University of Chicago Press reissued it in 1979, and it has been in print ever since.

6. Gayle S. Rubin, "Introduction," in *Renée Vivien, A Woman Appeared to Me*, trans. Jeannette H. Foster (Reno, NV: Naiad, 1976), iii–xxxviii.

7. Gayle S. Rubin, "The Traffic in Women," in *Toward an Anthropology of Women*, ed. Rayna R. Reiter (New York: Monthly Review, 1975), 157–210. This collection is foundational in feminist anthropology.

8. We referred to the conference as the Moulin d'Andée after the plushy cultural center in Normandy at which it was held. While it is not central to my story, what happened at the conference should not have been forgotten. Organizing it and getting it funded was quite an accomplishment, an attempt at getting feminist scholars (most of whom were lesbians but that was not public since at that time it was impossible to get academic or foundation funding for gay or lesbian scholarship) in America and Europe to engage in face-to-face dialogue. Carroll has told me that she still keeps in touch with quite a few of the European participants, and Gayle Rubin has three folders of documents pertaining to it. Here is what I wrote in my journal: "We met at Le Lieu Dit, a bookstore café, to talk about the program for the [Moulin d'Andé] conference. The organizing group was Carroll Smith-Rosenberg, Claudia Koontz, Cynthia Secor, Harriet Lutsky, Marie-Jo Bonnet, Gayle, Dominique, Rayna Rapp, and Lillian Robinson. It soon occurred to me that Gayle was going to play the role of the Young Turk—she made a lot of noise about having a separate workshop (aside from the general "woman," one) on lesbians, and recast another into her framework of the moment: the historical evolution of sexuality. . . . Want to record that at every meeting so far—i.e., dinner here, cocktails at Judy's, and yesterday at Le Lieu Dit, there's been tension and several clashes. Everyone's incredibly nervous, afraid of looking stupid, of having such a high-level conference, or everything connected with the big time, in fact." I never wrote about the actual conference. I was utterly miserable because Dominique, for whom responsibility equaled anxiety, completely ignored me.

9. A few years later, Amber Hollibaugh and I visited Gayle and her then lover

in their San Francisco apartment. I was curious and somewhat apprehensive about how these two stars of the leather world lived in private. They greeted us in flannel nightgowns and fuzzy slippers and offered us the tea with honey they were drinking, much to my amusement.

10. Julie is now a professor of English literature at Sarah Lawrence. I found this brief description of the Barnard conference to be accurate: "The Barnard Conference on Sexuality is often credited as the moment that signaled the beginning of the Feminist Sex Wars. . . . It was held at Barnard College on April 24, 1982, and was presented as the annual Scholar and Feminist Conference IX, an integral part of the Barnard Center for Research on Women. The theme of the Conference was Sexuality. The Conference was set up as a framework for feminist thought to proceed regarding topics that many felt uncomfortable talking about. As Carole Vance, the Academic Coordinator of the Conference, wrote in her letter inviting the participants, 'Sexuality is a bread and butter issue, not a frill'" (See https://en.wikipedia.org/wiki/1982_Barnard_Conference_on _Sexuality). For the original document that came out of the conference, see http://www.darkmatterarchives.net/wp-content/uploads/2011/12/Diary-of-a -Conference-on-Sexuality.pdf. Many more scholarly articles have been published about the meaning and influence of this conference.

11. Ann Snitow, Christine Stansell, and Sharon Thompson, eds., *Powers of Desire: The Politics of Sexuality* (New York: Monthly Review, 1983: 394–405).

12. Ann Snitow, Christine Stansell, and Sharon Thompson, eds., *Powers of Desire*, 398–99.

13. Carroll went on to a distinguished career at the University of Michigan. She is now emerita (retired).

14. Caroll Smith-Rosenberg and Esther Newton, "La Lesbienne Mythique et la Nouvelle Femme," in *Stratégies des Femmes: Livre collectif*, ed. Marie-Claire Pasquier, Françoise Ducrocq, Geneviève Fraisse, and Anne-Marie Sohn (Paris: Tierce, 1984).

15. Esther Newton, "The Mythic Mannish Lesbian: Radclyffe Hall and the New Woman," in *Margaret Mead Made Me Gay: Personal Essays, Public Ideas* (Durham, NC: Duke University Press, 2000), 176–88. The essay was originally published as Esther Newton, "The Mythic Mannish Lesbian: Radclyffe Hall and the New Woman," *Signs* 9, no. 4 (Summer 1984): 557–75. I had been thinking about Hall since reading *The Well of Loneliness* as an adolescent and had thought about writing her biography. I once had the pleasure of meeting Janet Flanner in her old age, and when I told her my plan, she dismissed Hall as stuffy. Whether to support her case or to soften it, she added, smiling, "She was the perfect gentleman."

16. Some heavy-hitters were part of the group, including John Boswell and George Chauncey (both of whom were at Yale, George as a graduate student). Martin's original plan was to institutionalize CLAGS at Yale (which he had attended), but he and Boswell fell out, and Yale failed to act. When CLAGS became

part of the CUNY system, I was dropped as co-chair and Martin became the sole director. My demotion was attributed to my not being part of the CUNY system. Later, under the leadership of Jill Dolan, I was invited to give the Kessler lecture that led to this memoir and invited to join the CLAGS board, on which I served for two years. There are many documents from the period before CUNY in my personal papers.

BIBLIOGRAPHY

Abbott, Sidney, and Barbara Love. *Sappho Was a Right-On Woman: A Liberated View of Lesbianism.* New York: Stein and Day, 1972.

American Biographical Library. "Women of the Century: Runkle, Bertha." In *The Biographical Cyclopaedia of America, Volume 2: Daughters of America*, 166. New York: J. T. White, 1892.

Brinnin, John Malcolm. *The Third Rose: Gertrude Stein and Her World with Photographs.* Boston: Little, Brown, 1959.

Butler, Judith. *Gender Trouble: Feminism and the Subversion of Identity.* New York: Routledge, 1990.

Freud, Sigmund. "The Psychogenesis of a Case of Female Homosexuality." *The International Journal of Psychoanalysis*, Vol. 1 (1920), 125–59.

Gagnon, John H., and William Simon. *Sexual Deviance: Readers in Social Problems.* New York: Harper and Row, 1967.

Hall, Radclyffe. *The Well of Loneliness.* New York: Covici Friede, 1929.

Harris, Bertha. *Confessions of Cherubino.* Ithaca, NY: Daughters, 1972.

Hughes, Holly, Carmelita Tropicana, and Jill Dolan, eds. *Memories of the Revolution: The First Ten Years of the WOW Café Theater.* Ann Arbor: University of Michigan Press, 2015.

Illich, Ivan. *Deschooling Society.* New York: Harper and Row, 1971.

Johnston, Jill. *Lesbian Nation: The Feminist Solution.* New York: Simon and Schuster, 1974.

Johnston, Jill. *Marmalade Me.* New York: E. P. Dutton, 1971.

Johnston, Jill, Esther Newton, Florence Rush, and Bertha Harris, eds. *Amazon Expedition: A Lesbian Feminist Anthology.* New York: Times Change, 1973.

Keil, Charles. *Urban Blues.* Chicago: University of Chicago Press, 1966.

Kennedy, Elizabeth Lapovsky, and Madeline D. Davis. *Boots of Leather, Slippers of Gold: The History of a Lesbian Community.* New York: Routledge, 1993.

Koestenbaum, Wayne. *The Queen's Throat: Opera, Homosexuality, and the Mystery of Desire*. New York: Poseidon, 1993.

Miller, Isabel. *Patience and Sarah*. Vancouver: Arsenal Pulp, 2008.

Millett, Kate. *Flying*. New York: Alfred A. Knopf, 1974.

Millett, Kate. *Sexual Politics*. Garden City, NY: Doubleday, 1970.

Mishler, Paul C. *Raising Reds: The Young Pioneers, Radical Summer Camps, and Communist Political Culture in the United States*. New York: Columbia University Press, 1999.

Newton, Esther. *Cherry Grove, Fire Island: Sixty Years in America's First Gay and Lesbian Town*. Durham, NC: Duke University Press, [1993] 2014.

Newton, Esther. *Margaret Mead Made Me Gay: Personal Essays, Public Ideas*. Durham, NC: Duke University Press, 2000.

Newton, Esther. *Mother Camp: Female Impersonators in America*. Chicago: University of Chicago Press, 1979.

Newton, Esther. "My Best Informant's Dress: The Erotic Equation in Fieldwork." *Cultural Anthropology* 8, no. 1 (1993): 3–23.

Newton, Esther. "The Mythic Mannish Lesbian: Radclyffe Hall and the New Woman." *Signs* 9, no. 4 (Summer 1984): 557–75.

Newton, Esther, with Paula Webster. "Matriarchy As Women See It," with Paula Webster, in *Aphra, the Feminist Literary Magazine*, vol. 4, No. 3, Summer, 1973.

Newton, Esther, and Shirley Walton. *Womenfriends: A Soap Opera*. New York: Friends Press, 1976.

Pearce, Jane, and Saul Newton. *The Conditions of Human Growth*. New York: Citadel, 1964.

Radicalesbians. "The Woman-Identified Woman." In *American Queer*, ed. David Schneer, 232–35. Boulder, CO: Paradigm, 2006.

Reiter, Rayna R. *Toward an Anthropology of Women*. New York: Monthly Review, 1975.

Rubin, Gayle S. "The Traffic in Women." In *Toward an Anthropology of Women*, ed. Rayna R. Reiter, 157–210. New York: Monthly Review, 1975.

Runkle, Bertha. *The Helmet of Navarre*. New York: Century, 1906.

Runkle, Bertha. *The Island*. New York: Century, 1921.

Runkle, Bertha. *The Scarlet Rider*. London: Andrew Melrose, 1915.

Runkle, Bertha. *Straight Down the Crooked Lane*. New York: Century, 1921.

Runkle, Bertha. *The Truth about Tolna*. New York: Century, 1914.

Shteyngart, Gary. *Little Failure: A Memoir*. New York: Random House, 2014.

Smith-Rosenberg, Caroll. "La Lesbienne Mythique et La Nouvelle Femme." In *Stratégies des femmes: Livre collectif*, ed. Marie-Claire Pasquier, Françoise Ducrocq, Geneviève Fraisse, and Anne-Marie Sohn, 274–311. Paris: Tierce, 1984.

Snitow, Ann, Christine Stansell, and Sharon Thompson, eds. *Powers of Desire: The Politics of Sexuality*. New York: Monthly Review, 1983.

Solanas, Valerie. *SCUM Manifesto*. London: Verso, 2004.

Sprigge, Elizabeth. *Gertrude Stein: Her Life and Work.* New York: Harper and Brothers, 1957.

Stein, Gertrude. *The Autobiography of Alice B. Toklas.* New York: Literary Guild, 1933.

Stein, Gertrude. *Four Saints in Three Acts: An Opera to Be Sung.* New York: Random House, 1934.

Toklas, Alice B. *What Is Remembered.* New York: Holt, Rinehart and Winston, 1963.

Troubridge, Lady Una Vincenzo. *The Life and Death of Radclyffe Hall.* London: Hammond, Hammond, 1961.

U.S. Department of Labor, Office of Policy Planning and Research. *The Negro Family: The Case for National Action.* Washington DC: U.S. Department of Labor, 1965.

Vivien, Renèe. *A Woman Appeared to Me.* Reno, NV: Naiad, 1984.

Webster, Paula. "Matriarchy: As Women See It." In *Toward an Anthropology of Women*, ed. Rayna R. Reiter, New York: Monthly Review, 1975.

West, James. *Plainville, U.S.A.* New York: Columbia University Press, 1945.

Wittig, Monique. *Le corps lesbien.* Paris: Éditions de Minuit, 1973.

Wittig, Monique. *The Lesbian Body.* New York: William Morrow, 1975.

INDEX

Page locators in italics refer to photographs

Abbott, Sidney, 154
abolitionists, 40–41
abortion, 94–95, 96, 97
Abraham, Julie, 242, 246, 259n10
abstraction, 247
academia, 136, 174–75; European faculty, 141; fellowships, 138; French system, 142; "no departments" era, 143–44; open admissions, 141; personal life separate from, 114; teaching, 138–39; tenure process, 141–42, 154, 160–62
affiliation-versus-descent controversy, 110
African Americans, 4, 105–6
African anthropology, 102
African Queen, The (film), 102
age differences, 171
"aggressives" (AG), 4
Aggressives, The (film), 4
Al-Anon, 126
Alice Hunting (unpublished manuscript, Newton), 118, 192–93, 199–200, 202–3, 208–9, 214, 219, 228–29, 232, 235–36, 247, 254n
allies, 136
Amazon Expedition: A Lesbian Feminist

Anthology (Johnston, Newton, Rush, Harris), 155, 163
American Anthropological Association, 142, 158, 238
American culture, 112–13, 200
American identity, historical context, 19–20, 37
American Kennel Gazette, 33
anarchist feminism, French, 225
Andy (geographer), 142
Anger, Kenneth, 219
anger, strength through, 67, 75–76
Anthropological Research Group on Homosexuality (ARGOH), 238, 242, 258n3
anthropologists, queer, 238, 242, 258n3
anthropology, 77, 102–18; of American culture, 112–13; on black single mothers, 109; primitive matriarchies, 158
anti butch-femme ideology, 17, 241
anti-Semitism, 30
antiwar movements, 135, 157
Apfelbaum, Ben, *107*
Arnold, Skip, 112, 114, 116
arts, 125, 146, 193, 221, 227
As You Like It (Shakespeare), 99

Austen Riggs mental hospital, 84–85
Autobiography of Alice B. Toklas, The (Stein), 229

"baby butch," 90
Bachelors for Wallace, 67
Bacon, Deborah, 96, 251–53n2
Ballance, Charles, 38, 47
Ballantine, John, 77
bar culture, 2, 90–92, 109, 130, 257n1 (ch.9); butch as compulsory, 4
Barnard Conference on Sexuality, 241–43, 241–44, 259n10
Barney, Natalie, 239
Bash, Bertha Runkle, 37–40, 48, 51, 55, 72–75; *The Helmet of Navarre*, 43, 250n5; novels by, 43, 74
Bash, Louis Hermann, 38, 40, 43–44, 44, 46, 48, 72; death of, 51
Bauer, Richard, 33, 36, 54
Beasley, Mary, 68, 69
Belgian Village Camp for Girls, 68–70, 70, 79, 148
Belli, Marvin, 77
Benedict, Ruth, 158
Bennington, 88
Berman, Marilyn, 100
Bernhardt, Noah, 61
Beth, 194–97, 200, 215, 216–17
Bilignin (Stein and Toklas summer place), 202
Birkby, Phyllis, 145, 146, 155, 165, 220–21
bisexuality, 88–89, 136
black single mothers, 109
Blackwood, Evelyn, 238
blues singers, 112
bohemia, 125
Bonnie and Clyde's, 193–94, 257n1 (ch. 9)
Boudin, Kathy, 69
Brinnin, John Malcolm, 98–99
Brontë, Emily, 216
Brooklyn Dodgers, 66
bullying, permanent damage from, 83–84

Burma Shave road signs, 53
butch: body markers, 8–9, 90, 237–38; defined, 1, 4; as gender identity, 4, 10–11; mannish lesbian role, 245–46; masculinity, 1, 3–5, 10, 81–82, 91, 228; postmodern, 5; skills stereotypes, 4–5; transmen and, 10–11
butch/femme, 121, 130, 176, 193–97, 232–33, 240; feminist views of, 149; Hollibaugh and Moraga's essay, 243–44
Butler, Judith, 254n3

Calhoun (Lucia's husband), 40
Calhoun, Carol, 146, 167
Camp Woodland, 69
career, 1–2, 236; butch appearance and, 90; class and gender issues, 2; feminism and, 137; hiding sexual orientation, 3; vs. marriage, 98; obstacles to, 3; as second best choice, 98
castration complex, 212
Cherry Grove island vacation enclave, 117, 118, 128, 182, 247
Chicago, 105
Chicago, Judy, 221
Chicago Anthropology Department, 103–4
Chicago Tribune, 45–46
childhood experience, 4
children, gender identity and, 9–10
CIDOC, 179–80
City University of New York (CUNY) system, 137, 246
Civil War, 40–41
Cixous, Hélène, 227–28
class, 2, 7, 201–2, 207–8, 217–19, 227; decadence, 217–18; middle-class lesbians, 120–22, 130–31, 138; working-class lesbians, 3, 195–96, 201
closet, 17, 104, 108–9, 140–41, 237
clowns, 111–12
Club 82, 90, 118
co-dependency, 126
Cohen, Dobie, 23, 31, 59

Cohen, George, 22, 26, 27, 59
Cohen, Maishe, 25–26, 29–30, *31*
Cohen, Minnie, 22–23, 28
Cohen, Saul. *See* Newton, Saul (Cohen)
Cohen, S. K. (father of Saul Newton),
    24, 25–26, 28–30
Cold War, 67
Colfax, Schuyler, 41
college, 2, 12, 44
colonialism, 113
Columbia University, 140
coming out, 80, 215
coming out stories, 12–17
Committee on Lesbian and Gay Studies
    (CLAGS, CUNY), 246, 259–60n16
communal living, 131, 194
Communist Party, 2, 19, 45, 47, 67, 133,
    250n1(ch.3)
competition, 174
complementarity, 233
Confessions of Cherubino (Harris), 231
confidence, 72
Congo Reform Society thesis, 100
consciousness-raising groups, 146, 152,
    158, 184
consensus decision making, 155–56
Cook, Blanche Wiesen, 239
Coss, Clare, 239
Cottrell, Cal, 108–9, 111
counterculture, 131, 138
creative writing, 175
cultural capital, 43
culture, female impersonators as,
    112–13, 117–18
Cuthbert, Melinda, 246

Dann, Mary-Ann, 152–53
Daughters of the American Revolution,
    37–38
Davy (sheltie), 73
de Beauvoir, Simone, 234
de Neven, Anne, 174
DeLarverie, Stormé, 118
des Femmes press, 226
Deschooling Society (Illich), 179

desire, 163
deviance, social, 115, 117
"deviants," 115
Dillon, Michael, 9
Dinner Party (Chicago), 221
Dirty Dancing (film), 5, 7
dog breeding, 33–36, 51, 93–94
Donne, John, 99, 100
double gender-consciousness, 8
Douglas, Helen Gahagan, 157
Downtown Community School (DCS),
    61, 63, 69, 79
drag kings, 118, 254n9
drag queens. *See* female impersonators
    (drag queens)
"The Drag Queens: A Study in Urban
    Anthropology" (Newton), 116
Dreyfus, Alfred, 173
DSM-IV, 8
Duberman, Martin, 246, 259–60n16
Dworkin, Andrea, 175

Edwards, Mary, 143–44, 158, 161, 166,
    194
Eliot, George, 216
Elizabeth (friend), 122, 126, 146, 166
Ellis, Havelock, 245
embattled community, 26
Emmanuelle (film), 217
emotions, 63–64
encounter groups, 138
End of the World, 130
entitlement, sense of, 55

father figures, 18–22
father-mentors, 103
Feeley, Jill, 132
female chauvinist, 63
female impersonators (drag queens),
    8, 17, 112–15, 241; Mummers Parade,
    145; transitioning, 9
feminine women, nonlesbian, 7
feminine-feminine couples, 6
femininity, 108; rejection of, 57–58,
    59–60, 63

feminisante, 212

feminism, 10, 126–27; accomplishments and failures, 136–37; anti-pornography, 242; lesbianism compared with, 241; Miss America pageant protests, 132–35, 137; mystical side, 174, 240; nineteenth-century, 133; as scholarly perspective, 162; second wave, 136, 156, 158–59; women's groups, 132–36

Feministes Revolutionaire (FR), 225–27, 231

femme lesbians, 6–8, 195; equal relationship, desire for, 7–8

Fenichel, Otto, 108, 109

Fiedler, Leslie, 174

Fiedler, Margaret, 174

Film about a Woman Who . . . , 219–20

first-person writing, 200

Fischler, Stan, 127, 152

Fishman, Louise, 124, 145–48, 147, 163–67, 170, 193–94, 219

Five Lesbian Brothers, 118, 254n9

Florida Everglades, 44–45

Flying (Millett), 200

Ford, Gerald, 183

Fouque, Antoinette, 224–27

France, 101, 149, 167; Nazis in, 173–74; past, American focus on, 201, 235; tendance differente, 224

Freeman, Jo, 134

French feminism: anarchist feminism, 225; lesbian feminists, 218–19, 222; la parole, 227–28

French Gestapo, 173

Freud, Sigmund, 4

Freudian psychoanalysis, 162–63

Friedan, Betty, 104

Friedlander, Judy, 164, 167–68, 184, 218

gay liberation, 3, 10, 125, 137–38, 147, 151–52

Gay Liberation Front (GLF), 138

gay men, 112–14, 238, 240

Gay Pride Week, 1971, 151–52

gay women's groups, 152–53

Geertz, Clifford, 116

gender dysphoria, 9–10, 17, 118

gender expression, 5

gender identity, 223–24, 228–29; butch as, 4, 10–11; origins of, 62–63

genealogical trees, 37–38

Ghent, Manny, 89

Gilbert, Lucia. See Runkle, Lucia Gilbert

Gilbert and Sullivan operettas, 53–54, 111

Glass, Bob, 142

Gluck, Laszlo, 18–19, 47

Goffman, Erving, 115

Goldschmidt, Wally, 103

graduate schools, 2–3, 97–98, 103–5

Grant, Ulysses S., 41

Great Depression, 45

Greeley, Horace, 41

Greenwich Village, 17

Grey, Jennifer, 4–5

Gross, Larry, 238, 242, 257n1 (ch. 11)

Growing Up Trans (film), 9–10

Hall, Radclyffe, 8, 157, 245–46, 247, 259n15

Hall, Stuart, 5

hands, as erotic organs, 120

Harper's, 41

Harriet (novelist), 229–31, 234–35, 247

Harris, Bertha, 146, 155, 165, 166, 170; Confessions of Cherubino, 231

Harrison, G. B., 99

Harry Stack Sullivan, 80

Hart, Lois, 138

Harvey, Joan, 66, 95

Hélène, 206–10

Helmet of Navarre, The (Runkle), 43, 250n5

Hepburn, Katharine, 102

heterosexuality, 107–8; disruption of normative gender roles, 7

Hollibaugh, Amber, 144, 243–44, 245

Holmes, Dr., 93
Holocaust, 174, 178, 194, 201
homosexuality, tragic, 88
Hoover Tower, 133
Howard, John, 161–62, 165–66
Hughes, Holly, 246

Illich, Ivan, 179–80
Indian Hill music and arts camp, 84
institutional structures, 3
"inversion," 4, 8, 245
Islas Mujeres (Island of Women), Mexico, 168, 181
It's All Right to Be Woman theater, 135, 146

Jewel Box Revue, 118
Jewish identity, 5, 18–32, 59, 201
Johnson, Philip, 143
Johnston, Jill, 154–56, 163, 165, 200
Jorgensen, Christine, 9
Joyce, James, 209

Kansas City, 116
Kaplan, Abbot, 165
Kay (friend), 182
Keil, Charley, 112–13
Kennedy, Flo, 134
Kennedy, John, 106
Kennel Gazette, 52
Kerr, Deborah, 102
ki-ki dykes, 90, 92
King Solomon's Mines (film), 102
kinship studies, 110
Kite Film, The, 221
Koestenbaum, Wayne, 56
Koonz, Claudia, 245

La Pyramide (restaurant), 208
Lanza, Bianca, 145, 146, 167
Lavalle, Céline, 231–32, 235, 247
Lavender Menace, 146, 256n7
Lawton, Catherine, 167, 168–69, 174
Le corps lesbien (Wittig), 213
leadership and "stardom," 156, 158

leftists, 61; French, 201; male-dominated, 179–80
Les nouvelles lettres portugaise, 224–25
lesbian domestic life, 121, 148–49
lesbian feminism, 164, 220–21; anti butch-femme ideology, 17, 241; lesbian-feminist template, 5; sexuality, views of, 175–76, 190–92, 215
Lesbian Nation (Johnston), 154
lesbianism, feminism compared with, 241
Leser, Frederica, 145
"Letters from Next Door" (Gilbert), 41–42
Lévy, Dominique, 168–74, 176–81, 184–93, 194, 197–217, 198, 219–20, 221–25, 228–29; final breakup with, 236, 237; photos of, 172, 203, 205, 239
Lévy, Dr. Sophie, 173, 203–9
Lewin, Ellen, 11, 142, 238, 258n4
LGBT studies, 113, 132, 175, 244–47; Committee on Lesbian and Gay Studies (CLAGS), 246, 259–60n16
Librairie des Femmes, 225–26
literature, 98–99
Lone Ranger, 62
Love, Barbara, 154, 155
Love, Iris, 145
"lovers," 147
Lowen, Abbot, 87, 89
Lower East Side, 61

Madeira School, 88
Maeder, Hans, 87
Mafia protection, 116
male impersonators (drag butches), 118
Manhattan, 148–49
mannish lesbian role, 245–46
marginalized/minority experience, 247–48
Mariposa papillons, 54
Marmalade Me (Johnston), 154
marriage, 109–10; vs. career, 98; feminist views of, 133–34; lesbian commitments, 146–47, 163; nineteenth century, 42–43; pressures, 3

marriage equality movement, 146
masculine-masculine couples, 6
masculinity, butch, 1, 3–5, 10, 81–82, 91, 228
matriarchies, primitive, 158
matrifocal families, 109
Mattachine Society, 67
maturity, 98, 119–20
Mayflower, 37, 38
McCarthy, Joseph, 67
Mead, Margaret, 140, 250n1 (ch.3)
medical intervention, 8, 9
Meggitt, Mervyn, 140
Mehegan, Gretchen, 87, 92
memoirs, 247–48
"Men, Women and Status in the Negro Family" (Newton), 109
mentors, 88, 103
Meyer, Sybil, 194, 221
Michigan Women's Music Festival, 151
middle-class lesbians, 120–22, 130–31, 138
Milice Française, 173
Miller, Isabel, 146, 254n7
Miller, William H., 18–19, 47–48, 71
Millett, Kate, 200, 220
Miss America pageant protests, 132–35, 137, 255n5
Mitchell, Joni, 130
Mitchell, Juliet, 179, 212
mommy-daddy priorities, 219
monogamy, 164, 219
Moraga, Cherríe, 243–44
Mother Camp: Female Impersonators in America (Newton), 1, 17, 113, 132, 150, 161, 238, 254–55n3, 254n2
mother-daughter ties, 36, 51, 53, 54–57, 86, 163, 205–6
motherhood, psychological theories of, 23–24
Mouvement de Liberation des Femmes (MLF), 257n4(ch. 9)
Ms. Magazine, 156
Mummers Parade, 145
Munt, Sally, 4, 8

Murra, Johnny, 102–3, 104
"The Mythic Mannish Lesbian: Radclyffe Hall and the New Woman" (Newton), 3, 245–46, 259n15

Nazis, 173–74, 202
Near, Holly, 135
Negro Family, The: The Case for National Action (Moynihan Report), 109
Neuberger, Roy, 143
Neuberger Museum, 143
New Age concepts, 174
New Woman generation, 245
New York City, 19, 87; financial crisis, mid-1970s, 183–84
New York Tribune, 41
Newton, Esther: academic regrets, 174–75; double journal with Walton, 149–50;; Freudian analysis, 157, 162–63, 181, 193; "Heavy Combat in the Egological Zone" journal entry, 155; journal writings, 81, 84, 148–57, 169, 177–78, 184, 203, 220, 225, 235–36; Kessler lecture, 254n(ch. 7), 260n16; lesbian and gay studies career, 244–47; Mexico trips, 127, 167–81; move to California, 51–52, 72–80; in Paris, 99, 149, 198–236; photos of, 11, 62, 78, 107, 115, 117, 124, 147, 172, 203, 239, 242, 245; psychoanalysis, 162–63, 181; public readings, 156; at Queens College, 137–43; tenure granted, 165–66, 194; tenure process, 160–62, 165–66, 184; as "the Biographer," 192, 211; writing with Walton, 158; Zena Road experiment, 131–32; Works: *Alice Hunting* (unpublished), 118, 192–93, 199–200, 202–3, 208–9, 212–14, 219, 228–29, 232, 235–36, 247, 254n; "The Drag Queens: A Study in Urban Anthropology," 116; "Men, Women and Status in the Negro Family," 109; *Mother Camp: Female Impersonators in America*, 1, 17, 113, 132, 150, 161,

238, 254–55n3, 254n2; "The Mythic Mannish Lesbian: Radclyffe Hall and the New Woman," 3, 245–46, 259n15; *Womenfriends* (with Walton), 127, 150, 157, 220, 226, 254n1

Newton, Rob, 21–22

Newton, Saul (Cohen), 19–30, 48–50, *49*, *60*, 85–86, 100–101, 227; in Catskills, 30–32, *31*, 45; feminism, support of, 133; financial support, 64; name change, 24, 250n6; return from military service, 57, 59; wedding incident, 24–25

Newton, Virginia Bash, 19–20, 33, 34–55, *47*, *58*, 91–92; arrest at demonstration, 45–46; disinheritance, 48, 55, 94, 126; divorce, 50–51; maternal literary heritage, 39–41, 52–53; move to California, 51–52, 72–80; *The Papillon Primer*, 55; at University of Chicago, 45–46, 105–6

Nin, Anaïs, 154

Nixon, Richard, 157, 200, 211

normalcy, attempts at, 12, 35, 76, 94–98, 127

Northern California Papillon Club, 54

nurture vs. nature debate, 6, 249n3

Oberlin College, 40

Odile, 212

Oedipus complex, 163, 170

oil shock of October 1973, 183–84

"old gay," 152

one-upmanship, 10

open relationships, 138, 164–65

oppression, feminist views of, 150–52

Ortner, Sherry, 111, 253n2

O'Wyatt, Jane, 155

Packard, David, Jr., 77

Palo Alto, California, 72; high school social hierarchy, 76–79

Papillon Primer, The (Newton), 55

papillons, 33, 54

Paris Conference, 1979 (Moulin d'Andée), 239, 241–44, 258n8

la parole, 227–28

Patience and Sarah (Miller), 146, 256n7

patriarchy, 135–46, 155–56, 158, 164, 175, 242

Patsy, 121, 126, 130–31, 144–45, 144–46, 166, 194–95

Paul, Bobby, 111

Pearce, Jane, 21, 50, 63, 64–65, *65*–66, 80, 95, 103, 108

Père Lachaise Cemetery, 202, *203*

Perkins, Tony, 171

"The Personal Is Political" slogan, 135

pet people, 33

Phaedra (film), 171

Pilgrims, 37

Pitt-Rivers, Julian, 104, 116

Plainville, U.S.A. (West/Withers), 103

police raids, 92–93

political correctness, 241–43

"political lesbians," 152

polyamory, 166

poodles, 31–32, 34–36

Popular Front, 173

pornography, 217–18, 242

Powdermaker, Hortense, 103

pregnancy, 151

primitive matriarchies, 158

"private" life, 114

Progressive Party, 67

progressives, 125

Provincetown, 70–71

Psych et Po group, 224–27

psychoanalysis, 2, 83–84, 162–63, 181

"The Psychogenesis of a Case of Homosexuality in a Woman" (Freud), 4

puberty, 9–10

Purchase College (SUNY system), 142–44, 160–61, 165–66, 194

Putney Work Camp, 79–80

Queens College, 137–43, 150

queer anthropology, 108, 132

Rachel, 164–67, 170, 176, 183
Rainer, Yvonne, 219–20
Rankin, Bertha, 68
Rantz, Berta, 87
Rapp, Rayna, 242–43
Reed, John, 252n2
Reed Report, 252n2
relatives, vs. family, 20
revolutionary attitudes, 157
Riis Park, 121
Robinson, Jackie, 66
Rockefeller, Nelson, 143
Rollins College, 44
Rosett, Jane, 24
Roth, Debbie, 194, 211, 221
Rougier, Nicole, 185–86, 198–99, 231
Routsong, Alma, 220–21
Roz (friend), 124
Rubin, Gayle, 10, 239–44, 242,
    254–55n3, 258–59n9, 258n8
Runkle, Bertha. *See* Bash, Bertha
    Runkle
Runkle, Cornelius, 42
Runkle, Daniel, 42
Runkle, Lucia Gilbert, 39–40, 43, 55,
    69, 133, 250n2; "Letters from Next
    Door," 41–42; on marriage, 42–43;
    novels by, 74
Ruth Benedict Collective, 158, 164, 167,
    194
Rye House, 194

sadomasochistic (S/M) sex, 240–41
Sagaris, 256n13
Sappho Was a Right-On Woman (Love
    and Abbott), 154
Sayre, Nora, 219–20
Schnebly, Julia, 38
Schneider, Aby, 104, 116, 253n2
Schneider, David, 103–4, 106, 113–14,
    115, 132, 238; Newton's thesis de-
    fense, 116–17
Schwartz, Susan, 231
Scorpio Rising (film), 219
SCUM Manifesto, 146, 256n7

Second Congress to Unite Women, 146,
    256n7
second wave of feminism, 136, 156,
    158–59; *Feministe Revolutionaire* (FR),
    225–27
segregation, 67
separation, 98
Service, Elman, 102–3
Seuil press, 224–25
"sex change," 9
sexologists, 245
Sexual Politics (Millett), 200
sexual predator stereotype, 4
sexual violation, 59–61
sexuality, 122–24, 213–16, 222; Barnard
    Conference on Sexuality, 241–44,
    259n10; first encounters, 12–17;
    heterosexual as act of domination,
    175; lesbian feminist script, 175–76,
    190–92, 215, 240; open relationships,
    138, 164–65; sadomasochistic (S/M)
    sex, 240–41
Shelley, Martha, 133–34, 152, 156, 157
shtetl stories, 24
Shteyngart, Gary, 6
Siamese cats, 47
Signs journal, 246
Silber, John, 125
Silver, Betty, 89–90, 121, 243
"Silver, Betty," 12, 13
Silverman, Martin, 110–11
Silverman, Sydel, 139–40, 141
single room occupancy hotels (SROs),
    148–49
sisterhood, dream of, 126, 135, 158–59
Smith, Hilary, 97, 99, 105, 126
Smith, Nancy Rae, 80, 88–89, 120–26,
    123, 144, 167, 177, 234
Smith-Rosenberg, Carroll, 239, 240,
    244–45, 258n8
Snyder, Elise, 162
social justice, family historical context,
    41–42, 45–46
Society of Lesbian and Gay Anthro-
    pologists (SOLGA), 238

sociology, 113
Solanas, Valerie, 256n7
Sontag, Susan, 177
sororities, 12
Spanish Civil War, 21, 22
spoiled identities, 115
Spyer, Thea, 145
St. Mark's Church, 61
State University of New York (SUNY) system, 142–43
state-sponsored terror, 237
Stein, Gertrude, 7, 98–99, 119, 137, 149, 196, 202, 208–9, 234–35; America, view of, 157; fan credentials, 229–30; grave site, 202–3, *203*; influence on Newton's writing, 180–81; on not being born a woman, 5, 244; portraits of, 209–10
Steneck, Margaret, 251–53n2
Stevenson, Adlai, 106
Stigma (Goffman), 115
Stockbridge School, 86–87, 251n1
Stone, Lucy, 134
stone butch, 120
Stonewall riots, 137–38
Story of o, The, 217
student protests, 140–41
Sullivan Institute, 80
surgery, 10
Susan (women's group leader), 214–15
symbolic anthropology, 117

Teena, Brandon, 8
tendance différente, 224
Theresa, St., 230, 234
"Thinking Sex" (Rubin), 242–43
Third Rose, The (Brinnin), 98–99
Thompson, Clara, 50, 70
Toklas, Alice B., 7, 99, 119, 149, 180–81, 202, 234–35; grave site, 202–3, *203*; sacrifice for Stein, 228–29
tomboy identity, 57–58, 63–64
Towar, Barbara, 152–53
"The Traffic in Women" (Rubin), 239
Transcontinental Railroad, 41–42

transgender, 8–11; evolution of movement, 10–11
transition, 9
translation, 212–13
transmen, 8–9
Troubridge, Una, 157
Truman, Harry, 67
Trump, Donald, 137

"unfit mother" gambit, 165
University of California, Santa Cruz, 143
University of Chicago, 45, 102, 105–6
University of Michigan, 89, 96–97, 251–53n2; police raids, 92–93
Upper West Side of Manhattan, 148–49
Upper West Side WITCH, 135
Upsurge, The, 46

Vance, Carole, 241–42, 259n10
Vassar College, 40
Victorian novels, 216
Vietnam War, 136, 157, 183, 200
Virginia Tech shootings, 141
Vivien, Renée, 239
Voyage Out, The (Woolf), 180

Wallace, Henry, 66–67
Walton, Shirley (Fischler), 12–16, 89, 92, 126–30, *129,* 131–32, 136, 148–54, 157–58, 165, 252n2; broken ankle, 167; double journal with Newton, 149–50; Mexico trip, 168; pregnancy and motherhood, 151–52; *Womenfriends* (with Newton), 127, 150, 157, 220, 226, 254n1
Washington Heights, 144
Weather Underground, 136
Webster, Paula, 158, 167–68, 174, 179–80, 184
Weinstein, Faith, 101
Well of Loneliness, The (Hall), 13, 82, 157, 245–46, 247, 259n15
Westminster Kennel Club, 133

"What We're Rollin' around in Bed With" (Hollibaugh and Moraga), 243–44
White, Preservèd, 37
Whitehead, Harriet, 108, 110–11, 119–20
Wilde, Oscar, 62
William Alanson White Institute, 50, 64, 70, 80
Windsor, Eddie, 145
Withers, Carl (James West), 103
Wittig, Monique (Théo), 213, 218, 224–25, 227, 231
"The Woman-Identified Woman," 146, 150–51, 256n7
Womenfriends: A Soap Opera (Newton and Walton), 127, 150, 157, 220, 226, 254n1
"women's culture," 240
women's groups, 214–15
Women's International Terrorist Conspiracy from Hell (WITCH), 133–35
Women's Liberation, 132–34, 138
Woodstock Festival, 132
Woolf, Virginia, 180, 233
working-class lesbians, 3, 195–96, 201
World War II, 22
WOW Café, 118
writers, women, 39–42, 74, 216, 229–31
writing, 99–100

Yourcenar, Marguerite, 137